Child Care Choices

Child Care Choices

Balancing the Needs of Children, Families, and Society

EDWARD F. ZIGLER

and

MARY E. LANG

THE FREE PRESS
A Division of Macmillan, Inc.
NEW YORK

Collier Macmillan Canada
TORONTO

Maxwell Macmillan International
NEW YORK   OXFORD   SINGAPORE   SYDNEY

Copyright © 1991 by Edward F. Zigler and Mary E. Lang

The Free Press
A Division of Macmillan, Inc.
866 Third Avenue, New York, N.Y. 10022

Collier Macmillan Canada, Inc.
1200 Eglinton Avenue East
Suite 200
Don Mills, Ontario M3C 3N1

Printed in the United States of America

printing number
1 2 3 4 5 6 7 8 9 10

Library of Congress Cataloging-in-Publication Data

Zigler, Edward
    Child care choices: balancing the needs of children, families, and society / Edward F. Zigler and Mary E. Lang.
      p. cm.
    Includes bibliographical references and index.
    ISBN 978-1-41-657333-3
    1. Child care services—United States. 2. Child development—United States. 3. Infants—Care—United States. I. Lang, Mary E.
II. Title.
HQ778.7.U6Z54 1991
362.7—dc20   90–37737
                                                  CIP

This book is dedicated to H. Smith Richardson, Jr.
and to his children
Peter Richardson *and* Adele Ray,
in recognition of
their efforts on behalf of our nation's children.

Contents

Preface

A great many people today think of child care as a service bought by mothers of preschoolers so they can go to work outside of the home. Until the early 1980s, much discussion about supplementary child care focused on whether or not it was really necessary and how it might affect children. People debated—in private, in educational and scientific journals, in the media, and in the halls of Congress—if mothers should raise their children exclusively at home until school age or could safely leave them in a child care setting during the workday. Magazines targeting mothers published countless articles on the subject, some offering reassurance to those using child care services, others warning of possible harmful effects.

Several assumptions underlying these debates are now being questioned—and so they should be if we are to make true progress in solving the child care problems of America's families. First, it was taken for granted that child care was a service for mothers, not for families or children. Mothers, after all, were the ones who opted to use child care or to stay out of the labor force while their children were small. It was also assumed that choices between the two options were made privately by families—primarily by women—without the input or influence of the larger society.

There is some indication that the American public is now beginning to realize that child care choices are not determined by families alone and that families alone cannot solve all their child care problems. In June of 1989, Ethel Klein of Columbia University, with the help of a grant from the Ms. Foundation for Education and Communcation, analyzed the results of public opinion polls on family issues during the past decade.[1] She found that during this time more and more Americans have begun to believe that business and government should help families with child care concerns. For example, in 1981 only 34% of the respondents to a Washington Post/NBC poll thought that federal spending on child care for the working poor should be increased; by 1987, 57% of the respondents thought it should. Similarly, other polls are showing that more of the public has come to expect that businesses will provide their employees with some kind of child care assistance. In addition, over 200 bills designed to address the child care needs of the nation's families have been introduced into Congress, most of them during the last two years, and child care has gained more and more attention in the media. It is clear that the American public is looking for help with increasing the supply and improving the quality of child care. But there is as yet no national consensus on what kind of help should be given and who should give it: federal, state, or local governments; private agencies; or the business sector.

Another assumption made until recently was that child care was a problem mainly for parents of preschoolers (children from about three to five years old). Yet the demand for services now comes from families with children ranging in age from a few weeks to 12 or more years old. When planning for child care programs, communities most often overlook children at the extreme ends of this age spectrum. Yet the oldest and youngest children have specialized needs that cannot be met by the same kinds of services offered to preschoolers. Therefore, we have devoted several chapters in this book to the child care needs of infants and toddlers and those of school-age children.

Perhaps the most erroneous assumptions about child care that have been made in the past concern the nature of child care and its purpose. Child care is not just a service for working parents; it is a setting that constitutes a significant portion of the total environment in which our nation's children are developing physically, intellectually, and socially. Nor are child care services part of a unified system that is subject to regulations sufficient to protect the interests of all the children it serves. Child care environments are neither consistent nor routinely evaluated in many communities. Child care services are also not readily available to all families who need them. Arrangements available in the local community and parents' abilities to pay for them both determine access to child care.

Neither is child care an alternative form of child rearing that can simply be contrasted with parental care in the home. Because the majority of children are experiencing child care as a supplement to parental care during some part of their formative years, comparisons between child care and home care as though they were separate systems have become less meaningful and less relevant. Child development occurs both in the home and in child care settings. What remains meaningful and relevant, however, is continued exploration of the variety and the quality of child care environments and their impact on children.

In this book, we explore relationships between the whole society and child care. We discuss how social and economic changes create a demand for child care and how the quality of child care actually available affects children, their families, the society, and the economy. Our observations and recommendations are driven by the belief that society needs to make two basic commitments in regard to child care. First, every child deserves a total environment—including home, school, and child care setting—that is of high enough quality to support healthy growth and development. We believe that the nation as a whole has both the ability and the obligation to provide such environments for its youngest citizens and that it ignores this obligation at its peril. Second, a democratic society must guarantee parents, who have always had and still have the major responsibility for raising children, that they will have real choices in how they balance work life and family life. When families are able to achieve the balance that best meets their individual circumstances, the nation will be better able to balance the needs of its children and their families with all of society's other needs.

Edward F. Zigler
Mary E. Lang

Acknowledgments

This book would never have been written without the invaluable assistance of a number of organizations and individuals, each of whom made unique contributions to our thinking and rethinking about the issues we presented. We thank the Ford Foundation for their financial assistance and support. We benefited greatly from the experience and advice of Matia Finn-Stevenson, who provided us with new insights and concrete information in many areas, especially the current School of the 21st Century model and the child allowance trust fund. Deborah Phillips reviewed much of the book and made invaluable suggestions for alternate interpretations of research data and for appropriate revisions. We also thank Suzanne Martinez for reading Chapter 2 and giving us additional information and perspective on the recent history of child care issues at the federal level.

The Wellesley School-Age Child Care Project, especially Dale Fink, were very helpful in supplying advice and resources for the chapter on school-age child care. We drew on the expertise of Dana Friedman and Ellen Galinsky on business and child care issues. We also appreciate the work of our editor at the Free Press, Susan Milmoe, who made many suggestions for improving the manuscript.

The staff of the Yale Bush Center in Child Development and Social Policy gave us a great deal of support on this project. Sally Styfco contributed the bulk of the writing of two chapters, carefully read and heavily edited each of the other chapters, did substantial research, and helped us to improve the manuscript at every stage of revision. Karen Linkins did research on the feasibility of a children's allowance, and Adrienne Opalka developed the scenarios and tables for that chapter. Pamela Ennis helped with the initial research for several chapters, and gathered together a number of resources before taking a leave to care for her infant son Ariel. Claire Timme did an excellent job quickly and accurately typing each chapter and making the multiple revisions required. Sally, Pam, and Claire managed their own family/work life balances very effectively, and we are very grateful to them and to their families.

We thank our own families for their support and encouragement: Bernice and Scott Zigler; Bruce, Kimberly, and Joel Neild; Rebecca McFarland; and Frances and Hubert Lang.

E. F. Z.
M. E. L.

1

—◆—◆—

The Mixed System
of Child Care

Just a generation or two ago, the term "child care" referred to all the duties performed by parents while raising a family. Supplementary care, referred to as babysitting, was arranged when parents needed to shop, meet appointments, or pursue social and civic activities. Assistance with child care while parents worked was common only among low-income families, although many wealthy families also relied on paid caregivers to help with child-rearing responsibilities. In the last two decades, more and more middle-class families have also come to require supplemental care for their children on a regular basis. Today the meaning of "child care" has evolved to imply nonparental care—it is understood as the customary care given to children by adults other than their mothers or fathers while parents work, seek work, or attend career-related school or training programs. Child care is distinguished from babysitting, typically an informal arrangement made when parents hire a caregiver for a brief period of time. It also differs from formal education, including nursery school and early childhood intervention programs, where operating hours may or may not accommodate parental work schedules and goals are much narrower than child rearing.

Although the term child care has not yet been entered in most dictionaries, it is now part of the vocabulary, just as child care itself is part of the daily schedule of the majority of children growing up in the 1990s. Each workday, more than two-thirds of American mothers go to work outside of their homes. And while they work, their children—ranging in age from two weeks to about thirteen years old—are cared for by someone else. Many are cared for by unrelated caregivers in their own homes, by staff in day care centers, or by other adults—almost all of them women—who take children into their homes during the workday. Others are cared for by grandparents or other relatives who are unemployed, employed at home, or working night shifts. Some children—and we will never know exactly how many—are cared for by "relatives" who are actually other children too young to care even for themselves. The school-age children (five to thirteen years) are supervised during school hours, but somewhere between 2 and 10 million of them are alone in their homes or on the street for several hours before and after school and on school vacation days. For some families, it has become necessary to make complex arrangements combining two or more of these scenarios, depending on the day of the week or on the time of day.

Never before in the nation's history have so many children, at such young ages and for so many hours of their lives, been placed in such a wide variety of caregiving environments. Concerned observers have noted that our society has embarked on a broad social experiment in child rearing, one in which parents continue to raise their children, as they always have, but with a significant difference—mothers and fathers have turned over the supervision of a large part of their children's waking hours to a vast mixed system of child care. The system is subject to few controls, has lacked sustained national commitment, and varies significantly in quality from excellent to harmful. We have very little information about how well this system is serving parents and children, but there is growing concern about its effectiveness in providing even the minimal environment necessary to support the healthy growth and development of the nation's future citizens.

In this book, we will explore the American child care system as it currently exists and as it might evolve in the future. We will consider the history of the system and the policies and social attitudes that perpetuate it. We will examine what constitutes adequate quality in child care settings, and how it can be achieved. Our main concern will be the developmental needs of American children and ways in which child care experiences meet or fail to meet them. We will also examine the needs of the special populations—infants, ill and handicapped children, and school-age children—who are most poorly served by the current system. The responsibilities of the child care system to children, working parents, employers, and society have become so broad that together we must insure it can fulfill them. We will offer our suggestions on how to design an integrated child care service that benefits the children and adults who depend on it.

WHY MOTHERS WORK

> Once upon a time, women had their babies and stayed home
> with them. Once upon a time, one paycheck paid the bills. Once
> upon a time, husband and wife lived happily ever after.[10]

To understand the current need for child care, one has to look at the role today's mothers play in the family economy. Just a generation ago—during the "baby boom" years following World War II—most women waited to enter or re-enter the work force until their children were nearly grown. Recent labor statistics indicate that the pattern has changed significantly. In 1987, 67% of women with children under the age of 18 were in the out-of-home work force,[32] as compared to only 39% in 1970.[13] Predictions are that by the year 2000 the rate of female participation in the work force will be identical to that of men, with most women working during their years of childbearing and child rearing.[27]

Part of this change is accounted for by the increase in the number of single-parent families headed by women who are divorced, separated, or who never married. In 1970 there were 7.5 million such families, but by 1988 there were 13.5 million.[30] Given the current divorce and out-of-wedlock birth rates, the actual percentage of children who will live in a single-parent home for some period during their childhood is probably higher than 50%. Divorce usually brings a dramatic fall in financial status for women and their children. Many single mothers must work to help support their households; in the frequent cases where child support payments from fathers are irregularly or never made, mothers must provide the full support of their families.

In two-parent families many mothers also need to work outside the home. In a 1983 *New York Times* poll, 71% of working mothers who responded said that they work "not for something interesting to do, but to support their families."[4] Married mothers whose husbands' incomes are low to moderate are more likely to work outside the home than those whose husbands enjoy higher earnings. Sixty-eight percent of mothers married to men who earn $15,000 to $19,000 annually are in the work force, as opposed to 53% of those whose spouses earn $50,000 or more.[30] Of the working mothers of preschoolers, nearly 60% are married to men who earn less than $25,000 per year. It is clear from these numbers that the majority of mothers in the 1990s work for the same reasons fathers do: to adequately feed, clothe, and shelter their children.

Even in more advantaged families, there are as many reasons for women to work during the childbearing years as there are for men. Both parents may work to provide more than the immediate basic necessities for their children—a home of their own or savings for college tuition, for example. They may work in order to put to use their own expensive college educations. They may work to keep abreast of changes in their professions, knowing it will be difficult to return to the job market when their children are older unless they are well-versed in the current thinking and latest technology of their fields. Many wives see the current divorce rate and fear the economic consequences should they not maintain the potential to support themselves and their children. Like men, women also work for personal fulfillment, to contribute to the society, and to feel valued for that contribution.

For whatever reasons they work, married mothers do contribute substantially to their families' and the nation's economies. According to the Select Committee on Children, Youth and Families,[30] they contribute an average of 41.3% of total family earnings. The Committee[29] cites a Congressional Budget Office report indicating that the median income of American families (halfway between the poorest and the richest) rose 20% from 1970 to 1986. Much of this increase can be attributed to the contributions of working mothers.

The increase in median family income does not indicate that all families were better off in 1986 than they were in 1970. The Select Committee[28] reports income for the poorest two-fifths of families with children actually decreased 12% during that 16-year period, after adjusting for inflation. Poor single mothers and their children have suffered the most; in 1986, approximately 40% of all single-mother families had incomes below the poverty line. Incomes for the youngest families—those whose heads of household were under 25 years old—also fell behind. Overall, the median income for these families in 1986 was 43% below that for comparable families in 1970. The figures for black and Hispanic families were even worse. Clearly, most families today need more workers in the household than did families a generation ago.

Regardless of whether a mother chooses to work or has to work outside the home, the fact is that mothers do work and will continue to work. As the current shortage of labor intensifies, estimates are that two out of three new jobs created within the next 10 years will have to be filled by women, most of whom are of childbearing age and will become mothers during their working lives.[27] Their children will need supplementary care in increasing numbers. As a nation we must deal with the inadequate supply of child care at present, but we must also begin to plan for the future.

We would not need a child care system, of course, if mothers or fathers were willing and able to stay home and care for their own children. Arguments by some conservative groups that children and society would best be served if women recognized their responsibility to stay home with their children are faulty for two reasons. First, the majority of mothers cannot choose whether or not to work. It is unrealistic to think that society could do without their labor or that most families could make do without their financial contributions. Second, it is highly inconsistent for a democratic society that professes to value diversity and freedom to dictate to families what kinds of financial and social choices they should make while rearing their children. Although raising children entails many moral obligations on the part of parents, it also entails moral obligations on the part of society: obligations to be sure that parents have the support they need to perform their duties, and obligations to be sure that decent, safe, and nurturing environments are maintained for children.

THE CHILD'S TOTAL ENVIRONMENT

The most important part of a child's total environment is the family. This is as true today as it was before mothers entered the work force in such significant numbers. Families, not schools or day care centers, rear children. The family is still responsible for the majority of the expense, the choices, the work, the joys, and the worries of rearing children.

Yet with the advent of supplementary care for the children of working parents, a major part of the child's daily environment is no longer under the direct observation or control of the family, even before school age. To understand how important this fact is, we must broaden our thinking about what influences children as they grow and learn. Developmental psychologists once thought that the child-mother relationship was the primary determinant of the course of psychological growth. Later they began to look more closely at the child-family relationship and the influence of peer groups on children. Today many have expanded their view to include the relationship of a child with the total environment.

To take this kind of ecological approach, advocated by Urie Bronfenbrenner[1] and others, is to understand the child first in the context of his or her family. The family itself is not seen as an isolated entity but as part of a community of families, employers, and government agencies. Everything that happens in a community that affects parents affects their children in some way. Thus, a factory closing influences the lives of many growing children, because it has tremendous impact on the financial status and emotions of their families. The opening of health clinics influences the lives of children who previously lacked adequate health care. Pollution, we have only begun to discover, has negative effects that last beyond childhood. The perceived quality of school programs affects even those children too young to attend them, as parents develop positive or negative feelings for the local schools and the community and decide to deepen their roots there or move elsewhere. Thus, for children to develop adequately, the community must provide an adequate environment for the entire family unit, not just for the child.

Although all aspects of the community have an impact on the growing child, three elements can be said to affect children's development the most. (Another is the health care system, which we will not discuss here.) First and foremost is the family, which has the most direct and continuous influence. Next is the school, the most organized and systematic of the three. At least as influential as the school is the child care system. We bestow such import upon child care not only because children spend so much of their lives within it, but also because it so closely resembles the function of the family. These three elements are of course interrelated and simultaneously affect the course of the child's development. In the best of circumstances, when the family, school, and child care environment are all operating well, the child's development will be optimized. While no environment is perfect all the time, this does not necessarily mean development will be compromised. Children are resilient, and most have high degrees of stamina. However, they are subject to what Edward Zigler has called an environmental threshold.

Picture child-rearing environments as a continuum, ranging from the best of conditions to the worst. Along most of this range, the environment will be adequate to support children's development. That is, children will develop as they should and at the proper rate in the physical, intellectual, emotional, and social spheres. Below the threshold, however, the environment drops below a critical level of quality, and the child's development will be compromised in one or more of these spheres. For example, if the child does not receive adequate physical care and love from the family, we suspect that his or her intellect, personality, and ability to form close relationships in the future will somehow be damaged. If the school fails to instill basic skills and a love of learning, we worry about the child's course in adulthood. If the child care environment does not provide for the child's various needs, we fear that developmental damage will ensue.

Above the minimum threshold of environmental nutrients, we can expect children to thrive. But that threshold must be maintained in all systems that influence the child, because the child's total environment is what ultimately determines development. For example, consider the importance of consistency in the life of the child. Most of us would consider inadequate a school that employed a new teacher for the same class every few months or that changed teaching methods, grading practices, or hours of operation frequently. We would not tell ourselves that our children would do well in this environment because their home lives were predictable and stable. We would expect bad results from this kind of haphazard education.

By the same token, an environment in which a baby or preschooler spends a good part of the day has to have some consistency from day to day, patterns and people that the child recognizes, and some harmony with the home life experienced the rest of the time. Unfortunately, for the small child whose environment includes a child care setting, consistency such as this is rare. Child care centers often experience high turnover rates and rotate staff among various age groups. In smaller, less formal child care arrangements, providers go in and out of business frequently, and send parents scurrying to find replacements. In the many communities where there are inadequate and fluctuating sources of child care, some parents simply cannot secure environments that are above the minimum threshold necessary for adequate child rearing. What has developed in America is a two-tiered system of child care: advantaged families can afford adequate environments for their children; poor and many middle-class families cannot.

FINDING A CHILD CARE ENVIRONMENT

Today newspapers and popular magazines are filled with true stories about the problems parents have had in their search for good child care environments. Sandra and Mark (not their real names), who reside in a suburb of Birmingham, Alabama, tell of an experience that is typical of many couples living anywhere else in the nation.

Sandra and Mark thumb through a stack of unpaid and partially paid bills and realize that their family income definitely needs a boost to ward off any more delinquency notices. Sandra has not worked since the birth of their daughter, Mandy, a year ago, and the couple had not foreseen how difficult it would be to live on just one income or how expensive baby clothes, formula, and pediatrician's visits could be. They reluctantly agree to place Mandy in child care so that Sandra can search for a job. She would prefer a part-time position because she is reluctant to leave the baby for very long. Armed with two recommendations from friends, Sandra begins a quest for a loving, caring environment for their bright, happy, and energetic little girl.

As she enters the first center—where her neighbor's 18-month-old son is enrolled—Sandra is overwhelmed by the stench of urine and the sound of crying infants. The center director leads her into a room packed so tightly with 10 cribs that a person cannot squeeze between them. An unsmiling woman in a white uniform (no, the director tells her, she is not a nurse), lifts a baby over the foot of his crib, mechanically changes his diaper, and without a word places him back on the wet sheet and props a bottle in his mouth. Seeing no open floor space, Sandra asks where the infants play. She is told that since none of the babies is walking yet, they have no need to play. The mother wonders a bit about this, since several of the children in the room, including her neighbor's son David, appear to be well over a year old, and she knows that David has been walking for some time.

Sandra asks to see the toddlers' area. She is ushered into a dingy room, devoid of any decoration on the walls, with a dirty, peeling linoleum floor. She is again met by the smell of urine and the sound of crying. There are 11 children ranging in age from about nineteen months to three years. One is in a corner sucking her thumb, a few are wailing or walking aimlessly, and several are on the floor squabbling over three toys. Another white-uniformed woman, as expressionless and voiceless as the first, lifts a two-year-old girl onto a changing table, removes her soiled diaper, and replaces it with a dry one without ever cleaning the child. Sandra notices that the child has uttered only three distinct words during this encounter, while Mandy, who is much younger, is the only one in the room babbling continuously.

Sandra has counted 21 children so far and two caregivers. This does not include the director, who is dressed in a business suit and has not touched or spoken to a single child since they began the tour. The director quotes a daily rate which seems reasonable but is almost half of what Sandra's part-time pay will be. The mother begins to doubt that child care will really be in Mandy's best interest.

The second recommended center is already expecting them, and Sandra tries to quell her discouragement as she drives toward it. When they arrive, they see the front hall decorated with drawings done by some of the children in attendance. The floors are covered with clean carpeting and the walls are brightly painted and filled with colorful pictures and seasonal decorations. The infant room is staffed by women dressed in casual clothing. One is rocking a small baby while the others are sitting on the floor encouraging older babies to explore the spacious room and to play with the stacking toys, washable dolls, and musical toys that litter the floor. The director did not meet Sandra at the door; she is occupied reading a story to a small group in the toddler room. When she sees Sandra and Mandy enter, she smiles first at Mandy and invites her to play with blocks while mother and director talk.

There will not be a space for Mandy for three months, when one of the toddlers will be "graduating" to a preschooler group. The daily rate is exactly the same as that of the first center. Yet there are many more caregivers, each watching fewer children, many more toys that cover the wide range of interests and abilities that characterize developing children as they progress through infancy and toddlerhood, and certainly much more cheer. Sandra decides that it will be worth the wait to secure a space in this nurturing environment for her precious little girl. She is not happy about the fee, but decides that the half of her salary left over will at least help them make a dent in those bills.

When a family does decide that the mother must work, they immediately encounter two major problems that illustrate the current national child care crisis: finding care they can afford and choosing from an array of child care options that vary tremendously in form and quality. The issue of quality, which will be discussed in greater detail in Chapter 3, is not always as apparent as it was to Sandra, since differences between settings are usually more subtle. Issues of cost, availability, and type are more likely to be confronted first.

Affordability

Affordability can be a major obstacle for families seeking child care. Nationwide, averaging across age groups and location, a common estimate is that full-time care costs an average of $3,000 a year, making child care the fourth largest household expense after housing, food, and taxes.[26] Yet there is considerable disagreement about the actual range of child care costs, largely because fees vary greatly according to age of the child and geographic location. For example, the following are the results of some surveys conducted during roughly the same period of time. According to the Children's Defense Fund, in 1987 the national average cost for child care was $3,000 per year ($58 per week).[3] However, parents of preschoolers in Washington, D.C. must pay $100 a week or more for quality care.[17] The U.S. House of Representatives determined the cost of infant care to be up to $130 per week.[4] Although infant care costs up to $200 weekly in New York City and its immediate environs, it can be obtained for as little as $80 in some places in nearby Long Island.[18, 21] In New Haven, Connecticut—just outside the area considered metropolitan New York—the cost of infant care is about $150 per week. These figures can be expected to rise somewhat in the coming years, although past increases have been modest after adjusting for inflation.[14]

In many cases, middle- and low-income parents spend less on child care than do higher income parents. However, they must spend a greater proportion of their earnings. In an analysis of child care costs, Sandra Hofferth[12] noted that whereas families who are not poor allocate, on average, 10% of their income to child care, poor two-parent families spend 22%, and poor single mothers up to 32% of their income for child care. Take the case of a single mother earning $15,000 a year (about twice the minimum wage) and living in any of the areas mentioned above. At the lowest rate for infant care ($80), over one-fourth of her salary would be required; at the highest rate ($200), more than two-thirds of her gross income would be used. At the national rate of $58 per week, a single parent working full time at minimum wage would use 45% of her income for child care.[5] Such a mother has no access to child care; no matter what facilities exist in the community, she cannot afford them.

Availability

Another factor limiting access to child care is the sheer lack of available spaces for the number of children in need of care. Actually, there is some confusion and disagreement as to the issue of the availability of care. Some researchers contend that child care is difficult to find and that there is more of a demand for services than there is supply. Others, pointing to the expanding supply and diversity of services that exist, note that the child care market is working well and that there is no shortage.[12] Even among those with this opinion, some qualifications and exceptions are noted: shortages in child care do exist in some communities, and in at least two segments of the market—namely, for infants and toddlers and for school-age children—the demand for services far exceeds supply.[31] It is also acknowledged that although parents may be finding child care, there is no guarantee that the environments they are finding are adequate to support the child's development.

Another point over which there is no dispute is that the demand for child care is going to increase in the next decade and beyond. The demand for services will be fueled by the continued presence of mothers in the labor force and the increase in the number of working mothers expected to occur as the result of the Family Support Act of 1988. The expected increase in demand will coincide with the tightening of the labor market. Economists predict that there will be fewer workers in many fields, including child care,[27] thus widening the gap between the need for and availability of care.

Some studies have been undertaken to estimate the number of licensed child care facilities throughout the United States. Results are not always comparable because investigators vary in the types of facility they choose to include. The National Association for the Education of Young Children (NAEYC)[24] found that there were approximately 60,000 licensed centers and almost 168,000 licensed day care homes available nationwide in 1985. Gwen Morgan of Work/Family Directions, Inc. found a similar number of centers, but approximately 10,000 fewer licensed homes.[22] Using these and other data, the Congressional Research Service estimated that there were fewer than 3 million regulated child care slots in 1986–87.[33] At the same time the U.S. Bureau of the Census revealed that there were 25.2 million children (8.2 million of them under the age of five) whose mothers worked and thus might need full- or part-time care.[35] Although there are discrepancies between the numbers, clearly there is a shortage of regulated child care slots for children who need them. Of course, many children are cared for by babysitters or relatives—types of care that are typically not regulated. The U.S. Department of Labor[37] found that so many children were in such informal care arrangements that it declared no shortage exists. We disagree. When a state as progressive about child care as California finds it is meeting only 9% of the need (in the words of Robert Cervantes of the Department of Education, "for every nine kids, there are 91 more waiting at the gate"), a major lack of supply is indicated nationwide.[19] The millions of children who are not accounted for in the national surveys are likely being cared for in unregulated homes or are caring for themselves.

Complicating the shortage problem is the fact that not all child care spaces are available to children of certain ages. In particular, some communities may have adequate slots for preschoolers but lack sufficient facilities for the numbers of infants and school-age children who need care. Fifty-two percent of mothers of infants work outside the home,[2] and these mothers are re-entering the work force at a very high rate;

the need for infant care is especially pressing. Currently, 62% of school-age children are enrolled in some kind of child care, but the demand is estimated to reach 77% of that population—or 30 million children—in 1995.[13] If parents can find child care for a three-year-old but not for the toddler or the seven-year-old in the same family, we cannot really state that the family has access to child care.

The availability of child care is also limited by the location of facilities and their hours of operation. Is the child care setting near enough to work, to home, or to public transportation? Do the caregiver's hours correspond to the parents' work hours? A parent who has to add an hour of extra commuting time to drop off a child at the only facility where space is available may nominally have access to child care; one who has no car and is not near a bus route to that facility has no access. Parents whose work hours do not correspond to standard nine-to-five or eight-to-four o'clock shifts may find themselves literally locked out of child care.

Information and Referral

The lack of available child care spaces, coupled with the problems of affordability and accessibility, mean that parents are finding themselves with few child care options. Helping them to learn about all available options is thus the only way to widen their limited range of choice. One important initiative dedicated to this part of the child care problem is the resource and referral (R&R) system, sometimes called information and referral (I&R) services. Some R&R agencies are supported by businesses to help their employees find child care. Others are sponsored by nonprofit groups to assist parents as well as caregivers in the entire community.

One of the main goals of R&R agencies is to help parents find child care; the other is to help increase the actual supply by informing community planners—and potential providers—of the number and type of child care spaces needed in a given area. The success of such services can perhaps be measured by their popularity among parents. In a 1976 national survey,[36] parents were asked to rank those programs for which they most wanted to see government funds allocated: R&R services were high on most lists. Congress responded to this popular support in 1984, when the Human Services Reauthorization Act, or Public Law 98–558, was passed. The act included a provision allowing federal Block Grant money to be channeled into state and local R&R agencies to provide dependent care information.

Although R&R agencies cannot supply child care slots where there are none, they can fill the information void that parents face when they look for child care. Besides offering information about the type, location, cost, and hours of licensed facilities in an area, some agencies also provide instruction on how to judge quality in a caregiving setting. Others can tell parents about sources of child care subsidies and explain eligibility rules and how to apply. Many R&Rs also assist new or potential providers, giving them information on start-up procedures, licensing requirements, and local training resources. Some R&R services actually provide caregiver training or actively recruit for family day care home providers within the community. Finally, a few R&R services advocate policy development for child care regulation and funding within their states or geographical areas.

THE VARIETY OF CAREGIVING SETTINGS

Affordability, location, suitability for the age of the child, and hours of operation are all considered when parents choose a child care environment. Within these restrictions, they might be able to choose what form of child care they prefer. There are basically three broad categories of child care options to choose from: in-home care by relatives or nonrelatives, family day care homes, and day care centers. In 1982, the U.S. Bureau of the Census reported that 25.7% of children under six whose mothers worked full time were cared for in their own homes by fathers, other relatives, and nonrelatives; 43.8% were cared for in another home by relatives or nonrelatives; 18.8% were in group care centers; and 11.8% were in arrangements classified as "other."[34] Within the "care in home by relatives" category and the "other" category are probably a number of children—under six years old—who are left to care for themselves; at least one-half million are cared for by a neighbor or relative under the age of fourteen—many considerably younger.[30] It must be remembered that these figures were gathered by census takers and represent self-reporting by parents. Parents who leave small children to fend for themselves, whose children are cared for by illegal aliens, or who keep older children out of school to care for younger ones are unlikely to report these circumstances to an official representing the federal government.

In-Home Child Care

The category generally referred to as "in-home child care" actually includes a host of different kinds of arrangements, some of which are not child care by our definition. For example, in some families the mother works different hours than does the father, so that one parent is usually at home when the children are. Because child care is supplementary care provided by someone other than a parent, this is a form of shared child rearing, not child care. We mention it here because some families alternate such convenient arrangements with supplementary child care, and because many surveys include fathers when they count the number of children cared for by relatives. For example, in the Census figures cited above, the 25.7% of children cared for at home include those cared for by fathers. Of all children whose mothers worked full time in 1982, 10.3% were cared for by their fathers, the same percentage as in 1965. When mothers work part time, a greater proportion of fathers of children under six are involved in caregiving during the mothers' work hours: 20.3% in 1982, down from 22.9% in 1965.[34]

The advantages of care by parents are obvious. There is usually no cost outlay or transportation hassle. The most important benefit is that children are being cared for in a familiar, consistent environment by their own families. The disadvantages of being a "split-shift" family are many, however. Parents who limit their work hours also limit their earning potential and advancement opportunities. If one parent works days and the other works evenings or nights, there is very little family time during the week and precious little time for mother and father to spend even an hour alone. This can put a strain on a couple's relationship. Changes in the demands of the work place, such as the need for one parent to work overtime or to change shifts temporarily, are a problem in any child care arrangement. However, the split-shift family has an even more delicate balance in scheduling than do most working parents.

Another in-home care arrangement that is not true child care involves a parent who is self-employed or performs paid employment at home. A parent may have a cottage industry, do free-lance work, or be able to do work from the office at home. The advantages of this kind of parent care are similar to those of care by split-shift families. The disadvantages are obvious to anyone who has ever tried such an arrangement. Infants, toddlers, and preschoolers need constant attention and frequently interrupt the parent's concentration. The equipment or tools needed for some kinds of at-home work may be dangerous to children, and papers and employer-owned equipment must be kept out of inquisitive hands. Only a few kinds of employment can be done at home for an extended period, and few families can arrange such care. Often, they must purchase occasional child care to fill in the gaps.

When adult relatives other than parents, such as grandparents, aunts, and uncles, care for children at home, this may be considered in-home child care. Sometimes relatives are paid directly; sometimes there is a barter arrangement, such as child care in exchange for room and board. The benefits of any kind of in-home care by relatives are that children remain in their own familiar homes with familiar, committed people, and usually—but not always—parents can trust that their own child-rearing values will be preserved. Such arrangements are not always ideal, however. Whether the relative is paid or not, he or she may suddenly find another job, knowing the child's parent "will understand." Family squabbles may be taken out on the child. We have no idea how many grandparents—who worked hard most of their lives raising their own children and earning a living—are spending their golden years caring for grandchildren because parents do not trust or cannot afford someone else to do it.

In-home care may also be provided by nonrelatives such as professional nannies, full-time babysitters, or live-in caregivers. They may be teenagers who are recent high school dropouts, mothers with older children, or elderly women who need the income or wish to keep busy. They may be totally lacking in skill and experience, or they may be fully trained and experienced professionals with good references. Although the advantages of having the child cared for at home (familiar environment and no transportation problems) are good ones, the main disadvantage is that this type of arrangement is the most expensive form of child care. There is also a tremendous range in the quality of caregiving. After extensive searches and interviews, parents may find the ideal person. They can also unwittingly choose a caregiver who is not suited for the work, who ignores or mistreats children, or who is simply unreliable. In most places, in-home caregivers need no license. Some work through agencies that supply nannies or babysitters, but often the only requirement for employment by an agency is that they be bonded. This protects the family's valuables from theft, but it does not protect the children from the caregiver's inadequacies. Even when an in-home caregiver is good, and many are, turnover is frequent. Because in-home caregivers are generally not licensed or registered, no statistics on turnover are available.

In the past, care in the child's own home was the most popular choice among families with very young children. For example, in 1965 49% of children under three were reportedly cared for by relatives if their mothers worked; another 21.5% were cared for by nonrelatives in the child's own home.[34] In total, approximately 70% of children receiving child care once did so within the umbrella category of in-home child care, compared to the approximately 49% reported by the Census Bureau for 1982, the last year for which such statistics are available.[13]

As stated above, the statistics concerning the types of care children receive are neither totally reliable nor consistent; however, it is clear that while in-home care arrangements are still popular, they are much less dominant than they were 25 years ago. Care by relatives has decreased as more aunts and grandmothers join mothers in the work force. Many people no longer live near extended family, because of increased social mobility and the unavailability of jobs or the high cost of housing in some areas. In-home care by nonrelatives has become prohibitively expensive for many families because of increases in the minimum wage and the social security tax. In addition, arrangements with even the most reliable in-home caregiver can go awry. If the caregiver is ill or has to cancel for other reasons, parents are left without a replacement. Many working parents understandably prefer secure arrangements that they can count on every day.

Family Day Care Homes: The Cosmic Crap Shoot

According to the U.S. Bureau of the Census,[34] family day care homes are the most popular form of child care for children under six years of age, especially infants and toddlers. While in-home care by relatives and nonrelatives has decreased since 1965, the number of families who enrolled their children in family day care homes increased by 50% in the same time period. The exact definition of a family day care home varies from state to state, but all are private residences where care is provided to a limited number of children—typically four to six. The caregiver may or may not be related to the child, and she (family day care providers are almost always women) may or may not have children of her own at home. Depending on state specifications, some family child care businesses may serve a larger number of children (typically up to 11 or 12) if they have additional caregivers. These may be classified as group day care homes or small child care centers.

The main reason for the family day care home's popularity is the "home-like" atmosphere parents believe it provides. There is no guarantee, however, that such a home will resemble the child's own home in any way, except that it is a private residence. Edward Zigler has called family day care a "cosmic crap shoot," because choosing such a setting is a gamble; a child may win the very best or lose to the very worst type of care. This phrase became the title of a *New York Times* editorial,[8] which noted the death of two children and injury of six others after a fire in an unlicensed family day care home. The editorial writer went on to comment that there were fewer than 2,000 licensed family day care providers in the entire city of New York, and suggested that children in the 25,000 unlicensed homes might not be in safe hands. Certainly a very large number of family day care homes are operated without registration, licensing, or monitoring by the states (the reasons are discussed in Chapter 3). Estimates range up to 90% or more.[6] Since the vast majority of family day care homes operate unofficially, it is impossible to say with any certainty what this type of child care is really like.

There is probably no typical family day care home. Some family caregivers park the children in front of the television set while they go about their housework, while others organize activities and interact and play often with the children in their care. Some take the children on family errands or on outings to the library or the park. Some providers care for children of several ages, while others accept only infants and toddlers or only preschoolers.

One of the reasons we know so little about what actually goes on in family day care homes—beside the fact that most of them operate underground—is that they are so widely dispersed and so heterogeneous that they are very difficult to study. In one study, *Windows on Day Care*, Mary Keyserling observed that the worst kinds of neglect and abuse are possible in such environments.[16] More recently, a few researchers have taken a closer look at the actual experiences of children in family care. One of these studies, conducted in British Columbia, revealed that children in homes rated high quality engaged in more structured activity, more fine and gross motor activity, and more reading, music, and art activities than did those in low-quality homes.[11] The Canadian researchers noted that licensed homes were generally of higher quality than unlicensed homes. Children in unlicensed homes engaged in solitary play significantly more and watched television twice as much as those in licensed homes. This might be partly explained by the findings of another study,[7] which showed that unregistered providers had less training and knowledge of child care and cared for more children than did providers who chose the registration route.

Many parents are attracted to family day care arrangements because they believe the small group setting allows the caregiver to give individual attention to children. Yet, on at least one measure of caregiver and child interaction, the British Columbia study seemed to show that children in both licensed and unlicensed family day care homes get less rather than more direct contact with the caregivers compared to children in child care centers. Workers in family day care homes engaged in fewer informational activities with children. Informational activities were not defined as formal lessons in any sense, but as informal episodes in which the caregiver conveys information, such as pointing out the name of a bird or discussing how to tell by the clock when parents are scheduled to arrive. Such informal interactions with children are believed to assist in their social and intellectual development, especially the acquisition of language.

Daily events in a family day care home in the United States probably follow patterns similar to those observed in the Canadian study. Yet even in licensed family day care homes in this country, the main consistency is that we can expect them to be inconsistent. Most states regulate family day care to some extent, through either licensing or registration. In two states, however, there is no regulation of family day care homes; in five states only homes that provide subsidized care must meet established guidelines; in three states registration is offered only on a voluntary basis.[22] In addition, 26 states that do regulate family day care limit only the number of unrelated children who can be cared for. For example, Arkansas defines family day care as one provider who cares for four to six unrelated children. A caregiver who watches three children in addition to her own and a few nieces and nephews would not even be required to obtain a license.

During the past few years, the media has devoted a lot of attention to child abuse in day care centers and family day care homes. For this reason, the lack of screening and monitoring of day care providers and the total lack of regulation of the majority of family day care homes concern the public, who fear that children are at greater risk of abuse and neglect in this type of setting. Although any incidence of child abuse is too much, the actual risk of abuse in any child care setting is a fraction of that in the child's own home. What ought to concern us more is the very real possibility that many children in family day care homes are experiencing not open abuse or flagrant neglect but a daily environment that drops below the quality threshold necessary to sustain and encourage optimal development.

Certainly many family day care providers deliver excellent care, but they do so in the face of many serious difficulties. For one, liability insurance has become a scarce and expensive commodity. In 1985, insurance for child care providers was transformed from a routine cost of running a business to an impeding problem. Throughout the fall and summer of 1985, NAEYC received approximately 200 calls *each week* from child care providers whose liability policies had been canceled or not renewed, whose rates had more than doubled, or whose coverage had been cut back dramatically. Many child care providers could not find replacement policies at any price.

The cause of the crisis was primarily within the insurance industry. In the early 1980s, when market interest rates were high, insurance companies were more than happy to sell child care providers policies because they stood to gain a lot from investing these funds. When interest rates dropped around 1985, insurance companies found that it was no longer profitable to insure many types of clients, so they dropped a large number of them and raised the rates for others. Child care was included among the industry's list of unprofitable businesses for two basic reasons. First, sensational headlines about child abuse in child care settings heightened the perceived risk in insuring this type of business. Second, children are able to sue up to the age of majority for events that happened to them in early childhood (this is referred to as a "long tail")—which makes actuarial predictions very difficult.

The insurance crisis of 1985 has now subsided, thanks to compromises reached between insurers, lawmakers, municipalities, and other parties that also benefited caregivers. A new crisis looms for child care providers, however, as the result of a tax reform law that took effect in 1989. Because of the "long tail," insurance companies often put money in reserve for "potential" claims that may not be made until years after an incident occurred. Now all of this reserve money is taxable. Thus, insurance companies may find that insuring day care operators is no longer as profitable as it once was.

To show how these crises have affected the industry, James Strickland reported that before 1985, the average cost of insurance in centers was $7 per child per year.[9] After that time, the premium per child multiplied to ten times that amount. The current average is between $35 and $70. Strickland, executive director of a child care research and training center, says that most of today's policies also cover less than they did when they cost $7. For example, a common exclusion is child abuse. If a caregiver is charged with child abuse, even if she is later found innocent, "many policies will not even cover [her] attorney fees," Strickland asserts.[9]

Although insurance woes have afflicted all child care facilities, family day care providers have perhaps suffered the most. Their incomes are typically small, so any increase in the cost of doing business will decrease already meager earnings. Family providers, whether licensed or not, run the risk that if a child suffers any accidental injury or illness while in their care they may be sued, with the possibility of losing not only their small businesses but also their family homes.

Some of the other difficulties that plague the family day care provider are long hours, isolation from other adults, difficulty coordinating vacations with those of the families they serve, and clients who neglect to pay. Although licensing or registration in most states is not costly, the expense of renovating to meet state or local requirements can be in some cases. As a result, the system of unlicensed and unmonitored care in family day care homes continues to be the norm.

In some communities, family day care providers have formed organizations and networks to improve the quality of the care they provide and to enhance their own working conditions. These networks link licensed providers to one another and sometimes to a central agency that provides substitute caregivers when a provider is ill, on vacation, or pursuing additional training. Some networks sponsor social and educational activities where providers can get together to meet and share with colleagues. Others circulate newsletters with information on efficient business and accounting practices, insurance, places where materials or activity plans may be obtained, and instructions for applying for the Department of Agriculture's surplus food program or other assistance. Providers who participate in such networks are likely to be interested in improving the quality of children's lives. Unfortunately, only a tiny percentage of licensed family day care providers belong to networks. The concept is relatively new, but it is a promising means to improve the lot of children and providers in family day care.

The family day care "system" nationwide, then, is so heterogeneous that attempts to assess its quality are extremely difficult. As a part of the child care service in this country that many parents continue to prefer, it will require closer observation than it has received to date. More study is needed to determine the special needs and contributions of family day care providers and how to help them better serve the families and children who depend on them.

The Day Care Center

Day care centers provide the most popular form of child care for Americans age three to five. In 1982, approximately 40% of all preschoolers whose mothers were employed full time were enrolled in day care centers, compared with about 15% of children under three.[13] Centers provide group care for 12 or more children in buildings ranging from modern facilities to church basements and unused schools. Some centers specialize in infant and toddler care, but the majority do not serve children under the age of three. A growing number serve mixed age groups and offer before- and after-school care as well. Such mixed facilities can be complicated to administer, because state standards for staff-child ratios vary for different age groups.

Day care centers differ from family day care homes in aspects other than size. In many states the director must have training in early childhood education, and staff members are more likely to have such training than are family day care providers. There are likely to be more child-oriented furnishings and play materials in a center than in a private home. Organized group activities—story reading, field trips, art and music activities, and the like—occur more frequently in centers than in family day care homes. The type and number of educational activities offered depend on the philosophy of the individual center. The better day care centers resemble good nursery schools (some call themselves such); the only distinction is that these centers have longer operating hours and include time for meals, nap, and outdoor play.

Although all the states have regulations regarding safety, space, staffing levels, staff training, and program in day care centers, these vary so widely that no universal description can be made. Because it is difficult to keep a large operation like a day care center hidden from authorities, most centers are licensed. Degree of monitoring varies, however, and in some areas it is relatively easy to operate without complying with all state standards for the long periods between inspection visits.

There are two subcategories of day care centers: for-profit and nonprofit facilities. For-profit centers include large national or regional chains, such as LaPetite Academy, Kinder-Care, and Gerber Children's Centers, and also comprise small "mom and pop" businesses run by families and other small partnerships. Nonprofit centers may be operated by churches, parent cooperatives, community centers, and YMCAs; some are operated by businesses for the benefit of their employees, or by the employees themselves (see Chapter 8). Some parents may be lured by a for-profit center's advertising claims, which usually promise educational benefits. Other parents may feel that charitable organizations are more likely to operate in the child's best interests.

Professionals themselves appear divided about whether the quality of care differs markedly in for-profit and nonprofit centers. Kagan and Newton[15] found the care in government nonprofit centers to be superior to that delivered in for-profit facilities, but they judged the quality in both to be acceptable. The authors did caution that the state where they conducted the study has fairly stringent standards, so their findings should not be generalized nationwide. The National Child Care Staffing Study included centers in five metropolitan areas from coast to coast.

The authors likewise reported that nonprofit centers provided better quality care than for-profit centers,[38] but they found the care delivered in both to be of marginal quality overall.[25] Interestingly, while 21% of the nonprofit centers contacted declined to participate in the study, 42% of the for-profit chains refused. The authors attributed the differences in quality to the fact that nonprofit facilities devoted 62% of their budgets to staff salaries and benefits, whereas for-profits allocated only 41–49%. Meisels and Sternberg concluded that "profit absorbs funds that might otherwise be devoted to improving services."[20] It seems safe to say that among child care centers, regardless of auspices, there are excellent, mediocre, and poor ones—just as with other types of child care arrangements.

The major benefit of center care as opposed to family and in-home care is that it is the most reliable of all child care options. A sitter, grandparent, or family day care provider may, for reasons of illness or other emergency, cancel at the last moment, causing disruption of parents' and children's routines. This does not happen in centers that have more staff members and find it easier to hire temporary workers as substitutes. A center offers the preschooler a larger variety of playmates and experiences. Although some centers are more expensive than family day care homes, they are more often able to offer family rates or sliding fee scales for parents of lower income, because the expense is spread out over a greater number of families and because more types of government assistance are available to them.

Parents who prefer arrangements other than day care centers notice the faults: centers tend to be noisy, bustling places where the needs of the individual child may sometimes be overlooked. This is of particular concern to parents of infants and toddlers (see Chapter 4). Fixed hours of operation mean security for some parents; other parents have odd or irregular work hours and long for more flexibility in the schedule. Many centers are open only during the school year, so alternate arrangements must be found for the summer. Parents may feel less comfortable relating to a professional caregiver than to a family child care provider. The latter is more likely to have time to stop and chat and perhaps develop a friendship with the parent. The trade-off between organization and informality is a decision not easily arrived at by parents.

WHY THE MIXED SYSTEM IS NOT BETTER ORGANIZED

It is clear that women are in the work force to stay, that their numbers will increase as the beginning of the next century is approached, and that their children need care while they work. It is also clear that available child care in our simplest understanding of that term—number of licensed spaces—is not sufficient even to meet current needs. What is available may be too expensive or too distant to be truly available. Finally, the quality of care is as mixed as the system itself. The only explanation for this sorry state of affairs is that as a nation we have been unwilling to spend the time, the energy, and the money to make good child care a reality for every child who needs it. The historical and political reasons for this are complex, and will be discussed in Chapter 2. There are some social reasons for the current child care crisis, however, particularly in American attitudes toward child rearing and the function of the family.

Americans correctly perceive the family as being the central environment and resource for the child from birth to about age five. Popular sentiment also assigns the family the role of sole provider for the young child's educational, moral, social, and physical development. We have traditionally hesitated to intervene unless parents are for one reason or another unable to perform their functions. The general assumption is that society has no responsibility for children until about age five or six, when suddenly communities are expected to provide the educational part of the environment for all children. As long as any kind of societal assistance in the education and rearing of children under five is perceived as usurpation of the family's rightful role, Americans will have mixed feelings about supporting such assistance.

In its sole provider role, the American family has had to absorb the shock of the many social changes over the last few decades, including the rising divorce rates and increased maternal employment mentioned earlier. Yet popular child-rearing models are based on an assumption of uniformity in families that no longer exists. A family is supposed to include a father and mother and children. In the old model, the father's primary role was that of breadwinner. He played with his children on weekends and perhaps in the evenings, but he had little direct effect on their growth and development, especially in the preschool years. The real influence on the young child's development was thought to be the mother, so it was important that she be available to the child almost all the time. Within this idealized family structure, the state had no identified function in child rearing for those younger than school age, except to allow wage earners small tax deductions for each child and to supply the most destitute with income supplements.

Being flexible and adaptable, individual families have risen to the occasion by attempting to forge new models. The ideal "family man" of the 1940s and 1950s has now been replaced by the ideal "new father," who is expected to take some part in the physical, emotional, and intellectual nurturance of his child from birth on. Exactly how many fathers actually fit this new mold and do have greater involvement in direct care of their children is unknown. Census Bureau figures, cited earlier in this chapter, indicate that the percentage of fathers caring for children while mothers work has not risen since 1965, although the actual numbers no doubt have. And even in families successfully negotiating new models of parent care, the old models of noninvolvement by the rest of the society are as strong as ever.

Another attitude that contributes to the lack of society's involvement with child care before school age (and even before and after school hours) is the mistaken notion that given all these changes in the family, the needs of children have somehow changed too. Infants are now placed in their parents' arms immediately following birth so they can begin to form close bonds. Apparently these bonds are thought to form quickly, because a close daily relationship with a person highly invested in them is no longer guaranteed to infants beyond the newborn stage. Children in grade school, previously thought too young to care for themselves, are now thought to be more sophisticated and responsible than children of earlier generations. This is evident in the push for earlier schooling, the introduction of academic subjects in lower grades, and the number of children now left in self-care. Yet there is absolutely no scientific evidence that psychological development has somehow sped up in children born in recent years. Nor, we submit, will there be any, because children are still children.

Not only have child-rearing models not sufficiently adapted to the needs of children, but they also have not adapted to the needs of families. Sources of societal support in the form of close neighborhoods and nearby extended families have all but disappeared in many cases, with few new social forms emerging to replace them. Our inattention to the child care crisis is not only a symptom of our inability to see the needs of children and the needs of families raising children, it is perhaps part of the cause of that inability. In our efforts to preserve the primacy of the family in child rearing, we may be undermining its ability to perform that function.

There are some general principles to be kept in mind when proposing ways and means of integrating new and traditional forms of child care for the 21st century:

- Children of all ages are raised by families, not by schools and not by formal and informal caregivers who assist families. Thus we should not think of child care as a substitute for parental child rearing, but as a supplement. Children of the next century, like those of all ages past, will be their parents' primary responsibility and concern.

- Child care should not be confused with intervention programs, such as Head Start, the primary goal of which is to enrich environments made inadequate because of economic status. Although child care environments for low- and middle-income children alike should meet the minimum requirements of the environmental threshold, child care alone cannot be expected to make up for inadequacies in the rest of children s worlds.

- Although it is the case that families, not institutions, raise children, they never do so in a vacuum. The society's formal and informal institutions—including the family—are subject to the ebb and flow of social change.

- What happens in the economy affects the lives of children and families; what happens in the lives of children and families eventually affects the economy. Productive families feed the economy as much as they are fed by it. In an age when we are fearful that the United States is losing ground as an economic power and technological leader, we would be wise to keep this in mind.

- What becomes of our children in the long run will determine the society of the future. We have reasons other than altruistic ones for insuring the future of today's children, the adults of the 21st century.

- There are no magic ages of childhood. Although a good start in infancy is absolutely essential to the developing child, so is adequate care at each stage through adolescence. Environmental supports for each stage vary in detail, but not in importance.

- In spite of the increased knowledge we will have about the details of child development, the children of the next century will develop in approximately the same way as do the children of today. Babies are not any more intelligent than they were because we now know they begin to learn at birth. A seven-year-old is no more or less capable of supervising a younger child alone than were those in the early 1900s. Despite the coming of "toys that teach" and computer games, children are not suddenly going to be able to survive on their own without adequate adult care and attention.

- Because children will remain the same, we can accurately predict what the needs of the child of the 21st century will be. What is more difficult to predict is the means society will employ to meet those needs.

If we accept as a society that the family has the primary responsibility for child rearing, it follows that it is of the utmost importance for all families to be as strong and as capable as possible. Whether the family poised at the brink of the 21st century is actually strong enough to live up to its responsibilities or whether it is deteriorating to the point where it can no longer serve its essential function of raising children seems to be a matter of political rhetoric rather than of actual fact. The facts themselves, including the high divorce rates in recent years, the separation of the nuclear family from its multigenerational extended family of the past, and the increase in mothers working outside the home might suggest a weakening of the family. Yet our personal belief is that families are strong and adaptable; otherwise, they would not continue to form and survive as they have.

The question in relation to child care is not whether or not families can continue to exist, or even whether or not they should continue to have primary responsibility for raising their children. Of course they should. The question is, how can we make the mixed system of child care in the United States an effective social institution that supports families in their responsibilities?

Today it is safe to say that the child care system has become a social institution, but only by default. As will be shown in the next chapter, the institution is fragmented and disorganized because it developed without our awareness that it was developing. In the 21st century, perhaps we will plan for the total environments of all our children as we have planned for their partial environment in the public school.

This does not mean we will be institutionalizing child care in the sense that it will be required for all children. Parents who can arrange to stay home with their children will never be obligated to use the system. But the system is now the reality for the children of at least two-thirds of American families. Whether it is a viable and helpful one or a weak and problematic one does not depend on our rhetoric about child care and the proper role of the government in the family. It depends upon our willingness to shape and adapt the institution to the real needs of children and their families, just as we have shaped and adapted the American public school.

2

◆ ◆

Where Is the Child
in Child Care?

At various times during our nation's history, child care outside the home has been seen as an aid to the economy, as part of the war effort, and as a means of advancing family social or financial status. Child care systems have been instituted to reduce the number of children cared for in crowded orphanages, to integrate immigrants into American society, and to save on welfare payments to single mothers. Child care has been treated sometimes as a women's issue, sometimes as a social welfare issue and, depending upon prevalent trends in political and popular thought, as an issue related to "traditional" versus "new" family values and as pro- or anti-democratic. For some, child care is regarded as a potentially profitable consumer market. Of late it is coming to be viewed as a way to help the private sector become more productive by enabling mothers to enter the work force. Most of these disparate approaches to dealing with the child care "problem" have one thing in common. They focus primarily on the effects of child care on adult society in America and only secondarily on the environment of the child.

Although we pointed out in Chapter 1 that child care does affect the whole society, both in the long and the short term, a shift in focus toward the needs of children and of the families who raise them is necessary in an era when so many children, at increasingly younger ages, experience care by people other than their parents for large portions of their waking hours. For, as ungainly and unworkable as it is now, the supplementary child care system has become a permanent one and an integral part of the daily environment in which we raise American children. Children are the ones who stand to lose or gain the most by how we shape this service. As a society, we have refused to establish control over this hodgepodge institution partly because of our attitudes about children and child rearing and partly because the system has developed mainly as a response to the prevailing currents of social reform and society's economic needs rather than to the timeless needs of children.

A BRIEF HISTORY

Two threads entwine in the development of the supplementary child care system in America: the history of the purposes of child care services and changing philosophies of education. These histories did not develop independently, yet we need to examine them separately in order to understand current practices and policies for the care of children whose parents cannot be at home for them all day long. Of course, the reasons that families needed assistance with child care, and the various forms that that assistance took, did not follow an orderly chronological progression, just as the educational system did not develop in clearly demarcated stages. Social change is a gradual process, so there is considerable overlap in the time line of the events chronicled here.

During the 17th and 18th centuries, parents rarely had sole responsibility for their children. Arlene Skolnick points out that our romantic notions of a multigenerational family in which grandparents were always on hand to assist with child care is not completely accurate, because the life expectancy of adults was much shorter in the 1600s and 1700s than it is today.[22] Yet parents in early America were generally assisted by large extended families, most of whose members worked and lived in or close to the family home. If both parents had to be away, there were adult relatives and older siblings or cousins to watch the young children.

During the 19th century, the Industrial Revolution, internal migration, and the flow of immigrants into the United States began a process of change for many families. Young pioneers and immigrants often moved into a new territory or a new city where job opportunities existed, leaving relatives behind. Because family units became smaller and were no longer self-sufficient, the labors of both parents and older children were needed to secure the basic necessities. In cities in particular, emerging industries required more and more laborers and long working hours to meet production needs. Mothers who needed the income but had no one to watch their children could not take these jobs; both families and employers suffered. Some mothers had no choice but to leave children by themselves so they could work to provide for them.

One response to the problems of undernourished and unattended children came from the charitable and social reform movements of the 19th century.

In some locations part of the solution came in the form of infant schools, where education and daytime care were provided to young children from poor families. These schools were based on the popular European models of Johann Pestalozzi and Robert Owen. Pestalozzi was a Swiss-born educator who believed that education held the "power for regeneration of society."[24] He founded several schools to help young beggar children lead better lives, with limited success. His theories of education and teacher training, however, were embraced by educators from around the world. In Great Britain, where rapid industrialization had forced many mothers to work outside the home and left them little time to care for and teach their children, reformers established at least 55 infant schools similar to Pestalozzi's in just one year.[6] Owen was instrumental in founding the British infant school movement. As manager and part owner of a cotton mill in Scotland, he had opened an infant school for the workers' children around the turn of the century. This school was part of his utopian vision to create a new social order by bringing education to all classes, but he acknowledged that the school served the additional purpose of freeing mothers and older children from child care responsibilities so they could join fathers in work at the mill.[6]

A group of evangelical women brought the concept of early childhood education to America in 1828 with the opening of the Boston Infant School—believed to be the first day care center in the nation.[15] The school accepted children from eighteen months of age to about four years old. As many as four additional schools were soon opened in the Boston area, and similar efforts were mounted in cities such as New York and Philadelphia.[6] The purpose of the infant schools was not only to provide child care to enable poor mothers to seek employment or to protect the children of those already working. Their religious founders designed the schools to provide "moral education" to poor children. We should note that during the early 19th century, poverty was not considered so much an economic problem as a moral one. There was fear among the deeply religious that, lacking financial and ethical resources, poor people would easily succumb to temptations and vice. The main objective of infant schools was to offer training in religion, morality, and character building. This instruction was seen as a foundation which would enable children to escape from poverty when they grew older. Further, it was hoped that the children would introduce this training into their homes and thus redeem their families. The schools were in session long hours to allow parents to work harder toward improving their lives.

Infant schools had a very short life in America. By the early 1830s some educators were questioning the value of education for the very young. One asylum director, Amariah Brigham, went so far as to proclaim that the effect of too early learning "is nearly always disease," both physical and mental.[3] At about the same time, there was a revival of the traditional belief that small children—even poor ones—are best nurtured and taught by their mothers at home.[6] This may be one reason why the entrance age for primary schools—just being established in New York City and other northern areas—was placed at four or five years of age. Donations to the infant schools diminished, as did the vision that poor young children could be guided toward a successful life through a comprehensive child care program.

The infant school movement highlights many issues that have repeatedly emerged in our nation's efforts on behalf of young children. First, these schools were founded to provide *both* care and education—not one or the other. Second, they show the longevity of beliefs that education can be a tool of social reform.[6] The fact that they were started for families in poverty, however, represents the seed of the two-tiered system of child care that continues to flourish today.

Poverty, of course, did not cease along with the infant schools. Some mothers still had to work and their children still needed care. Those who could not enlist the help of a neighbor or afford to pay someone to watch their children had little choice but to leave them alone. Many such "abandoned" children were placed in orphan homes, either permanently or temporarily. Although most orphanages were run by charitable groups, some mothers paid "baby farms" to take their children until adoptive homes could be found. These for-profit agencies operated in New York City from the mid-1800s to as late as 1910, in spite of public outcry against them. The infant mortality rate in orphanages or foundling asylums was sometimes as high as 85–90%; the rate must have been at least as high, if not higher, in the baby farms.[26]

It was a profitable business for the baby farmer, however. Mothers were charged a "surrender fee"—$50 in New York, for example—and potential adoptive parents could have one of the few surviving infants for as little as 25 cents. Although poor mothers were often suspected of sending their infants to baby farms as a form of de facto infanticide, an 1880 editorial in the *New York Times* recognized that some of the women who did so were "poor widows who desire to go out . . . to do . . . housework, where they find it very inconvenient to be incumbered by very young children."[17]

One way that society provided child care, then, was by taking children away from their parents. The specter of the orphanage or baby farm, where many died of disease, malnutrition, or lack of love—what we now know as "failure to thrive syndrome"—is one that disturbed the reformers then. This old specter of institutional care is still invoked to haunt many discussions of supplemental child care today.

One solution was to have the mothers stay with their infants in the foundling home at night and go out to work by day. In 1871, for example, the New York Infant Asylum changed its practice of taking in foundlings only. By accepting the babies' mothers as well whenever possible, they reduced infant mortality from 80% to 18%.[14] During the same period, an alternate solution based on the French creche—or day nursery— was brought to America. Unlike the infant schools, which sought to redeem poor children through proper care and education, day nurseries were more directly meant to provide daytime care for children while their mothers worked. (The first creche was founded near Paris so mothers could labor in factories but be close enough to their infants to nurse them.)[6] A day nursery opened in New York City in 1854, and charitable agencies quickly moved to establish more. The number of nurseries soared in the 1880s and 1890s as European immigrants and rural Americans flocked to industrial centers.[15]

The philosophy of day nursery care was basically hygienic—children would be fed, kept clean, and protected from injury for as long as 12 to 14 hours a day while their mothers worked. The facilities organized into the National Federation of Day Nurseries in 1898 in an attempt to promote high standards, but the quality of care remained variable. And, just as in the 1980s, the need far exceeded the supply. Overcrowding resulted, so many of the nurseries could offer care that was little more than custodial. Nonetheless, the existence of the nurseries at least prevented the children of widows and other women who had to work from being taken away from their families.

Although the primary goal of the day nurseries was physical care of the child, their secondary purpose was to alleviate poverty through self-help. Mothers who were freed of child care responsibilities could become self-supporting and less dependent on charity. Most of the nurseries provided parent education in skills such as homemaking and child care and also helped with job placement.[15] Although a few offered education and health care for the child, most existed for the benefit of the mother. Ironically, concern for the mother eventually led to the end of the day nursery. Worries about the poor unskilled woman, toiling endlessly at work and at home, sparked efforts to allow mothers to remain at home. Around 1911, mothers' pensions (the precursor of Aid to Families with Dependent Children, or AFDC) were provided to pay women to care for their own children. The pensions were minimal, and few families received them, but by then day nurseries were losing popularity. Although the nurseries had been started as a means of keeping families intact, they were now viewed as a threat to the family unit since they allowed for the separation of mothers and children.[6]

One influence in the decline of day nurseries early in the 20th century came from the growing profession of social work. Social work, long the domain of religious women, philanthropists, and volunteers, was becoming a discipline for educated and trained professionals. This new field was influenced to some degree by psychiatry, and some social work students were taught clinical casework methods. This training did much to change the idea that poverty was a problem inherent in the structure of society, thus deserving of societal solutions, to the idea that poverty was the fault of the individual. Some social workers were trained in the philosophy that the poor needed assistance to achieve the mainstream lifestyle—one in which the mother tended the children at home and the father provided for them. Child care should not be a permanent remedy, but a temporary, emergency measure to be used only until the family was on its feet. Only the "worthy" poor—those ready, willing, and able to work—were to be served. Screening was designed so that "lazy" fathers could not use the facilities to avoid their parental responsibilities. The fear among social workers and laypeople alike was that the poor would become overly dependent on social assistance and would fail to achieve independence.

The day nursery set the tone for attitudes about child care that linger today. As Emily Cahan has aptly noted, the original day nursery was an early form of social welfare, so the history of child care is tied to the welfare system more than to the education system.[6] The later involvement of newly trained social workers bolstered the stigma associated with child care. Judgments about the worthy and unworthy poor, and the view of nursery care as an emergency intervention, began the formulation of child care as a poverty issue.

Of course, throughout the 19th and into the 20th century, poor families were the only ones who desperately needed assistance with child care. More affluent mothers rarely worked, and if they did they bought or hired nannies to oversee their children. Women who were widowed, abandoned by fathers, or whose husbands were ill or not very good workers had to depend on themselves to support their families. Many could not depend on the availability of child care services, however, because even at their height infant schools and day nurseries were not that widely available in America. The majority of these facilities were located in and around large cities and were never numerous enough to serve all those in need. European countries, where these programs originated, were already working to institute national child care systems to insure universal accessibility (see Chapter 5), but in this country many poor children were left to wander the streets and suffer the consequences of lack of supervision. Distressed reformers frequently reported on the alarming number of children, including toddlers, who were unattended during the workday, and called for action to stem the increasing rates of accidental injury and death among them. Noting that "with disquieting frequency children are ground up under street cars," a 1904 New York Times editorial suggested that motormen, drivers, and chauffeurs receive stiff penalties for killing or maiming a child.[18] Yet most newspaper accounts of the period blamed children themselves for their reckless behavior, or they blamed mothers for not being able to do the impossible—work and attend to their children at the same time.

Child care was generally viewed as a poverty problem and a mothers' problem until the Great Depression, when the federal Works Progress Administration (WPA) funded centers for needy children of unemployed workers. The goal was not to provide child care while parents worked, as many parents had work infrequently. Instead, the WPA centers were designed to create jobs for unemployed people, especially schoolteachers laid off by budget cuts. The emphasis was on meeting basic health and nutritional needs, but it is likely that the educators who worked in the centers offered instruction and general emotional support as well. Still, it is portentous that our government's first financial commitment to supplementary child care was not really to serve children, or their parents for that matter, but to get the unemployed off the welfare rolls.

As American involvement in World War II approached, unemployment declined and the WPA centers were about to be dismantled. However, once we were at war the situation became similar to that at the height of the Industrial Revolution. Mothers were again needed in the work place. Their labor was essential in the war effort to fill jobs abandoned by men who were called into military service. All segments of society were called upon to make changes in their daily routines and lifestyles, such as limiting automobile travel, restricting the consumption of certain foods through food rationing, and doing without new appliances, rubber goods, and other consumer products whose raw materials were needed for war supplies.

Again, children were affected by the needs of adult society. Many had to cope with an absent father; and with their mothers going away to work each day, life at home was not at all as it previously had been. At the beginning of World War II, there was little formal child care available, and the neighbor or relative who used to watch the child on occasion was likely to be at work herself. Consequently, many children, like their predecessors of the Industrial Revolution days, were left unsupervised at home or in cars outside the factories where their mothers worked. By this time, Americans had a much lower tolerance for this sort of thing. In 1942 legislation was hastily enacted to continue and expand the WPA child care operations in areas close to war industries. When the entire WPA program ceased, funding for the nurseries was continued by the Federal Works Agency (FWA) under the Lanham Act (which established many social programs during the war). Soon 1,150 of the original WPA nurseries were being supported by Lanham appropriations, although the other 550 were permanently closed since they were not in war-impacted areas.[8]

Faced with pleas for more child care programs, the FWA began to grant Lanham funds to local communities, which could then meet the need for child care for women employed in defense plants. According to James Hymes, Jr., president of the National Association for the Education of Young Children shortly after the war, the vast majority of the Lanham centers were located in public school buildings; thus funds were only required for caregivers and for materials, not for expensive construction projects. The communities had to provide half the operating costs, however, and faced the bureaucratic nightmare of having their applications reviewed by seven different agencies. These logistical difficulties, and the persistent attitude that young children should be cared for by their mothers at home, may explain why the war need for child care went largely unmet. At the most, federal funds helped support about 3,100 centers serving approximately 140,000 preschool and school-age children, although officials estimated that federal assistance was needed for the care of one million children.[6,8]

President Roosevelt helped a little by allocating $400,000 to help communities set up child care facilities. The fact that no operating funds were provided reflects our government's continual ambivalence toward becoming involved in child care.[6] Indeed, throughout the war the FWA was constantly threatened with termination of funding. To escape this confusion, some private businesses used their own and non-FWA federal funds to set up on-site care for children of employees. For example, the Kaiser Shipyards in Portland, Oregon used money from the U.S. Maritime Commission to operate their own child care centers. In addition, they offered health care services and prepared meals to be carried home by mothers too busy and tired to cook after working long shifts.

Our government's involvement in child care was not without its critics. At the beginning of the war, agencies as diverse as the Children's Bureau, the Labor Department, and the War Manpower Commission all recommended that mothers of young children should remain at home. Later, a group of social welfare departments which included the Children's Bureau and Office of Education attempted to gain control of the child care program, arguing that the FWA knew nothing about the needs of children. The agency's primary concern was to reduce the labor shortage in wartime industries, and it supported child care only because it would enable mothers to work. These efforts to move the service to agencies traditionally involved with children failed, and responsibility for child care remained with the FWA.

It must be remembered, as Gilbert Steiner states in *The Children's Cause*, that child care was a "win-the-war program, not a save-the-child program."[23] A child care system was established only because parents' efforts were diverted to serve a nation in crisis. The day care center all but disappeared when the troops came back home and "Rosie the Riveter"—and Rosie's mother—returned to private life. There was a widespread belief—or yearning—that the "good old days," when mothers stayed at home with children and fathers were the breadwinners, would return. The truth, however, is that all mothers did not leave work in the post war years. Shortly after the end of the war over 4 million women did leave their jobs, but some 16 million remained—over 2 million more than were working before the war.[8] By 1950, there were three times as many mothers working outside the home as there were in the prewar years.[15] The number of employed mothers steadily increased over the next decade, much faster than the number of child care facilities.

A few cities continued their Lanham Act centers for a brief period after the war. In addition, a very few of the older day nurseries, such as the Leila Day Nursery in New Haven, Connecticut, have remained continually in operation. A notable exception is California, where the Lanham centers were continued by the state to enable women to serve in the area's growing economy. Had the system of child care established during the war remained in place, the nation would now have a formal child care institution advantaged by decades of cultivation and experience. (Indeed, California "was and remains the lead state in its responses . . . to the need for child care provision."[12]) Yet by the mid-1960s, most communities did not even have full-day programs. As long as the majority of mothers (75% in 1965) of preschool children did not work outside the home, community pressure did not mobilize for child care services, and whatever arrangements were already in place were considered adequate.

The winds of change were already blowing, however. During the late 1960s, the fledgling feminist movement argued that mothers, regardless of economic status, had both the right to work and the right to child care. This argument began to shift child care gradually out of the ranks of poverty issues and into the ranks of women's issues, positions it simultaneously occupied throughout the 1970s.

Despite popular perceptions that feminists were responsible for sending women out of the home and into the work place, the real growth in need for supplementary child care was not among welfare mothers, who were being subsidized to stay home, nor among educated and professional women, who justly demanded the right to compete in the work place on an equal footing with men. The main demand for child care came from those women who simply needed income. By 1978, 30% of working families with children consisted of two wage earners who, if the mother had not worked, would have had incomes in the poverty range. Also in that year, 25% of working families were supported by a single parent who had no other source of income.[25] Through the 1980s, the increase in the number of women in the out-of-home work force continued unabated. The rise was particularly steep among mothers of young children. By 1987, the Bureau of Labor Statistics reported that over 53% of mothers of children under age six held outside jobs.[4]

Child care services grew quickly but irregularly in an attempt to meet the growing need. That the system now in place remains inadequate is partly a result of the haphazard history of child care, initiated by various elements of society at various times for various purposes. The government's tendency to avoid child care altogether, except in times of national emergency, has proven to be a practiced habit. The current hodgepodge of formal and informal arrangements, described in Chapter 1, is a result of the lack of a unified commitment to the care of young children. At the end of the 20th century, the range of services available is based on the three types of care developed to serve American children during the first half of the century: the neighbor or relative, the day nursery, and, as we will now discuss, the nursery school.

EDUCATION: THE FAVORED SYSTEM

Concern with providing schooling for all children began the day the colonists arrived in the new land called America. They feared their religious traditions would die in the isolation of the new world unless their descendants were educated to carry them on. By the time the U.S. Constitution was signed, several states already had free public schools, and the call for universal schooling throughout the new nation began in earnest. If we were to have government by the people, all the people had to be educated. Schooling was no longer a private luxury but a public necessity if the United States of America was to realize the aspirations of its settlers. Between 1776 and the Civil War, great debates were heard in every state and township over the need for universal education, who should pay for it, who should control it, and what should be taught. Despite the controversy, "Americans during those years forged one of the most revolutionary educational developments of modern times—their public school system."[5]

The development of educational programs for younger children, however, was not characterized by the same zeal for universality. As mentioned earlier in this chapter, when infant schools began in America their purpose was to educate and care for poor children. These benefits did not go unnoticed by wealthier families, who founded their own infant schools in scattered areas. Such schools were meant to provide enrichment for the child rather than to reform the family. The activities were designed to prepare children for formal schooling and to enhance their social skills.[6] Private infant schools were not very numerous, because the ethic at the time was that a mother's devoted care was the best nurturance for a growing child.

Middle- and upper-class preschoolers did not leave mother's side until the 1920s and 1930s, when child study institutes were founded in several universities. They needed children as subjects for their research as well as to train future teachers, so they began nursery schools which were soon filled by the children of the psychologists and educators who worked there. College-educated mothers also sought to enroll their children. The nursery schools were child-centered, offering varied educational and social experiences to supplement the child's home rearing.[6] Recall that at this time poor children were being cared for in crowded day nurseries where untrained women fed them and tried to keep them from harm but had no time to teach them the alphabet.

What can be seen in the first days of the nursery school, as was apparent a century before in the infant school movement and even earlier in the push for universal public schooling, was a growing recognition that children have developmental (including educational) needs separate from those of adult society. Until the middle of the 17th century, childhood was considered over when a child started school; now childhood was seen as a time of special needs that lasted throughout the years of schooling.[1] From the age of five or six, all children needed education in addition to that which their parents could provide. Even ten- and twelve-year-olds did not belong in factories; they belonged in school, where they would learn to be fully participating citizens of the democracy. This long-term goal was often in conflict with the immediate needs of adults, who relied on children's labor.

Debates about restricting the minimum age and maximum hours children could be employed were so intense that they led to the first federal child labor law being declared unconstitutional in 1918, two years after it was passed. Children's advocates, educators, labor unions, employers, and politicians argued over the type of jobs children should be allowed to perform, but they eventually agreed that work should not interfere with school attendance. The Fair Labor Standards Act of 1938 stipulated that children could work at most types of employment at age 16, but 14- and 15-year-olds could not be employed during school hours. Compulsory school attendance statutes also forced employers and parents who were not convinced to conform to what society believed to be the proper place for children in America.

The conflict between the needs of the school-age child and those of the adult society seemed settled by the 1940s; however, it will be seen in Chapter 6 (school-age child care), that it was a rather uneasy truce. As a nation, we had yet to come to terms with the educational and developmental needs of infants and young children, except when emergency conditions like those resulting from the Depression and war existed. A gap began to develop between our concept of what a school-age child is entitled to, no matter what the prevailing social conditions, and what a preschooler, infant, or toddler is entitled to. The sense that the needs of these two groups were somehow different resulted in their artificial segregation into two systems: one highly organized and socially supported system to oversee the development of those of school age; and one highly scattered, poorly funded system that was hastily assembled in emergencies and dismantled as hastily when adults deemed the emergency was over or changed their minds about its resolution.

No one really knows why "school age" came to be defined as the sixth or seventh year of life. One reason may stem from the religious goals of education in colonial times. To many, education meant study of the Bible and principles of morality, lessons which could benefit only those who could read. Later, advocates of free public schooling argued that the ability to read, write, and "cipher" were the minimum requirements for making informed political decisions. Since most children become ready to read and develop the fine motor coordination needed to write at about the age of six or seven, instruction in these skills would be of little value before this. The first kindergartens did serve children younger than five, and Boston's public schools admitted toddlers as young as 22 months,[15] but these programs did not follow traditional educational curriculums. Young children were generally considered unformed, incapable of intellectual, religious, and moral learning as it was historically understood. Only when children attained the age of reason did they need to be educated for adult society by adult society.

Such views about the educational limits of young children should have eroded earlier in this century, when we felt the influence of Piaget and others who actually studied the development of the child before formal school age. It was discovered that children do not suddenly attain the age of reason and intellectual capability; instead, they develop in all areas, including the intellectual, socioemotional, and physical, by degrees or stages. It is easy to forget what a shocking revelation it was that the groundwork for education is laid long before the age of reason. By now we are aware that infants are born as organisms capable of responding to the environment—that is to say, learning—from the first day of life.

Tremendous energy has now been directed to researching the care and development of the child from birth through preschool. Much public information has been distributed by physicians, child psychologists, and various "experts" about the importance of early experiences in a child's life. A new set of ages has been nominated for the "magic years"—those from zero to three or zero to five—when the child's personality and intellect are supposedly shaped. This has had great impact on the practices of child rearing within middle- and upper-class American families, but it has had little impact on our views of society's role and responsibility in child care and less on the public schools. No matter how important these new magic years are, they are still considered of interest primarily to the families that raise children, not to the remainder of the society.

Until the early 1960s, then, the first five years of life were basically ignored in planning for the public education of children. By this time, most public school districts did offer kindergarten for five-year-olds, but attendance was (and in most places remains) optional. Private nursery schools proliferated, however, and became the educational mainstay of children from middle-class and wealthy families. Educators began to observe that children entered public school with a wide variety of educational experiences. While some had attended nursery school for a year or even two, others lacked any preparation that could support their academic growth in the public school. The latter children, usually from low-income families, were considered "deprived" in the language of the War on Poverty years. Project Head Start was conceived to give them literally a head start on their education. The program was designed to aid in all the aspects—physical, socioemotional, and cognitive—that had begun to be recognized as critical in the growth of the young child. The idea was that each child could be given assistance and experiences that would insure an equal chance at success in grade school and beyond.

The high hopes that people placed in the Head Start program echoed those of the social reformers who planned the infant schools. Early enrichment would lay the foundation for successful schooling, which would allow children to rise out of poverty in their adult years. President Johnson, in a ceremony announcing Head Start's first summer programs in 1965, proclaimed, "30 million man-years—the combined lifespan of these youngsters—will be spent productively and rewardingly, rather than wasted in tax-supported institutions or in welfare-supported lethargy."[11] Also reminiscent of the infant schools was Head Start's commitment to the total child—it offered health care and nutrition in addition to social learning and educational experiences. Both settings thus provided care *and* education as equal partners. Another parallel is that both preschools attempted to reach the family, although from different directions. The 19th century version hoped that children could reform their families, while Head Start believed that parental participation in the school program could help families help their children at home.

Government support of a preschool program was indeed a milestone in the history of education. Although the educational needs of older children had been acknowledged since the beginning of universal schooling, the needs of their younger siblings were seen as the province of the family. Governmental assistance was not deemed appropriate until the child had lived for six or seven years. Then the nation noticed that the family sometimes failed. Head Start, like the infant school before it, was designed to bring the influence and experience of society to bear on the growth and education of the young child only when we perceived that not all families had adequate resources to support that growth and education.

GOVERNMENT TESTS THE CHILD CARE WATERS

In the last two decades, there have been three major developments in the history of American child care. These developments show the increasing politicization of the issue, a politicization that has much to do with our traditional attitudes toward society's role (or nonrole) in child rearing.

Toward a National Policy

The first of these historic milestones was the Comprehensive Child Development Act of 1971, crafted by Congressman John Brademas and Senator Walter Mondale. Work on the bill actually began in the late 1960s, after the apparent success of the Head Start program led to its enthusiastic acceptance by the American public. Soon there was a desire to expand such efforts to more and to younger children. After months of study and expert testimony, legislators recognized that all preschool children needed atmospheres that enhanced cognitive, physical, and socioemotional growth. About this time the 1970 White House Conference on Children identified child care as one of the major problems facing the American family. Brademas and Mondale turned this insight into foresight and decided to deal with the current and anticipated need for child care. Thus, the provisions of the Comprehensive Child Development Act included $700 million for federal funding of high-quality child care for welfare recipients and $50 million for the creation of new child care facilities. The bill also extended child care services to single parents and working families on a sliding fee scale.

The type of care called for is suggested by the title of the Act. It was to be comprehensive care addressing all of the child's developmental needs. There were to be educational enrichment efforts, health and nutrition programs, and parental involvement and outreach. In other words, quality child care was defined as Head Start-like services. In fact, existing Head Start centers were to be folded into the new network of child care centers. Grants for the programs were to be distributed to local communities, and control was to be essentially at the local level (operating within federal guidelines).

In the meantime, the White House was diligently engaged in an unrelated effort to reduce the welfare rolls by placing recipients into training and employment programs. This massive effort, titled the Family Assistance Plan (FAP), was introduced in 1971 by President Nixon. The architect of the plan was Patrick Moynihan, then Domestic Counselor to the President (and later author of the 1988 Welfare Reform Plan). A major obstacle to getting welfare mothers to work was the lack of affordable child care. Hence the plan earmarked $750 million in the first year for child care services. A logistical problem was how to apply this money—should the government build its own facilities, subsidize existing ones, or directly pay providers of care? When the administration realized that Congress was mandating a network of child care centers through its Child Development Act, it found a ready-made solution to this problem. Combined, the child care funds from the two plans would have created a national institution providing quality care to young children.

Representatives of the Nixon administration thus generally endorsed the 1971 bill, because they needed the proposed centers to provide child care under FAP. They did argue that the very large number of grantees would be unwieldly, and suggested that fewer, larger geographic areas be used for purposes of grant making. There were few other points of disagreement. Congress never compromised on these differences, because lawmakers felt the bill was so popular its passage was assured. An election year was approaching, and they knew they would be making American voters happy: families would be getting the child care services they needed, and middle-class children would be given access to desirable Head Start services. They would also be making their president happy, because he saw the Act as a necessary vehicle to institute FAP. The Nixon administration's basically positive stance proved valuable in getting the bill passed.

The nation then witnessed a surprising turn of events. As the Act made its way through Congress, a few social elements had appeared offended by the notion that middle-class children needed comprehensive services: their parents did a good job of providing for them, and only poor families needed help raising their children. Then right-wing activists from the John Birch Society to fundamentalist church groups formed a coalition and sent thousands of letters claiming that the Comprehensive Child Development Act represented a large-scale "invasion of the family" on the part of the federal government. President Nixon, in a surprise veto message, quoted from the letters and op-ed pieces that opposed the bill. Among other things, he said that the bill was "the most radical piece of legislation to emerge from the 92nd Congress" and that it entailed committing "the vast authority of the federal government to the side of communal approaches to child rearing over against the family-centered approach."[19] There has been much speculation as to why Nixon vetoed this popular bill that he had basically supported. His veto statement shows that he heard the complaints from the right wing, although they were clearly the vocal minority. Perhaps the main reason is that by this time Moynihan had left the White House, and Nixon simply lost interest in FAP. If there was to be no FAP, there was no need for an expensive child care network.

The real sadness in the defeat of the Comprehensive Child Development Act was in the shrill tone of the veto message. Communal living and communist precepts were in no way suggested by the various services included in the Act. The bill merely represented a formal recognition on the part of Congress that children in the United States were being raised in an environment that increasingly included supplementary child care. Nor was there any way that families would be forced to use the national child care system, as the coalition charged. Families who were not poor could choose to use the system by paying for it, a fact that insured enrollment would be voluntary. Thus the bill is more accurately seen as Congress's response to already existing problems of child care in the United States, rather than as an attempt to intervene in the family's decisions about raising children.

Once the Child Development Act was defeated, child care bills became something of an albatross in Washington. Legislators would not risk introducing them for fear of the backlash of mail from conservatives they knew would inundate their offices. The election of Jimmy Carter not only brought a Democratic president to the White House, it brought his Vice President Walter Mondale—an author of the Act—back into the limelight. Senator Alan Cranston, concerned that the nation had made no progress on what had been called the family's number one problem nearly 10 years earlier, was encouraged to introduce the Child Care Act of 1979. The bill was similar to but greatly scaled down from its predecessor. Mondale graciously kept his distance for fear his support would rekindle the ire of the 1971 opponents. This time, however, there was another fatal surprise. The Cranston bill met defeat after testimony of an administrator *within* the Carter administration. Arabella Martinez, an assistant secretary in the Department of Health, Education and Welfare (DHEW), told Congress that not all working families needed or supported center-based child care provided by the government. Many preferred their own informal arrangements. This statement flew in the face of much expert testimony that communities were crying out for help in funding child care, and was contrary to Carter's own campaign promises to help. (According to Stuart Eizenstat, White House Domestic Advisor, the White House was just as surprised as Congress by Martinez's statement. Apparently there was so much disagreement between liberals and conservatives within DHEW on the need and cost for child care that the normal process for preparing testimony was not followed and the statement was never given presidential review.) In disbelief that Martinez really represented the views of the administration, a stunned Cranston withdrew the bill.

Carter attempted to make amends by supporting standards of quality in child care environments. As early as 1968, the Office of Child Development (OCD) had attempted to regulate in some way the care provided in child care facilities serving families enrolled in federally sponsored programs. The resulting Federal Interagency Day Care Requirements (FIDCR) seemed to require comprehensive services like those of Head Start, but they were not at all specific. As such, they were open to varied interpretations and defied monitoring. In 1971, OCD began to turn this rhetoric into more exacting standards for factors such as staff-child ratios and caregiver training. In 1972, when the Comprehensive Child Development Act called for standards for all federal programs providing child development services, the revised FIDCR almost found a home. The Nixon veto of the Act withdrew the invitation, although many in Congress and the administration were still concerned with regulating quality at least in those facilities receiving federal money.

By 1980 a new version of the FIDCR had been drawn up by the Department of Health and Human Services (DHHS, formerly DHEW), after considerable consultation with child development experts. The new standards were essentially the same as those proposed in 1972, which speaks to their inherent soundness. With the support of Eizenstat, Secretary of DHHS Patricia Harris accepted these 1980 standards and sent them to Congress. Although they did not affect the host of private for-profit and nonprofit child care arrangements paid for entirely out of parent earnings, resistance from the states led Congress to suspend implementation of the standards temporarily. At the request of the Reagan administration, they were permanently eliminated by Public Law 97–35 in 1981. The standards do remain in the *Federal Register* of 1980 as an example of minimum quality required for healthy environments for children—fire and safety regulations, meals that are nutritionally sound, staff trained to work with children and sufficient in number to meet their basic needs.[9] (A more detailed discussion of issues of quality control of child care environments will be found in Chapter 3.)

All remained relatively quiet on the child care policy front throughout most of the 1980s. However, there were hushed anxieties and distant rumblings which would explode into a nationwide clamor by the end of the decade. Followers of New Right activists Phyllis Schlafly and Jerry Falwell were still preaching that the mother's proper place is at home, but there were few mothers at home to hear them. Families, still recovering from the inflation of the 1970s, had found a second income to be a necessity. Young children were being cared for here, there, and everywhere. Some were receiving excellent care and others were experiencing horrendous care; many were receiving no care at all. The problems of affordability, availability, and quality continued to grow unabated.

Federal Financial Contributions

The government's role in child care did not expand in proportion to the growing need but in fact declined in some ways during the 1980s. Federal child care subsidies take two major forms: the Child and Dependent Care Tax Credit and the Title XX Social Services Block Grant. (A third and smaller program, the Dependent Care Assistance Plan, which enables parents to deduct child care expenses from their taxable income through their employers, will be discussed in Chapter 8.) The tax credit allows parents to deduct a percentage of child care costs from their federal tax liability. Currently the maximum credit is from $480 to $720 for one child and $960 to $1,440 for two or more children, with the higher amounts available to families with lower incomes. Prior to 1983, only taxpayers who itemized deductions could claim the credit—meaning that higher wage earners benefited the most. Reform achieved in 1983 allowed families filing short tax forms to use the credit, which helped lower- and middle-class families to some extent. Between 1982 and 1983, the amount of credits claimed on tax returns rose 37%.[10] By fiscal year 1988, expenditures for the credit were more than $3.9 billion.[15] Although this amount includes care for dependents other than children, the tax credit remains the federal government's largest commitment to direct child care assistance.

Despite expansion of the tax credit in the 1980s, it represents a minimal benefit to many American families struggling with the high costs of child care. The credit applies only to the first $2,400 spent on care each year ($4,800 for two or more children). This ceiling is far too low to cover the actual costs in some areas of the country and does not address the fact that fees vary according to the age of the child. Another problem is that a tax credit once a year does little to help parents come up with the cash to pay their provider each week. Finally, poor families who have little or no tax liability cannot benefit from a tax credit. Plans to make the credit refundable have been proposed from time to time, but for now families of very low income who need help the most cannot obtain it through this method.

Although the tax credit was increased during the 1980s, the other source of federal support for child care—Title XX—was greatly diminished. Title XX, part of the Social Security Act that provides states with funds for a variety of social services, was cut 20% in 1982. By 1987, Title XX appropriations were still less than they had been a decade earlier, and inflation had eroded their purchasing power to half of what it had been.[7] Because states spend a portion of this money for child care services for poor families, nearly half had to reduce the number of children they could subsidize. State and local governments in some areas applied their own resources to help needy residents with child care expenses. In most cases, however, changes in the tax credit did not help poor families very much, and changes in Title XX appropriations hurt them.

Child Care Rediscovered

Policymakers' avoidance of child care problems came to an abrupt end in 1988, when more than 100 child care bills were introduced in Congress. If it can be said that demographics ultimately drive social policy, then one look at the demographics will explain this sudden onslaught. By this time over 60% of mothers held outside jobs, making families with working mothers the clear majority in America. With the divorce rate hovering around 50%, many of these working women were their children's sole source of support. In these healthy economic times, business leaders were complaining they were unable to keep up with increasing demands for services and goods because of a serious labor shortage. They needed to woo more mothers from home, a move hampered by the lack of suitable child care. In the meanwhile, children's advocates were worrying aloud about the effects of supplementary care and the need to insure quality in the child care environment.

Child care became such a big problem that representatives of the people could no longer fear or ignore it. Among the bills introduced in the 1987–88 session of Congress was the Act for Better Child Care (ABC bill), sponsored by Senator Christopher Dodd of Connecticut with nearly 200 co-sponsors in the House and Senate. The bill was created by an alliance of more than 100 education groups, child advocacy and welfare associations, labor unions, and others. In one of its developing forms, it called for $2.5 billion a year, most of which would help families pay for child care. Other provisions in various versions had to do with improving the quality of care by establishing minimum standards and upgrading the training and working conditions of caregivers. This ambitious bill even suggested an expanded bureaucracy with an assistant secretary of child care to oversee the expanded financial and physical system.

A much more modest bill was introduced by Senator Orrin Hatch of Utah. His $300 million plan would be used to improve the quality of family child care facilities without imposing federal standards. It would also provide incentives to businesses to help with employees' child care expenses, and assist caregivers with rising insurance premiums. Perhaps the most significant aspect of Hatch's "Child Care Services Improvement Act" was that it was sponsored by a conservative senator from a conservative state. Hatch's open concern about the problem of child care, a problem conservatives had successfully swept under the legislative rug in 1971, encouraged many more lawmakers to enter the arena carrying the colors of working mothers, their children, and caregivers.

The many other bills introduced that session addressed various aspects of child care, from increasing services in rural areas to placing responsibility for child care within the expertise of the established school system. Despite the varied menu, or perhaps because of it, no major child care legislation was passed by the time the 100th Congress adjourned. (It did enact the 1988 Welfare Reform Act, which contained a child care provision only because it required welfare recipients to seek training or employment when their children were age three instead of the previous age six. Here again, child care was treated as a means of reducing social assistance rather than providing it.) Nineteen eighty-eight was a presidential election year, and prolonged debate over each proposal brought lawmakers to the late hour when they perceived it best to wait and see who their new leader and co-workers would be. The stillness did not last long. Even before the new president, George Bush, took the oath of office, he suggested a plan to help poor families with the cost of buying or providing care for their children.

Child care issues again took center stage during the 101st Congress, which is in session as of this writing. Although a bill has not yet passed as of May, 1990, national child care legislation is close to becoming reality. In 1989 the Senate passed a modified version of the ABC bill. In an unprecedented complication, the House passed two separate bills from two separate committees—one from the Education and Labor Committee and the other from Ways and Means—indicating in effect that representatives were agreeing on their lack of agreement. In November, 1989, a Senate-House conference committee worked out a final version of the legislation known as the Hawkins/Dodd child care agreement (after Connecticut Senator Dodd and California Congressman Augustus Hawkins).

Lack of accord within the House again surfaced as the chamber considered the compromise. Problematic issues included whether federal funds should be funneled through state-appointed child care agencies, be given more generally through Title XX increases, or go directly to parents or programs. The old debates over who should regulate child care quality—and whether there should be federal standards—also divided House members. Another major and complex issue was whether or not child care programs sponsored by religious groups should receive federal subsidies. The church-state controversy is extremely significant. The National Council of Churches estimates that one-third of the nation's child care programs are affiliated with or run directly by religious groups.[13]

Finally, on March 29, 1990, the House passed H.R. 3—the Early Childhood Education and Development Act of 1990. The bill is quite similar to the Senate version, which bodes well for passage of landmark child care legislation in the near future. Both bills authorize $1.75 billion in federal funds to be allocated to the states to help parents pay for child care and to improve its quality and supply. A large share of this money would go to expand Head Start into a full-day, year-round program. Public schools would also receive funds for before- and after-school and preschool child care programs. States would receive assistance to improve child care standards and upgrade caregiver wages. Parents would receive vouchers to purchase child care of their choice, including that provided by religious groups whose programs are not sectarian. Discrepancies between the House and Senate bills involve how to channel the child care appropriation to the states and how to alter existing tax credits. The House version would phase out the Child and Dependent Care Tax Credit and Dependent Care Assistance Plan benefits for families with high earnings. Both versions would increase the Earned Income Tax Credit (although in different amounts) to provide low-income families with additional earnings and support to some extent mothers who stay at home with their children. Although the differences between the two bills are relatively minor and compromise should be achieved, whatever legislation is eventually passed by both chambers will have to be signed by President Bush. He has repeatedly voiced his commitment to assisting American families with their child care needs, but his views about the best way to do this may or may not be reconcilable with those of Congress and may result in another fatal veto.

We thus see that the recent history of legislative concern with child care had three phases. First child care was a welfare mother's problem, a birthmark it continues to bear. Eventually it became a women's issue, although for the majority of mothers the choice between family and work was really no choice at all. Not until the late 1980s did child care become a national issue, one shaped at least in part by worries over productivity rates and international competitiveness. And only when it became a national issue did concern for the child's long-term developmental needs fully enter the picture. Our leaders began to worry that children who receive poor or inadequate care today will not become very productive citizens tomorrow.

The nation has been forced to acknowledge finally that, in fact, a change has taken place in the way young children are being raised in the United States. The history of the child care system shows that the changes rarely took place, as they did with Head Start, because society set out to improve the environment in which children develop. They took place because the nation responded to children's needs on an emergency basis. When we did attempt to legislate thoughtful plans, we failed because there was no corresponding change in our attitudes about the role of society in assisting families with the care and education of young children. If our perceptions of the private lives of families and our understanding of the public good continue to clash in social legislation, future failure is assured.

OLD HABITS DIE HARD

The histories of child care and education in the United States reflect and perhaps have reinforced our society's attitudes about family and children mentioned in Chapter 1. These attitudes, which have become unwritten rules, make it difficult for us to shift our emphasis away from the politics of child care and toward policies that meet the needs of children. At the eve of the 21st century, we still believe strongly that society is obligated to play a large role in the rearing of children between the ages of five and about eighteen. All the rearing that is done before those ages is in the province of the family, and after those ages both society's and the family's obligations cease. Between those ages, we accept the school's responsibility to enhance the family's effort to provide for the child's growth as a person—emotionally, physically, intellectually, and socially. In most places the entire community rallies to provide the best teachers, educational materials, physical education equipment, and classroom space it can afford for its school-age children. Charges that the school system is failing, heard in the days following the Russian Sputnik launch and again after the scathing *Nation at Risk* report,[16] bring federal, state, and local efforts to fund immediate reforms.

Despite occasional criticism, public schools remain unchallenged in their supremacy over the realm of the family in conducting the education of our children. In every town across the nation, families with children between the ages of about five and sixteen are required to send them to public school for a great portion of the day or to prove that they are providing an equivalent education privately. Education during those years is considered a child's birthright, and that right is protected by state and local laws as well as by historical tradition. The tradition dictates that adequate and universal education for all U.S. citizens both derives from and supports the democracy.

Meanwhile, the two-tiered system of quality, determined by the ability to pay, continues not only for those under the age of five, but also for those over eighteen. Although state and federal governments do sponsor higher education to some extent, they do not underwrite its cost to the same degree that they do primary and secondary education, and it is the rare state college or university that can match the endowments of the expensive private universities. In the same manner, the only time government gets involved with a preschooler's education is when that child needs extra preparation for "real" school; for example, poor children (and a handful of others) are offered Head Start, and those with physical or learning impairments are eligible for special services through the public school system. For the vast majority of young children, however, parents must purchase caregiving and pre-school environments whose quality is often correlated with price.

Nor is preschool education or higher education required in the same way that education for the five- to sixteen-year-old is. Legal action will be taken if parents consistently keep a ten-year-old out of school, but not if they refuse to subsidize a four-year-old's nursery school or an eighteen-year-old's college education. We are not suggesting that it is wrong for society to provide education for children in public schools; we are merely pointing out that we have developed arbitrary rules for deciding at which ages society has a role to play in the child's development and education and at which ages it does not.

The Invisible Education of Invisible Children

Because of our social attitudes about the ages and times of day when it is appropriate for society to help educate children, their education during most of childhood is virtually invisible to most of us. We do not intervene much in the lives of children under age five or while they are at home during the privileged years of public school unless they are being seriously abused or neglected. In Britain, the children are the "Queen's children" when they are at school, and the state has the right to make all kinds of decisions about their welfare. We have a similar policy, although it is not so succinctly stated, in that we assign to the local school board the care and feeding and education of our children—for about six hours a day. This is provided they have achieved the legal age for such care or that their needs occur before two or three o'clock in the afternoon. Before that age and after that hour, society assumes that families are providing suitable environments for their children. We give too little thought to the experiences that educate children during all those hours and during all those years when their parents are at work and they are not in school.

When asked about the children's activities out of school, most adults will respond with something like "they're only playing." Herein lies another unwritten rule that has hampered the development of child care as a bona fide establishment. We have drawn a clear distinction between what play is and what education is. Play is loose and fun and involves toys, while education is structured and involves books. Although teachers may strive to make it "fun," the majority of children would rate school much lower on the pleasure scale. Yet play *is* the work of the young child and has been found repeatedly to be an important stimulant to intellectual growth, as Barbara Biber and others have noted.[2] Consider for a moment a toddler's engagement in play: building and knocking down blocks teaches coordination, equipoise, and the foundations necessary to understand the law of gravity later on. An infant's encounter with a rattle teaches the baby that his or her motions have consequences. The third grader's backyard baseball game teaches sportsmanship, physical skill, rules, and how to work together as a team.

Clearly, in all of these cases play *is* education. Once the lesson is mastered, as when the baby has learned all the manipulations and functions of the rattle, it is no longer "fun" and is abandoned for more challenging activities. Perhaps the only real difference between education and "only play" is the degree of structure imposed by adults, although that backyard ball game is probably more structured than the most rigid classroom.

Our society has drawn a similar distinction between what education is and what child care is. Children go to school to learn and to the babysitter's to receive watchful care. In actuality, the school setting offers a high degree of child care. There is constant supervision of the child's activities, the physical plant and equipment are maintained to insure the child's safety, and the teacher offers emotional as well as instructional support. The good caregiver does no less. While she may not teach her younger charges to read, she will read to them and instill a love of reading. She will teach them new words by talking to them instead of by vocabulary lists. She, too, helps them learn to get along with others, to share and take turns, and communicates the events of their day with parents. Once we comprehend the notion that play is learning, then the caregiver's role as teacher becomes clear. Yet just as we elevate the school to the status of educational benefactor, we elevate the teacher to the level of professional. The caregiver, who spends the day watching children "only play," suffers from the lowly image of child care as what children experience when they are not doing something important, that is, when they are not in school.

An Equal Place for Child Care

It must be understood that parents also provide a great many of their children's learning experiences. In fact, some have called parents the first and primary teachers of children (a principle of the Parents as Teachers Program [PAT] operating throughout Missouri). But remember that the total environment—family, school, and now child care—combines to teach children not only necessary skills but also who they are, what their worth is to society, and what roles they will be able to play in the democracy. Like the three legs of a milking stool, school, family, and child care make up the total supporting environment for the education and development of today's children, just as the stool supports the farmer. The quality of support provided for each leg must be equal, or the stool will topple. Charges that social policies geared to increasing the child care supply and improving its quality represent intervention in either school or family are not only destructive, they are beside the point.

Unlike the 19th century reformers who invented child care, today's advocates of high-quality child care do not want to reconstruct the American family. They want to bring the third component of the environmental threshold—the child care environment—up to a level of quality sufficient to support the total education of children that also takes place in homes and in schools.

The debates that were heard about universal schooling in past centuries—who is to pay for education, who is to control it, and what its content should be—are echoed in debates about child care today. Concerns about the health and destiny of a nation's citizens are as applicable to children under five as they are to children of school age. America is losing ground as a leading industrial world power. We need a capable populace to develop and produce advanced technologies. That capability must be nurtured in all our future citizens, not only when they enter school, but from the day they are born. Once providing education was considered an investment in an informed electorate; today providing quality child care is seen as an investment in human capital. It is to be hoped that this concern with future employees will have the same impact on the child care system as concern with democracy had on the institution of the public school.

To supply child care of appropriate quality today and into the next century is not an easy task, but it can be accomplished. In the next chapter, efforts to determine the features of child care quality will be examined. As the consistency among the various versions of the proposed Federal Interagency Day Care Requirements demonstrates, there can be consensus about what quality child care environments are like, once we begin to see them as significant influences on the total education of children, rather than as poor substitutes for home rearing and formal public education.

3

The Search for Quality in Child Care: Attempts at Definition and Regulation

In the early phases of research on child care, social scientists attempted to answer a deceptively simple question: Is supplementary care harmful or helpful to children's development? As they worked on the problem in the 1960s, they began to realize that the issues were much more complex than they had imagined. For the next two decades they conducted countless studies to determine the aspects of child care that make a difference. The type of child care setting, the background and behavior of the caregiver, the background of the child and family, and a whole host of child behaviors that might be influenced by out-of-home care have all been examined. (Deborah Phillips has edited a very readable review of the research to date.[25]) By now this work seems to have raised more questions than it has answered. There is at least a general consensus that good quality child care does not harm preschool and school-age children. (The agreement is much less unanimous when it comes to infant care, a problem we will discuss in Chapter 4.)

But what exactly is "quality" child care? Many people tend to think of "quality" anything as a kind of luxury item, not as a basic necessity. In fact, back in the 1970s when the Nixon administration was planning to subsidize care for children of welfare families so mothers could go into training or to work, there was a group of administration officials who felt that quality care was just too expensive. They pushed instead for "custodial" care, or care that provides for the child's physical needs and safety during the parent's workday. They saw this as the most affordable route and one that would make the greatest number of child care slots available. At the opposite extreme were those officials who wanted child care programs designed to improve the lives of children.

They argued that "comprehensive" care, or care that meets all of a child's emotional, physical, and educational needs, was the only acceptable arrangement. Even if this were true (and this was long before researchers began to study quality), such care would be exorbitantly expensive. To strike a compromise between these opposing positions, Zigler devised the term "developmental" care. This is care that meets at least the minimum threshold that allows for the healthy, all-around development of children.

Developmental care is what we will mean when we speak of quality child care in this chapter and throughout this book. Quality care may not enrich but it will not compromise a child's development. It is not a luxury but an essential.

So what are the elements of the quality care that every child needs for sound development? Here again, there are no simple answers. This point is driven home by looking at the diverse range of child care regulations in place around the nation. Regulations represent attempts by various federal and state agencies as well as professional groups to define quality. There are close to 50 different definitions in the 50 states. Some are relatively demanding, while others border on the totally inadequate. Apparently good child care means many different things to different people.

Parents in search of quality care cannot study all the different regulations and then move to the state where standards mirror their own. They might look to a franchised operation, believing that quality will be assured just as it is in the fast-food chains that serve meals that taste exactly the same in every location around the world. They may be disappointed, however, because there is no equivalent quality standard for child care. For example, Kinder-Care is the largest for-profit day care chain in the nation; it has served more than a million children in 40 states since 1969. A spokesperson for Kinder-Care claims that such companies can "maintain standards and quality controls" superior to those of nonprofit agencies.[18] Yet Kinder-Care adopts the licensing standards set by each state in which it operates, failing to establish uniform quality in such important areas as staff-child ratios. Thus, Kinder-Care centers in South Carolina need only one adult for every eight infants, but those in Kansas and Maryland must have one adult for every three infants. Kinder-Care president Edward "Hoot" Gibson told a *New York Times* reporter, "You can read 20 different opinions of what's the ideal staffing ratio. And the states have made reasoned decisions about what is good child care. All we're doing is following their lead."[18]

The variations in standards from state to state do not exist because the people of those states believe their children have different needs from children who reside elsewhere. They do not exist because there are no adequate models on which to base reasonable standards. They exist because the federal government has in recent years all but abandoned responsibility for the quality of child care environments, even those in federally sponsored programs. As will be discussed later in this chapter, the reasons for this hands-off policy are largely political, but there are other reasons as well. The lack of consistency in research findings is certainly one of them. We now turn to the problems in the research to date; later in this chapter we will ponder how research can more authoritatively inform social policy in the future.

RESEARCH: A KALEIDOSCOPIC VIEW OF QUALITY

Well before supplementary child care was as widely used as it is today, social scientists were worrying about its effects on children. Results from the first studies on this issue seemed to allay their fears. Children in high-quality child care settings were not found to suffer any developmental damage; poor children in fact benefited from the experience. The problem with these studies, however, was that most were conducted in well-designed, well-financed university settings where most parents could never hope to place their children. To correct this limitation, researchers began to study more typical child care environments. They also expanded their views about the indicators of quality and about the types of consequences they should observe in children. As studies became more and more complex, the results became less and less straightforward.

This does not mean that we are still far away from describing quality in the child care environment. Child development experts and child care professionals have long agreed about the basic aspects of good caregiving. They know that the physical setting, group size, and staff-child ratio all relate to quality of care. They know too that caregivers must be adequately trained and willing to stay with their jobs long enough for children to feel secure and to have time to develop relationships with someone familiar. Although there is little disagreement in theory that these are all important indicators of the adequacy of a child care environment, the precise effects of these components on a child's development have not yet been pinpointed. Policymakers and regulators often demand hard data to help them form decisions and support policies.

Researchers are working to give them clear answers and to give scientific credence to the wisdom of the field.

Part of the problem researchers face is that much of what occurs in a child care setting can be readily identified and gauged, but much cannot, making studies less exacting than scientists might like. One way of sorting out the easily measurable aspects from those that are difficult to quantify is to separate in our thinking the physical environment from the social or "people" environment the child experiences in supplementary care. Such a separation is artificial, of course, and does not exist in actual child care centers or family day care homes. Aspects of the physical environment that are most easily measured (and therefore most easily observed and regulated) include the amount of usable space per child, safety features or hazards, sanitary conditions and facilities, and the number of toys and educational materials in relation to the number of children. Obviously everyone agrees that the physical environment must be sanitary and free of hazards, must be large enough to support children's active play and physical development, must have adequate light and ventilation, and must include toys, games, and other materials that are in good repair and in sufficient supply to prevent undue competition among children. Thus, most state regulations cover some if not all of these aspects of quality to some degree, and researchers include combinations of them in their work.

There are some aspects of the social or "people" environment that are also relatively easy to measure and can be made subject to regulation. These include the staff-child ratio for different ages of children, group size, and the amount of formal training and/or experience the caregiver has had. Aspects that are observable but difficult to measure and regulate include the quality of child-caregiver interaction, the appropriateness of the caregiver's training and experience to the ages of children served, caregiver's personality, whether or not the program is suitable to the developmental level of the children, the "mood" or ambiance of the center or home, the satisfaction of the caregiver with her work, and the prevalence and reasons for staff turnover. Certainly such features as caregiver personality and the prevailing mood of a child care setting could be noticed by a trained observer, as could an exposed electrical outlet. But measuring these intangible aspects makes for less precise research and poses difficulties in attempts at regulation.

Together these features of the physical and social environments— including both measurable and nonmeasurable ones—equal the total environment a child experiences during the hours he or she is in care. Some investigators have devised overall quality scales or indexes to rate the total environment in the caregiving setting. For example, the Early Childhood Environment Rating Scale[14] assesses aspects such as personal care routines, fine and gross motor activities, and the furnishings and displays in a child care setting. Studies of global ratings have generally shown the same results as those of more concrete elements: that is, overall good care is good for children.[26] The problem with such a conclusion is that it does little to help practitioners create a quality environment, defined by so many and sometimes nonspecific criteria. Looking at the total environment may also mask the effects of individual components of quality.[8] If researchers are going to be able to answer the question of which specific strengths and weaknesses of programs lead to positive and negative outcomes for children, they need to be able to consider each quality indicator separately.

Overall quality indexes are still informative and a promising avenue of study, because the positive features of a child care environment tend to "cluster" in individual programs. For example, a program with well-trained staff is likely to offer frequent child-caregiver interaction and much verbal stimulation. On the other hand, certain elements of quality may outweigh the lack of others. Thus staff with minimal training may be able to offer good care if the group is small, and a program that lacks funds for a large number of expensive toys may have experienced caregivers who involve the children in creative activities.

These examples of research dilemmas illustrate why empirical efforts to define quality have not yet produced a clear-cut recipe, even though the experts are clear about the ingredients. There are numerous elements to look at, each element can be measured in different ways, and each may be related to the others in different degrees. Social scientists must continue to examine individual features they think contribute to quality child care, see where these fit into overall impressions of a quality setting, and delve into the "interactive, compensatory, and additive influences" of specific quality indicators.[28]

EFFECTS OF QUALITY CARE: EFFECTS ON WHAT?

The point of efforts to define quality child care is to insure a place where children can continue their course of development while away from home. That is, they should progress in verbal, cognitive, and social skills, achieve appropriate developmental benchmarks, and maintain emotional and physical health. We would expect them to fare no worse than if they remained at home with their parents, and some proponents of quality hope they might even do better.

The complexity of choosing and measuring quality indicators seems deceptively simple when it comes to the task of choosing and measuring developmental effects. Development is multifaceted, and assessment tools are limited. Researchers can only focus on those domains for which assessment tools have been devised. One domain that seems to be of interest to everyone is intelligence. Let us state at the outset that most studies have shown that child care has little or no effect on intelligence. Some research, such as that reported by Clarke-Stewart,[7] suggests that high-quality care has a positive effect, but there are no long-term studies to see if reported cognitive gains are likely to last beyond the child care years. Because intelligence is a relatively stable trait[12, 34] and is determined in part by heredity, it is unreasonable to hope that quality child care will turn young children into geniuses.

This conclusion may come as a surprise to many readers, since the child care literature contains numerous references to the tremendous benefits derived from certain quality preschool programs. Many of these programs are comprehensive interventions, not to be confused with the typical child care center or home most children attend. Head Start, for example, is a proven success in that graduates do better academically and behaviorally, if not on IQ tests. But Head Start offers total health care, sound nutrition, a full educational program, and involves parents, so these benefits are extended beyond the school day and year. The Perry Preschool Program, another frequently cited reference for quality care, had comprehensive curricula and a highly trained professional staff, lasted for two years, and included biweekly home visits to educate parents. Even the more common nursery school format can be a far cry from the typical child care experience.

If the more usual varieties of child care do not necessarily bolster intelligence, this does not mean they have no effect on other important aspects of development. Researchers have investigated the impact of child care on language acquisition, social competence, attentiveness, aggression, independence, cooperativeness, and a host of other behavioral traits. Because scientists differ in the ways they assess these features, in the samples of children and settings they observe, and in the length of time they allow for the effects of child care to become evident, results are in no way comparable. They run the entire gamut from no effects or bad effects to favorable outcomes resulting from "quality" child care. For example, of five studies reported in the monograph, *Quality in Child Care: What Does Research Tell Us?*,[25] one found that children who had more experienced caregivers did better on measures of language and sociability; another found they were less aggressive and anxious but also less sociable; a third also found low sociability but high cognitive competence.[9] What can this mixed bag of results possibly tell us about the effects of caregiver experience on children? Clearly, the methodology of child care research needs refinement, and the design of studies needs some consistency, if we are ever to understand the importance of good child care.

The latest research on the effects of supplementary care has further widened the list of possible determinants. Workers who espouse the ecological model of studying children's development have come to realize that the effects of child care are not dependent on the child care setting alone. The child who arrives on the caregiver's doorstep has a unique personality and a family and home life that provide the major share of environmental influences on development. Thus it is simplistic to conclude that a large group size makes children more aggressive, or that caregivers who engage children in much verbal interaction stimulate language development, because aggression and language skills are influenced primarily by the home. Supplementary care may encourage or delay such traits, but it cannot assume full responsibility for doing so.

Educators have long recognized that how well a child performs at school is related to the quality of family life. It makes sense that this should be true for how well a child fares in supplementary care as well. Researchers have just recently begun to account for features of family structure (for example, marital status, parents' education, income, profession) and family process (parent-child interactions, parental stress, attitudes toward working and child care) in their studies of child care.[13] What they are beginning to find is that these family features have as much if not more to do with the results of child care than the quality of the care itself.[26] For example, supplementary care is more likely to have negative effects on children from stressed homes; apparently daily separation from parents combines with other stressors to put the child at developmental risk.[12]

It is also important to remember that parents choose their child care arrangement (although many do not have the range of choice they might like). Parents who are under much pressure or who are not tuned in to their child's individual needs might settle for a poor-quality setting or a caregiver who is not suited for the child. This bad care may be found to have bad effects, but they may have been predetermined by the circumstances in the home. On the other hand, parents who have high standards for their child are likely to search for the best quality setting they can afford. This good care will supplement the parents' good care and produce a positive outcome. Indeed, studies have shown that children in low-resource families are more likely to be enrolled in low-quality child care,[13,22] while more secure families tend to place their children in higher-quality settings.[3] Obviously, the amount of money a family can pay for child care is also a factor in the particular setting they choose. Since quality care generally costs more than poor care, higher-income families are able to purchase better care, while middle- and lower-class parents who cannot obtain subsidies often must accept care that is less desirable.[37] Hence when scientists compare children in high- and low-quality settings, they may also be comparing children of different socioeconomic backgrounds.

Many other factors can confuse a researcher's attempts to link quality indicators with positive developmental outcomes. One is the child. Children come with a large variety of backgrounds and temperaments, so they cannot be expected to respond uniformly to the same caregiving setting. Caregivers also come with a large variety of backgrounds and temperaments, and they cannot be expected to respond uniformly to the same training or to the same children. Development itself follows a unique course in each child, with the mastery of certain skills taking precedence over others at different stages of growth. For example, one child may excel in language but ignore fine motor skills until a later age, while another may do just the opposite. We thus see that the "effects of child care" is not a simple matter because there are many and varied determinants of each child's response.

The complexity of research on child care is in sharp contrast to the simplicity of common sense: good child care is good for children; bad child care is not. Studies have given us many solid clues about quality in the caregiving environment, and we do not have to wait until the last word is in to be able to describe a decent child care setting. We now turn to this process.

THE ESSENTIALS OF QUALITY CARE

In spite of the need for additional information about the impact of different quality factors on children's development, we can speak with certainty about what constitutes an adequate child care environment. Experts have traditionally relied on more than empirical studies to define good quality. They also rely on many years of observations of relationships between children and the environments in which they grow and learn. They depend, too, on knowledge about the principles of child development, and on common-sense judgments about what children need to thrive.

Of course, there are variations in professional opinions about the definition of quality care, but these opinions are more similar than they are disparate. For example, one child psychologist may differ from another on whether staff ratios in infant care should be one adult for three infants or one adult for four. We know of no psychologist or early childhood education specialist who argues that one adult can look after eight or ten infants. By the same token, several national standard-setting enterprises have agreed on the type of care that cannot harm children—all three versions of the Federal Interagency Day Care Requirements (FIDCR) are strikingly similar. They are also consistent with quality requirements set by professional organizations such as the National Association for the Education of Young Children, or NAEYC,[2] and the Child Welfare League of America.[4] Thus, it can be argued that although research must continue to examine the form and essence of quality features and their relationship to overall outcomes for child development, there is considerable agreement about which features of child care environments are important in creating minimum standards.

Staff-Child Ratio

Staff-child ratio refers to the number of adult staff members there are to care for the total number of children in a child care setting. This number includes caregivers regularly assigned to groups of children, those who may circulate among groups or conduct special activities, and the director or head teacher of a large center. Many states specify which staff may be counted toward staff-child ratios, typically excluding such personnel as cooks, cleaners, and secretarial staff who have no direct child care duties.

Most people would think that high staff-child ratios are indicative of quality care and thus are best for children. However, the results of the National Day Care Study[33] "called into question the intuitive preoccupation of the child care community with staff-child ratios,"[29] except in connection with infant care. The study seemed to indicate that small group size and appropriate caregiver training were more closely associated with positive outcomes for preschoolers. On the other hand, the National Child Care Staffing Study[27] did find that ratios were definitely linked to the overall quality of care, and we do know that good quality promotes good outcomes. Clarke-Stewart points out, however, that results of studies attempting to either verify or refute the connection between adult-child ratios and measures of behavior and development have been "underwhelming."[9]

Few researchers are ready to deny the importance of setting appropriate staff-child ratios for different age groups in child care; rather, some are advocating caution in applying research results (or lack of them) to decisions of policy. "We should avoid blanket statements about high adult-child ratios being good and low ratios being bad," says Clarke-Stewart, "until we have checked out the *limits* beyond which a low ratio is bad and the *outcome* for which a high ratio is good."[9]

For a state or federal agency charged with the responsibility for establishing child care standards, however, the issue of appropriate limits for staff-child ratio is a practical one that cannot be ignored. The problems dealt with by researchers, such as isolating the specific measures to be used to test a specific outcome of too few staff members per child, cannot be used as an excuse to condone insufficient staffing in a child care program. Because there is inadequate scientific evidence to support specific staff-child ratios (except in the case of infants, where there is close agreement in all recommendations), cost considerations may pressure public servants into allowing too few adults to care for too many children. Such a situation is counter to the instincts of professionals and child development experts, regardless of what the research has failed to show to date. From a strictly practical standpoint, how many children can one caregiver lead to safety in the event of a fire or other emergency? With how many children can one adult maintain the accepting and intellectually stimulating relationship that has been linked to positive outcomes in some areas of development? It is difficult to imagine one adult attempting to explain a project or game to more than eight three-year-olds, or being able to keep track of each child's interests and difficulties. Thus staff-child ratios such as those set by the NAEYC and the 1980 FIDCR make intuitive sense in that they allow caregivers to give the individual attention each child needs.

Another way to view the staff-child ratio issue is from the standpoint of staff distribution in the center or group family day care home. A child needs to relate to a limited number of adults in the course of a day, a number that increases with the age of the child. It might seem at first glance that having a higher number of adults in a child care environment might be difficult for children, especially the younger ones. In practical terms, however, when the staff is sufficient to the number of children served, caregivers can be assigned in a way that does not disrupt children's activities and their relationships with adults. For example, where there are two caregivers for a group of eight two-year-olds (a ratio of 1:4), one adult can attend to a child who needs help while the other reads a story to the rest of the group. By contrast, where there is only one caregiver available for a group of four two-year-olds, there is no relief for the caregiver and either the group or the individual child must be ignored with greater frequency.

In a large center, poorly planned staffing patterns may actually negate the benefits of having an adequate number of staff. Caregivers may rotate from one group to another, or stay with one function while the group rotates. In what Phillips and colleagues call "accordion staffing," programs add staff in the mornings as children arrive, but rearrange groups and reduce staff during the day as children leave.[27] Children thus change caregivers and groups frequently, denying them the continuity they need. Since the rate of caregiver turnover is so high to begin with, such staffing patterns may only make a bad situation worse.

Group Size

Group size refers to the number of children who form a cluster within a larger setting, such as a day care center. Groups may be in separate rooms or, more typically, in separate areas sometimes set off by furniture or movable partitions. Depending on the staff-child ratio, a group may have one, two, or more caregivers. The National Day Care Study[33] identified limited group size as one of the significant contributors to positive developmental outcomes. Later studies have failed to establish a clear picture of a causal relationship between group size alone and specific measures of intellectual and social growth. At this date, we are not even sure that group size is directly related to the quality of care children receive. For example, Kontos and Fiene[17] found that group size is one of the regulable variables in child care that seems to predict overall quality of a child care environment. They thought this may be due to the "clustering" effect mentioned earlier—that if a center is good in other ways, the director and staff are likely to pay attention to group size as well as to other features assumed important by child care professionals. In the National Child Care Staffing Study, however, group size was the only one of the quality indicators that did *not* predict whether the care was good or bad.[27]

Regardless of this stalemate, when one observes the actual day-to-day activities in a child care setting, the advantages of restricting group size become obvious. Entering a center where group sizes are too large, one is bombarded with noise, scuffling for toys, and a general sense of chaos. The small group size (six) for infants and toddlers called for in the 1980 FIDCR, paired with a staff-child ratio of one adult to three children, allows for the sharing of responsibilities for the group by two caregivers. This limits the handling of infants and toddlers to fewer adults and allows staff and children to get to know one another better. Infants and toddlers do not engage in much cooperative play and cannot share toys and other resources without adult intervention. Limiting the number of other children with whom babies must compete daily makes it easier for caregivers to see that children are getting the attention, resources, and rest that they need.

As children reach the preschool years, caregivers and parents value opportunities for sharing, playing, and conversing with a wider variety of children. Preschoolers enjoy and are able to participate in more large group activities, such as sitting for a few minutes to listen to a story, singing songs, or playing musical chairs. Groups of 12 two-year-olds and 16 three-year-olds are manageable when there are enough adults to supervise. It may be that group size restrictions based on developmental level allow caregivers to function in a more orderly manner within the coping abilities and needs of the children in care.

As in the case of staff-child ratios, we could surmise that staffing and grouping patterns have a greater potential for affecting the quality of a child's actual environment than do numbers alone. Are children grouped according to approximate developmental level—for example, crawling infants in an area separated from preschoolers in the same center? Do groups remain consistent over time, long enough for children to get to know one another, or are children constantly switched from one group to another over the course of the day or week? Are the group's caregivers relatively consistent also, or do children have to adjust continually to the differing styles and interests of several staff members? All these questions need closer examination. Nonetheless, restrictions on group size by age may help staff pay attention to the differing needs of children of various developmental levels. Thus the establishment of staff-child ratios and group size restrictions is necessary despite the limited knowledge base. Not only are these factors more easily regulated than staffing patterns, but they do contribute in some way to the quality of care delivered.

Caregivers: The Soul of Quality Care

The caregiver is the very center of the child's environment and experiences during the hours of supplementary care. She must protect, comfort, and nurture all of the children in her care, plan their activities, and, ideally, teach and love them as well. She must be able to recognize signs of illness or loneliness; know what children might like to play with; know when to play with them; and know when to intervene in conflicts between children. To do all of this properly, she must have some amount of experience and knowledge about child development.

We do not need an expert opinion or hundreds of studies to be sure that a positive relationship between a child and caregiver is an absolute necessity. Liking a child and being attentive to his or her needs are key ingredients in this relationship, but so are frequent and stimulating interactions. Certain aspects of child development, such as language acquisition and other evidence of social and intellectual growth, are known to depend on interactions between caregiver and child. In the research that tells us so, the caregiver was typically the parent, but there is no reason to suspect that the same developmental outcomes do not derive from interactions with other caregivers as well. Indeed, most studies that have looked at children's interactions with child care staff find them to have some effect on children, but how much and in what areas differ from one report to another. Nonetheless, since we know they are necessary for normal development, we would hope to insure that caregivers are motivated and qualified to engage children in stimulating exchanges.

Although no one envisions a system whereby the number of verbal and educational interactions between caregiver and child will be determined by research and then enforced by regulation, it is clear that caregivers do learn to interact with children in a positive manner through some form of training and/or experience. Scientists have looked at both experience and formal education to see what best prepares those who look after children in different age groups. As you have read before in these pages, the results are too mixed to be at all conclusive. One reason is that "not all experience is alike."[28] Experience can mean time spent working under careful supervision, or time spent in a disorganized program with minimal supervision, or simply time spent mothering one's own children. It is also unclear what the value is of different kinds of caregiver education, such as a two- or four-year college degree as opposed to shorter-term training targeted to child development.

Despite this list of unknowns, we can say with certainty that in order to provide for the basic needs of children, caregivers need some kind of practical training and supervised experience in quality settings. Undoubtedly we will adjust the minimum recommended training levels as research reveals more specifically what they should be. The need for this work is pressing. For one thing, 28 states do not require any training or experience for family day care providers,[20] partly because they are unsure what to require. Second, with the growing shortage of child care slots, the only solution is to expand the work force of caregivers. We must know how to train these people to assure America's children that their caregivers will deliver quality care.

One way we know to provide adequate training is the Child Development Associate (CDA) credential program. The CDA program was initially formed in the early 1970s by a collaboration of the early childhood development profession and the federal government. Its purpose was to certify child care workers based on evaluations of their abilities to meet the developmental needs of young children. Since that time, the CDA program has awarded credentials to over 30,000 child care workers—an extremely modest number. Several states mention CDA certification as one way of meeting state standards for caregiver training. Until the program receives greater publicity, and the cost to trainees is reduced or subsidized, this promising method for increasing the supply of qualified caregivers will never achieve its potential.

Administered by the Council for Early Childhood Professional Recognition under the direction of Carol Brunson Phillips, a new CDA program model will be available by 1991. It will provide two avenues by which child care providers can earn the CDA credential. One avenue for inexperienced workers will be training through a professional preparation program in child development and other necessary skills, followed by supervised experience and a final evaluation. The entire process will take approximately one year. The other route will involve the assessment of experienced caregivers through a national network called the Credential Award System. As of this writing, the Credential Award System takes approximately 12 weeks, although the time is adjusted to the needs of the candidate. The cost is $325. Candidates will also be required to have a minimum number of hours of formal training in child development. Evaluations for CDA candidates are competency based: they must demonstrate their ability to apply their knowledge of children to the specific skills of child care.

One of the main advantages of requiring a credentialing program for child care workers is that those clearly unsuited to caregiving by reason of personality and/or lack of ability can be observed and weeded out of the profession. Thus the chances of child care environments having the all-important feature of good quality care—a positive relationship between child and caregiver—can be increased. Certification also lends an air of professionalism to the job. Many people view caregivers as "mere babysitters" who watch children because they are not qualified to take on a more dignified job. We hope we have shown by now how important the many hours and years spent in supplementary care really are to the future of the child. It is time to accord the profession of child care provider the status it deserves.

Once earned, an attractive diploma must do more for the caregiver than brighten up a bare wall. Elevating the practice of child care also means better working conditions and wages. Consider the shocking fact that the annual rate of caregiver turnover in our nation is around 42%,[24] compared to about 18% in all occupations.[1] Only one-third of child care providers have been in the profession for more than three years.[15] Yet consistency of caregivers has long been thought to be necessary for the healthy growth of children. No matter how caregiver stability is measured—whether in terms of percentage of turnover, of the number of new staff in a center, or of the length of time a child has been with a primary caregiver—it always seems correlated with some aspect of social development in children. Caregiver stability combined with level of skill have been identified as primary ingredients of quality care, directly responsible for positive developmental outcomes in children.[38]

The importance of caregiver stability makes the high turnover rate a cause for dire concern. The reasons for leaving a specific child care position or for leaving the profession entirely begin with low pay. In *Child Care: The Bottom Line*,[31] Reisman, Moore, and Fitzgerald state that 60% of child care workers earn less than $5.00 an hour (in California even welfare recipients do not have to accept jobs that pay less than $5.07 an hour). In 1984 the median salary of child care workers was $9,200, about half the national median and $3,300 less than the salary earned by janitors. Many caregivers do not receive health insurance, overtime or vacation pay, or other benefits. The impressive National Child Care Staffing Study[37] reports similar findings for center staff, adding that the average teacher *with a bachelor's degree* in their sample earned only $6.88 per hour. These researchers concluded that of all the factors in the work environment, staff wages were the most important predictor of quality care.

Because so many family day care providers are unlicensed, their wage levels are harder to document, but it is safe to assume that their earnings are generally less than those of workers employed in centers. Of the private household providers we do know about, 90% earned below the poverty level in 1984.[6]

With such meager wages, it is a small wonder that so many family child care workers choose to operate without a license. Estimates of the exact number vary, but the figure of 90% is cited most frequently. Many do not want to bother with the hassle and cost of complying with state and local codes and regulations, and some do not want to see their small wages depleted by income and self-employment taxes. This excuse will begin to disappear now that the Internal Revenue Service requires parents who take the Child and Dependent Care Tax Credit to report the names and social security numbers of caregivers. Whether this new ruling brings more providers out of the underground or forces them to close remains to be seen. We take the position that licensing is desirable for the good of the child. Only when we know about caregivers can we invoke at least minimal standards to assure children of adequate care.

Licensing, improved training, credentialing, and better pay, benefits, and status will do much to improve the lot of the caregiver. The "Catch-22" is that they will also increase the cost to parents. Yet if we are to maintain a stable child care work force, we have to attend to the plight of the caregiver, for she helps to determine the plight of the child.

Further Questions

While we have much to learn about even those elements we already know contribute to quality child care, many other elements are beginning to appear as prime candidates. The relationship between the parent and caregiver is thought to be important to the impact of supplementary care on a child, but how important remains unknown. Whether child care can be an effective social support system, or part of one, and how this benefits the family and child are issues worth pursuing. We also need to know more about stability in the child care experience—not just in terms of staff turnover but in items like peer group turnover and how often a child has changed settings. We need to know if umbrella organizations or networks for private homes and centers do, as we suspect, help to raise quality and are an effective support for caregivers. A pressing need is for more longitudinal research to tell if any suspected effects of supplementary care—positive or negative—are permanent or transient.

We definitely require more evidence about the value of regulation. Is the care in licensed and/or registered facilities better than that in unregulated settings? There is a dearth of research on underground family day care homes (for obvious reasons), so we cannot quiet proponents of deregulation unless we prove that licensing is correlated with quality to some degree. A related question is whether or not higher standards translate into better care. Phillips, Howes, and Whitebook have presented some strong evidence to show this is true,[27] but more evidence of this type is required to make a convincing case for standards.

The list of what we do not yet know could go on and on. We have certainly come a long way from the simple question of whether child care versus home care is good or bad for children. Researchers have "accumulated a vast collection of results" over the years, but "this literature has driven home the true complexity of child care and the real challenges faced by those who seek to assess its effects on children."[26]

THE STRUGGLE FOR FEDERAL STANDARDS

Throughout the early history of child care, programs providing daytime care for children were routinely excluded from regulation by the states, which limited their regulatory functions to the care children received in residential institutions. During the sudden burgeoning of out-of-home care during World War II, however, new state standards were written, or institutional standards were expanded to include child care settings. The first federal interest in child care quality came in the form of a set of standards developed by participants in a 1941 Conference on Day Care of Children of Working Mothers and issued in 1942 by the federal Office of Education.[5] After a hiatus of nearly 20 years, during which time child care and its quality were largely ignored on the national level, the Child Welfare League of America (CWLA) issued its Standards for Day Care Service in 1960. These standards addressed the same areas as have been discussed in this chapter—group size, staff-child ratios, staff training—as well as child health.[29] Clearly, professionals and experts have long known the key ingredients of quality care, even before research could support or modify their assumptions.

In 1962, a child care program and a means of regulation were mentioned almost as an afterthought in conjunction with a piece of welfare reform legislation, Public Law 87–543. The reasons for the child care addendum "would become a familiar litany" in political circles from then on.[21] To reduce welfare costs, recipients needed training and employment, a goal dependent upon available child care. The reform bill required child care programs established under the legislation to obtain state licenses. The effect of this requirement was that states that had no licensing procedures for child care hastily established them, using about 40% of the $800,000 appropriated for the child care program to do so.[21] Most states applied the new regulations only to new programs, thereby allowing older, poor quality programs to operate and thwarting the creation of new ones. It is important to note that regulatory power for federally sponsored child care programs was (and remains) a responsibility given to the individual states.

The demand for federal regulation of these programs arose from a turf battle during the late 1960s between the Office of Economic Opportunity (OEO) and the Department of Health, Education and Welfare (HEW). Both agencies wanted to gain sole administrative responsibility for child care programs that had by now been established under various bills. The developmentalists at OEO (who ran the Head Start program) were seeking fairly stringent and potentially expensive regulations for all federal child care programs, and the welfare reform specialists at HEW wished to keep costs of their programs down by establishing a minimal set of guidelines. A Federal Panel on Early Childhood, established by HEW Secretary Wilbur Cohen, drafted the first Federal Interagency Day Care Requirements in 1968. Cohen and his panel were able to effect a compromise between cost and quality advocates, with the content of the 1968 FIDCR striking a balance between the high-quality Head Start model and the least expensive version. The vague language, subject to wide interpretation in areas such as which personnel should be counted in determining staff-child ratios, together with the provision that enforcement of the standards be split among three federal agencies, reflect the context of the turf battle which would continue through subsequent revisions of the FIDCR.

President Nixon's Family Assistance Plan and its child care component were discussed in Chapter 2. The newly established Office of Child Development, under the leadership of Edward Zigler, was authorized to revise the FIDCR and create a set of "realistic, enforceable child care standards"[29] to accompany the establishment of approximately 400 new child care centers. The 1972 revisions renewed the cost-quality battle, but the actual provisions represented an improvement over the 1968 FIDCR. First, the new regulations included in-home care in addition to family day care and centers. They were also more age specific, recognizing seven rather than the three age groups outlined in the 1968 version. A staff-child ratio of 1:3 for infants, an age group not covered previously, was added to the 1972 provisions, but staff-child ratios for other groups were somewhat more lenient. Competency levels to be demonstrated by child care staff were more clearly defined in 1972. On the whole, the 1972 FIDCR tightened some of the 1968 provisions and loosened others. Advocates of cost-effectiveness lamented the more stringent changes, while advocates of quality bemoaned the weakening of staff-child ratios for preschoolers. When the new child care centers never got off the ground, the Nixon administration eventually decided to bury the revisions.

Each time the federal standards debate was renewed, it was never an issue in itself but arose in connection with proposed bills which had child care provisions attached. For example, in 1974 the proposed Title XX amendments to the Social Security Act created a system by which funds for previously separate social service programs were to be given to states in the form of block grants. States could decide how to distribute the funds, within certain limits. When signed into law in 1975, Title XX contained a provision that child care programs that received funding must comply with the 1968 FIDCR. Another provision mandated a study of the general effectiveness of federal regulation of child care. The vigorous controversy that ensued—especially over the staff-child ratios—led to a series of postponements to give the states more time to meet certain FIDCR provisions. By 1981, however, the compliance mandate was rescinded, and this is as close as the FIDCR would ever come to being operationalized. The last revision of the requirements was published in 1980, but it, too, never became law. The standards remain in the *Federal Register*[10] as an appropriate model for states or for future tilts at the federal child care regulation windmill, but it is unlikely that they will ever be put into effect.

In fact, the years of consultation with researchers and child development professionals that resulted in the final version of the FIDCR were totally bypassed when child care regulation again became a federal concern in 1984. Quality child care per se was not the impetus to the Model Child Care Standards Act of 1985.[36] It arose out of pressure put on Congress to respond to reports of abuse, especially sexual abuse, of children in child care centers. While such abuse is deplorable, it is, fortunately, much rarer than the public supposed, because child abuse is much more likely to occur in the home, not in child care arrangements.[11]

The so-called Model Child Care Standards Act was not an actual model. Despite a congressional mandate to provide a set of minimum standards in specific areas, the Department of Health and Human Services chose to suggest "regulatory options" instead, presenting the standards developed by the National Association for the Education of Young Children (NAEYC) and the CWLA as an appendix. The document's focus was on background screening of candidates for child care staffing positions to weed out potential abusers. States were offered the carrot of caregiver training funds if they adopted the Act, but many saw no reason to do so because they did not want to give up their regulatory powers.

Cost considerations and turf battles are not the only reasons federal child care regulation has created such opposition. The antiregulatory climate prevalent in Washington from time to time—especially during the 1980s—has worked against federal child care standards. In recent years many regulatory functions have been dropped by the federal government and handed to the individual states. To request that control of child care quality be handed back would be a motion against the tide.

Even some groups that might be considered potential supporters of child care standards have been traditionally opposed. Although national professional child care organizations support high standards, some small "mom and pop" centers are wary of such measures as better staff-child ratios and stricter training requirements. These higher standards would increase the cost of child care services that already operate with minimal profits. Large child care chains are also opposed because they realize higher profits in states with loose standards than in those with more stringent regulations. State lawmakers may favor standards, but not if they come from the federal government with federal strings attached. In fact, the National Council of State Legislatures opposed the 1988 Act for Better Child Care because of its call for national standards. Parents are understandably confused by the discussions and arguments among researchers, politicians, and professional organizations. Their fears that higher costs will be associated with regulation are realistic.

Recent activity in Congress to assist American families with their child care problems will no doubt result in another standards controversy, and it is likely that the 1980 FIDCR will be reinvented. Barring unforeseen developments, however, it is unlikely that national standards will ever be enacted and enforced. Our best hope for the future is that national leadership will develop regulations in the form of goals for each state to work toward and will provide financial incentives for the states to improve regulation and oversight.

ASSURING EVERY CHILD OF QUALITY CHILD CARE

Given our priorities to guarantee a suitable environment for each child, adequate standards and enforcement of those standards are important. At present, controlling that environment is a buck that stops at the door of working parents. The movement for parent education in quality issues has been undertaken by a number of civic, R&R, and professional organizations, such as the NAEYC, which provide publications to help parents select appropriate child care environments. Yet although parents are perhaps the best judges of such issues as caregiver personality and other nonregulable features of child care, judging the many features of quality can be somewhat confusing. In addition, many beleaguered working parents are short of the time necessary to act as watchdogs over their children's supplementary care arrangements. Even if they are uncomfortable with the quality of the setting, they may avoid "rocking the boat," out of concern that they will lose the scarce slot they worked so hard to find or out of fear that they must maintain a good relationship with caregivers to assure their children a comfortable child care experience.

Elliot Richardson, former secretary of HEW, once argued that if the federal government can demand that nursing homes for the elderly meet certain minimum standards, we can do no less for the nation's children. Despite the many hard efforts of children's advocates, it now appears that Washington will not promulgate regulations to assure quality in child care settings. This does not absolve it of responsibility, however; the least it can do is provide adequate models and incentives to the states. Because of the centrality of the caregiver to the child's experiences in care, our state and federal governments need to focus more attention on the environment as experienced by the caregiver. Better pay, benefits, better staff-child ratios, and affordable professional training are some of the necessary supports for those who share with parents the job of nurturing a child. Expansion of the Child Development Associate credentialing program would not only help more caregivers to provide environments that meet the minimum threshold for healthy growth and development, but it would grant more of them an appreciation of their own value to the society. Currently, however, the fees required for certification are beyond the reach of many poorly paid child care workers. This nation has done much to assist potential schoolteachers in gaining the education required for their profession; child care providers deserve equal treatment.

In terms of actual standards, we as a society have no excuse for saying that we will wait to enact what we believe to be beneficial to children until researchers agree on every connection between a specific quality feature and a specific developmental outcome. Developmental psychologists themselves, while cautious of making pronouncements that cannot be backed by research, frequently express concern that much of the child care available in this nation today is of inadequate quality. They fear widespread ill effects will become evident throughout society as the current generation of children in care attains adulthood. Yet we already know enough about children's developmental needs to understand how to meet them. Leadership at whatever level must apply the wisdom of the field in crafting reasonable minimum standards.

Of course most states will call their existing standards "reasonable," but periodic reexamination and refinement are called for in an area where new information is surfacing at such a rapid rate. In the National Child Care Staffing Study,[27] the best quality care was found in the state with the most stringent regulations, and the poorest care was observed in the state with the most lenient regulations. Since the "best" care was not that good, these findings indicate that all states might tighten their standards. To do so would certainly benefit children, ease the minds of parents, and in fact assist those in the business of child care. James Strickland, an expert on the insurance problems in child care, suggests that better standards and state regulations will make insurance more available and affordable to providers by lessening the risk to insurers.[35]

Improved standards will not solve all the problems of child care, of course. State licensing standards tend to represent the floor of quality. Professional standards are typically higher and represent the goals of the profession.[19] Deciding between adequate care and good care is a choice citizens of each state must make, but not before they eliminate bad care. Another problem is that even the best standards do not automatically result in high-quality child care. Phillips and her colleagues found that the rate of compliance with standards had nothing to do with how lenient or stringent the standards were.[27] Adequate monitoring and partnerships between state agencies and child care providers are needed to enforce regulations. With proper training and reasonable caseloads, monitors can be more than enforcers; they can assist providers in putting the requirements into effect in a cost-productive way. Here again, however, cost is an impediment. For example, the Illinois Department of Children and Family Services has determined that a monitor should have a caseload of no more than 56 centers or 104 family day care homes. Yet the average worker is assigned 80 centers or 183 homes; in the city of Chicago each monitor is responsible for 237 homes— more than twice the recommended number.[30] Until states make a commitment to quality in child care, and support that commitment by providing funds for monitors and other resources, standards cannot do much to assure quality child care environments.

Of course, researchers must gather more hard data to continue to justify their call for quality standards. Some of this work should be pointed directly toward the concerns of policy makers who must pay attention to budgetary constraints and proprietary rights at the same time they care about children. For example, if standards are raised, will the benefits of the higher quality care outweigh the price of some facilities closing and others going underground? If reliable child care enables a low-income mother to secure employment, how does her working affect her children's perceptions of their own job prospects and future earning power?[23] Phillips also notes the need for more information on the cost-effectiveness of child care subsidies; we add the need for cost-benefit data on expenditures for quality care. Government assistance might not only reduce welfare dependency but may produce increases in income tax and social security revenues. Good care costs more than inferior care,[32] but investments in quality care may reduce expenditures for remedial education and juvenile justice and rehabilitation programs. Armed with this type of information, legislators can take the necessary steps to draft public policies that benefit the youngest members of the public.

4

The Caregiving Needs of Infants and Toddlers

The first caring environment a baby experiences is the family, and this surrounding remains the most central one throughout the developing years. The introduction of a child to the family, whether by birth, remarriage, or adoption, might best be described as a naturally stressful time. This does not mean that families are unhappy with the birth of a child—usually they are delighted. It means that there are considerable adjustments to be made by all family members. There are increased demands on the family's finances. There are increased demands on parents' time and energies. If the child is their first, parents may have varying degrees of anxiety surrounding their parenting skills. Radical changes in their schedules and lifestyle must be made. Even parents who already have children may be overcome with the awesome sense of responsibility for a new life. Their older children may feel displaced and compete with the new baby for their parents' affection.

Infants, too, undergo a period of physical and emotional adjustment to the environments in which they suddenly find themselves. From the darkness, warmth, and security of the womb, they now face brightness, noise, and activity. Where once their life-sustaining needs were automatically met, their respiratory and digestive systems must now function on their own. They must depend on someone to be sensitive to and attend to their needs. Adopted children have great adjustments to make also. They must adapt to new surroundings and people. They must get used to new sights, smells, and tastes, and they must overcome separation from their former environments. Clearly, for both a new member and the entire family, life is going to be very, very different from what it once was.

Given these drastic changes, it is easy to understand why many specialists in child development have long recommended that infants remain at home with a parent for some part of the first year of life. The Yale Infant Care Leave Project found that in spite of the increasing tendency to place infants as young as two or three weeks old into child care, most experts still believe that infants and parents need a minimum of three to four months together at home, and longer if possible.[25] Efforts to turn these recommendations into a national infant care leave policy will be discussed in the next chapter. The requirements of child care settings for infants older than four months and for toddlers will be described later in this chapter. Now we turn to the needs of infants in the first few months of life, a period during which, we believe, children need to be with their parents in order to get a healthy start in life.

THE INFANT'S WORLD

Infants are generally defined as children under one year of age; they may be called newborns or neonates for approximately the first month of life. The general needs of infants are very basic but not always easy to recognize. For the adults in a new baby's environment, discerning and meeting the child's individual requirements is an especially perplexing task.

Many of the needs of newborns are physical in nature and stem from their innate biological processes. Wayne, a computer programmer who returned to work after a week at home caring for his wife and their newborn daughter, was asked by his co-workers how the new baby was. He sighed and said, "Well, at this stage she's all input and output—no logic." Wayne's quip captures the externally apparent features of a newborn. Feeding must come at regular intervals, but the intervals are determined by the infant's individual cycle. Diaper changing must be frequent enough to prevent discomfort and rashes. It often seems to parents that this endless cycle of input and output, determined by the baby's instinctual needs, is all there is to a newborn in the first weeks of life.

Newborns also need a great deal of rest, and they exhibit widely varying sleep patterns. It is a rare newborn who sleeps on a schedule. Irregular "cat naps" totaling up to 20 hours of sleep a day are the norm, although some newborns sleep much less. Waking hours may be at an inconvenient time of day from an adult point of view, such as the middle of the night. Letting babies establish their own schedules versus encouraging parents to try to establish schedules for them is a matter of child-rearing "fashion." Just a generation ago, experts advised parents to follow a rigid schedule for feeding, bathing, and sleep. Meals, for example, were to be exactly four hours apart, and the baby who felt hungry sooner should be made to wait. Today many physicians instruct parents to respond to feeding and sleeping cycles "on demand," allowing the infant to determine his or her own schedule. Whatever parents attempt to do, however, a newborn's ability to follow a schedule set by adults is extremely limited. It usually takes several months for an infant to adapt to the sleep/wake schedule and meal times of the rest of the family. And it may be as soon as a few weeks or as late as a year before parents can expect their infant to let them sleep through the night.

Whether asleep or awake, individual infants also have differing responses to outside stimulation, such as movement, sound, and touch generated by the household routine and their own care. Thomas, Chess, Birch, and associates identified three general types of infant temperament: "easy," "slow-to-warm-up," and "difficult."[21] For example, although most infants indicate discomfort with sudden, loud noises by a jerk of the whole body and crying, a "difficult" baby may respond this way even to a radio playing softly in another room. An "easy" baby drops off to sleep while someone is running a vacuum cleaner or siblings are playing loudly in the same room. Babies classified as "slow-to-warm-up" take their time deciding how to respond to the bustle and the people in the household and need extra attention to draw them out and into the life of the family. Parents must learn to "read" their own baby to determine which kinds of sight, sound, or touch cause them to be alert and interested and which cause them emotional and physical discomfort. Learning to get along with their babies and to make the best of personality differences is one of the important ways parents can help their infants adjust to the world.

During the first six months of life, infants' immune systems are not fully developed. They are born with a natural immunity to some illnesses derived from their mothers' immune systems, but these protections deteriorate rather rapidly. The infant's own immune system takes over as it matures later in the first year. In an age of inoculations and the near eradication of many life-threatening childhood diseases, it is easy to forget that there are many illnesses to which infants are especially vulnerable and for which shots are either not available or not appropriate for use with infants. Common respiratory, gastrointestinal, and viral infections can pose serious health risks to a young baby. Besides being put on a regular schedule of immunization, infants need to be protected from exposure to disease as much as possible.

Physical development is very rapid during the first year. Babies typically double their birth weight in six months and triple it in a year. There are advances in large muscle coordination, such as gradual abilities to hold up the head, roll over, crawl, creep, sit up, stand, and eventually walk. Babies also develop in fine motor coordination, or the ability to grasp, release, and eventually control objects. These developments create another set of infant needs: space to move about, safe clean objects to manipulate, and protection from falls, poisons, and other hazards.

In spite of the seeming absence of what the programmer-father called "logic," infants are also developing cognitively—that is, learning—during the first days and months of life. One major cognitive goal is the refinement of the ability to perceive through the senses. Perception of external objects and events and of internal processes is the basis of all infant learning, as it is the basis of learning in older children and adults. Through perceiving the unique facial features, voice, touch, and behavior of a parent, an infant is able to separate that person from other persons in the environment. All infants need a variety of textures to feel (tactile stimulation) and a variety of objects to look at (visual stimulation). They also need auditory stimulation if they are to learn to discriminate sounds; infants are born with a preference for and attraction to the sound of the human voice. The connection between sensory stimulation and the development of learning, once discovered by researchers studying infancy, gave rise to a kind of panic among parents, who were afraid that unless they supplied mobiles and toys designated as "educational," their baby would not be intelligent. In fact, ordinary household objects or anything that stimulates an infant's interest in learning about the world, presented at the appropriate time by a caring person, will allow for intellectual growth.

Of course, if basic physical requirements of food, sleep, and hygiene are not met in a prompt fashion, infants cannot develop interest in learning about the world and the sense of trust they need to survive in that world. This brings us to the obvious conclusion that the infant's primary need is for someone who is "tuned in" to his or her needs for stimulation at one time and rest at another, who can differentiate between cries of hunger and cries of distress, and who, in Bronfenbrenner's words, is "crazy about that kid."[5]

For an infant, the first caregivers not only control the environment—they are the environment to a great extent. Much of the time that infants and caregivers spend together in the first half of the first year is taken up with hours and hours of reciprocal communication in which they learn about one another. The infant cries, the parent comforts. The baby smiles, the parent smiles back. The infant coos and responds to the parent jiggling a toy in front of him. The infant may attempt to grasp the toy, or he may look away, indicating that he is overstimulated and can absorb no more. Such smoothly orchestrated scenes, enacted between a parent and baby, take place in the span of a few minutes, but many times each day. Eventually the baby develops a sense that there is someone in the world who knows what the infant needs and will supply it. A secure attachment (popularly called "bonding") to the parent ensues. Communication fosters that attachment, and family time together is the key to its success.

Stern has coined the word "attunement" to describe the total verbal and nonverbal communication that parent and child develop together.[20] Attunement does not happen as a result of parental instinct or exceptional infant intelligence. Parents do not automatically know what their own child needs in the first few months; they learn. The first smile, the first bath, the first sound that resembles a word, and the first attempts to crawl across the rug all are social experiences as well as physical and cognitive ones. And all involve the mutual interaction between the child and the family member who cares most frequently for the child. Because this is a two-way partnership, parent and child need to be with one another. This continuous companionship is most easily accomplished in the home with few outside pressures on the parent.

ATTACHMENT AND THE SOCIAL-EMOTIONAL WORLD

Because of the importance of the infant's or toddler's relationship to parents and caregivers in promoting healthy development, it is this relationship that social scientists most often explore in their research on the effects of early supplementary care. Attachment is an emotional bond—a sense of security and love—that a child develops with the people who care for and love him or her. Newborns do not appear to care much about who meets their needs, as long as their needs are satisfied. Soon, however, they develop a preference for their primary caregiver (usually the mother). This preference grows stronger in the latter half of the first year. Securely attached one-year-olds often seek physical contact with their mothers, cry loudly when she disappears from sight, and actively shun strangers. Research has now shown that babies can form attachments to other significant people in their lives, such as fathers, grandparents, and siblings,[14] but the most central and important bond is almost always to the mother.

The importance of secure attachment is that it gives the child a sense of trust, a feeling that the world is a good place. From this foundation the child will be able to explore the world and learn about it, knowing that someone is always there to give protection and guidance. Infants who do not develop secure attachments may not feel safe enough to negotiate their environment. Learning will suffer, they may have difficulties developing relationships with others in both childhood and adulthood, and they are more likely to develop emotional or behavioral problems. These are only possible outcomes, of course, but they represent the opinions of most (but not all) of the scientists who have studied attachment. We now turn to their studies.

Research on Attachment

Before daily child care for very young children was as widespread as it is today, studies in residential institutions and hospitals showed that inadequate stimulation and attention, and disruption of close contact with their mothers, caused infants to suffer alarming and damaging effects. Infants institutionalized or hospitalized for long periods without much interaction with loving caregivers showed signs of depression and withdrawal. (See Zigler and Finn-Stevenson[25] for a review.) Studies conducted in laboratories with primates showed that interrupted maternal-child contact resulted in infants developing insecure attachments to their mothers and eventual psychological disturbances.[13] Although these early studies dealt with institutionalized infants and baby animals, the fear was that short-term separations of human infants from their mothers, such as those experienced in regular child care, might have similar negative effects on the development of secure attachments. Therefore, the most prolific research on infancy, seen by many as being most relevant to the question of the effects of early supplementary child care, has been in the area of maternal-infant attachment.

Attachment behavior is commonly measured by a procedure called the Strange Situation.[2] A child and mother enter an unfamiliar room; soon a stranger enters and the mother departs. How the child responds to the strange environment, the strange adult, and especially to the mother when she returns are used as indicators of the quality of attachment. Securely attached infants use their mother as a base of operations—they take brief forays to explore the new environment or make overtures toward the stranger, but they soon retreat to their mother and begin the adventure again. They greet her very positively when she returns from a brief absence. Anxiously attached infants will show distress in the unfamiliar room even while their mother is there, and they may resist her when she returns. Avoidant attachment is shown by infants who do not much care to explore the room but do not seek their mothers for encouragement. They show little distress when she leaves and may ignore her when she returns.

How quality of attachment relates to later behavior has become somewhat controversial. For example, Jay Belsky, who has long studied the topic, reviewed the research and concluded that insecurely attached infants become more aggressive, misbehave more, are less compliant, and are less liked by their peers when they enter school.[4] Other researchers are more cautious in their interpretation of the same studies, but do seem to agree that insecure attachment is a risk factor for later socioemotional difficulties.[19] Still others are not so sure.[6]

When it comes to the question of whether early supplementary child care promotes insecure attachments and later problems, the controversy becomes much more heated. Over a decade ago, Belsky reviewed the existing studies and concluded that out-of-home care has no adverse effects on infants. As the practice became more common and the research more prolific, he again reviewed the matter and came to the opposite conclusion.[4] For Belsky to change his position publicly indicates not only open-mindedness, but a very deep concern for the infants being placed in child care. Not all equally concerned professionals agree with Belsky, however. One article, in which he suggested that early nonmaternal care poses a risk for developing insecure attachments and eventual behavioral difficulties,[3] prompted numerous responses from scholars. Perhaps the harshest came from Phillips, McCartney, Scarr, and Howes, who criticized Belsky's selective use of studies and method of interpreting results.[17] These authors felt that the existing literature was simply not sophisticated enough to warrant drawing any firm conclusions about the effects of infant day care.

The controversy has shown no signs of subsiding. Belsky's most recent analysis, in the journal *Early Childhood Research Quarterly*, is followed by reviews of his review.[8] Again, none of the authors of these commentaries wholeheartedly endorses Belsky's conclusion that infants who experience more than 20 hours per week of supplementary child care in the first year of life are at risk of developing insecure attachments and later social-emotional problems. Yet most express cautious concern about the practice, remain uncertain about its effects, and agree with Belsky's call for more and better research.

Scientists attempting to explore the effects of out-of-home care on infants face the same problems as those studying child care for older children. As explained in Chapter 3, variations in child care settings, caregiver experience and behavior, and characteristics of individual children and families all affect the response to child care. Those who study infant care are further hampered by the general lack of suitable measures of social and emotional behavior in infants, and by rapidly changing theories of personality development in the early years of life.

Although the Strange Situation is generally considered to be of value in assessing quality of attachment, it is not appropriate for use with children over the age of about 20 months. Therefore it becomes difficult to compare early with later attachment behavior to see if it is altered by child care. Scientists have devised a few other measures and are working to construct more, but it will be some time before their validity and reliability can be established and researchers can begin to feel comfortable using them. Clarke-Stewart discusses some of these alternative measures after she questions the appropriateness of the most widely used measure—the Strange Situation—in child care studies.[6] Leaving a baby in a strange room with a strange adult, she argues, is not that uncommon an experience to an infant who is dropped off at child care every day. The situation is not as stressful as it would be to a baby who stays at home with mother. Therefore, behaviors such as avoiding contact with the mother when she leaves and returns may indicate the child's adaptation to daily separations rather than problems with attachment. If the child care infant's response differs from that of the home-reared infant, it may be that each has developed a response style that fits with the circumstances. In fact, infants with different experiential backgrounds (such as mother care or child care) may express their attachment in different ways, a point well taken in light of findings that children in different cultures (and hence backgrounds) display varying patterns of attachment (see Thompson[22]).

Theorists are also beginning to question some of the long-held views about attachment. Where once they believed that the parent-child bond developed in the first year of life, some are now beginning to think it continues to develop through at least the second and third years. Thus, all may not be lost if attachment is not secured early in life. Second, some developmentalists are beginning to wonder if attachment relationships classified as insecure are as ominous as once believed. After all, infants who are placed in supplementary care might be better able to adapt and cope if they develop attachments in addition to the mother-child bond. Their parents may also encourage independent behavior at an early age.[6] And if insecure attachments are more common in child care infants, the real cause may not be the daily separations but the ongoing parent-child relationship. Working mothers are understandably busy and may feel relatively high levels of pressure and stress. Thus they may not have the time or energy to devote to nurturing their relationship with their infants.

Finally, even the last bit of comforting advice experts once had for parents is now coming under scrutiny. For several years there was general agreement that infants form attachments to their parents, not to their supplementary caregivers (see Gamble and Zigler[11]). Evidence is now surfacing that infants do form attachments to their caregivers.[1] This attachment does not displace the bond to the parent, is of a different type, and may signal a healthy adaptation to the supplementary care experience.

Such indications that formation of an attachment to the caregiver is advantageous to the development of an infant in child care underscore the importance of qualified caregivers (see also Chapter 3). If such findings are replicated and explained by further studies, they will also have an impact on our perceptions of such issues as staff-child ratio and caregiver consistency. If, as we strongly suspect, the formation of attachment to the caregiver is necessary to a positive and healthy experience in infant care, then caregivers must be suitable partners, by nature and by training. Changes in caregivers during infancy and toddlerhood must be avoided, and the number of infants and toddlers with whom one caregiver can form appropriate relationships is necessarily limited. We will explore these issues further later in this chapter.

Research on the effects of early supplementary child care is clearly a long way from providing any definitive answers. The assessment tool most relied upon has come under attack, raising questions about the value of much previous work. Theories of attachment and personality development are undergoing drastic revision, making scientists wonder if they have been asking the right questions all along. Yet what seems to be a state of confusion in the scientific literature is really not that dire. Today, more comprehensive research has been spurred by this healthy atmosphere of challenges to assumptions and conclusions and by the sharing of research results and information among different branches of the scientific community.

What is dire about the lack of clear answers at this time in history is that so many infants are experiencing supplementary care—right now—and their development cannot be put on hold while the experts figure out the consequences. Thus there has been much pressure on scientists to apply the results of their work to the current reality of infant child care. At issue is whether social science research to date can be interpreted to say that child care for all infants puts them at risk of future problems in social development, or whether the negative outcomes that have been observed in some children can be attributed to any one or combination of other factors that enter into their lives, such as family stress, the child's gender, the age of entry into child care, the length of time in child care, the quality and stability of the setting, or a host of individual characteristics. Gamble and Zigler suggested that some of these elements constitute risk factors that have an additive effect.[11] For example, males appear to be more adversely affected by early supplementary care than do females. So are children whose parents feel high levels of stress. We know that children from single-parent homes or those whose families are financially insecure are more likely to show problems in development, as are those in poor-quality care. The more of these factors a child experiences, the more likely he or she is to be harmed by early child care placement. Thus, we can predict with certainty that a baby boy from a father-absent home, living below the poverty level, and placed in a poor-quality caregiving setting will not have a chance at optimal development. Gamble and Zigler recommend that a variety of options be available to all parents of infants so they can choose what they think is best for themselves and their babies. The problem, of course, is that these options are not widely available, and most parents do not have much choice about when and where they will place their infants into child care.

The increasing number of very young infants experiencing child care continues to alarm us and to leave many social scientists, whatever their theoretical views, questioning whether research to date can legitimately be used to justify or condemn such a momentous and massive change in the rearing of infants in American society. Thus the experts' conclusions are often expressed in very cautious terms. Belsky, we have noted, warns that "risks seem to be associated with extensive nonmaternal care in the first year."[4] L. Alan Sroufe agrees, with a somewhat stronger statement: "I personally believe that parents who can do so should delay full-time day care into the second year, but this is as much because of what we do not know as it is because of what we do know."[19] Others tend toward the opposite judgment. Fein and Fox state that current studies "have too many methodological problems and constraints to serve as a basis for alarm or negative conclusions about the consequences of early nonparental care."[9] Perhaps the most unequivocal conclusion comes from Deborah Phillips and her colleagues, who declare that in this case responsible scientists still need to say, "I don't know—the evidence is inconclusive."[17] And because we don't know, we must proceed with the utmost caution. Disagreements among experts about the specific outcomes of various factors in infant/toddler care ought to encourage us to eliminate all possibly problematic elements and to insure care of the best quality we can devise.

Does the Research Tell Parents Anything?

With the experts so divided, it is not surprising that the public does not comprehend what those reviewing the research are actually saying about the effects of early supplementary care. Journalists do not always understand it either, so when parents rely on secondary interpretations in the mass media, they come away with a jumble of contradictory advice. Some of the experts are interpreted as saying that all mothers should stay at home with their children at least until they are in school (to prevent disastrous effects), while others are understood to be advising that all children should be placed in supplementary care, the sooner the better, in order to give them a "head start" on the wonderful things in life that could be derived from early child care experience. In reality, neither of these extreme positions accurately represents the statements of any of the experts mentioned above.

Meanwhile, more and more families are being pressured by the necessity of two incomes and by the social pressure for educated women to return to the work place soon after giving birth to avoid interrupting their careers and their future earning potential. Single parents, whose numbers are increasing, feel not only pressured but also sentenced to work. Parents are thus caught in an unresolvable dilemma: everything from dire consequences to social and intellectual success is being predicted for babies in child care, while more and more families feel the necessity of child care for their overall welfare.

What parents should keep in mind when they hear of these debates is that there is tremendous variability in quality among child care settings in the United States (Chapter 1), a variability that makes research difficult and interpreting research even more complicated (Chapter 3). Researchers cannot simply compare infants in child care with those who are reared at home for the first year, because neither of these two groups is experiencing anything like uniform child-rearing practices. Further, not all of the research has been done; we should always keep in mind that the phenomenon is too new for researchers to have available for study large numbers of adolescents and adults who experienced child care—in all its various forms—during infancy. Thus, the research community must continue to study and debate the question at hand, but they must do more than that. They need to develop guidelines for understanding the studies that they conduct, guidelines that parents can use to make individual family decisions and that society can use to make policy decisions regarding supplementary care for infants.

Such a consensus or unified voice is developing under the aegis of the National Center for Clinical Infant Programs with the help of the Institute of Medicine of the National Academy of Sciences. The NCCIP recently brought 16 researchers and other experts together in Washington, D.C. to develop a clear statement on child care for infants. They hoped that the statement would represent a broad consensus of the field and would lay out an agenda of unresolved research questions and promising approaches. In a press release issued after this summit meeting, chaired by Edward Zigler, the scientists and scholars involved made the following statements:

> [W]hen parents have choices about selection and utilization of supplementary care for their infants and toddlers and have access to stable child care arrangements featuring skilled, sensitive and motivated caregivers, there is every reason to believe that both children and families can thrive. . . . [However,] inadequate care poses risks to the current well-being and future development of infants, toddlers and their families, on whose productivity the country depends.[15]

The statement went on to recommend goals and methods for conducting further research. Their message appears to have been heard. Under the leadership of director Duane Alexander, the National Institute of Child Health and Human Development has committed itself to a series of studies on infant/toddler care, coordinated by Henry Ricciuti. The panel also attempted to delineate the conditions under which infant and toddler child care can be considered adequate, a topic to which we now turn.

THE DEVELOPMENTAL NEEDS OF INFANTS AND TODDLERS

We have already expressed our belief that very young infants need to remain at home with a parent to begin the process of forming a mutual relationship. The developmental needs of older infants and toddlers can be met in an out-of-home setting if it is carefully designed to do so. Yet alarming but not unexpected news comes from preliminary reports from an as yet unpublished section of the National Child Care

Staffing Study by Phillips, Howes, and Whitebook. In 1989, at a meeting of the Society for Research in Child Development in Kansas City, Kansas, these researchers stated that large numbers of infants and toddlers in the United States who are in child care are not experiencing such carefully designed settings.[16]

The needs of this young group are much more varied than those of the newborn, both in scope and as dictated by the child's rapidly changing level of development. First we should explain why infants and toddlers are considered together when they are clearly so different. Child development specialists classify children by developmental level rather than by chronological age, because although all children mature in the same sequential stages, there is considerable variation from child to child in the ages at which these stages are entered and resolved. In the development of children in the first three years of life, these variations are even more pronounced. To establish guidelines for child care, however, approximate ages must be used for the sake of consistency. Thus, children under one year of age are considered infants, and children between one and about three years are considered toddlers. As the name implies, the developmental marker used to divide infants from toddlers is the first tentative attempts at walking on one's own. (In popular British usage, toddlers are called "runabout babies," an equally descriptive term.) Because most infants begin to walk any time between approximately nine and eighteen months, each will enter toddlerhood, strictly speaking, at a different age.

Of course, many other important developmental milestones are being achieved by the individual child during the first three years. Clearly, the care of a six-month-old, who needs to be diapered, fed, and carried about, is totally different from the care of a thirty-six-month-old who can run, talk, and be entertained by toys and books. Still, the rapid pace of development from birth to about the third birthday, which necessitates continuous changes in what constitutes an appropriate caregiving environment, is the rationale for linking these vastly different creatures together in discussions of child care for the very young.

The ages zero to three deserve special consideration in assessing child care for several other reasons. First, these years represent the time of laying groundwork for all the developmental tasks that follow as the child matures to adulthood. Infancy and toddlerhood are full of familiar "firsts": first tooth, first smile, first cold, first step, and first words and sentences. These stages also include essential milestones that mark the beginnings of the first definitions of self in relation to the world, including interest in the people and objects in it, special attachments for family members, and communication of emotions and ideas. During the first three years children begin the construction of complex social, psychological, and intellectual ideas—efforts that must be accomplished before they can continue their developmental progression to the next stage. The most important "firsts," upon which social-emotional as well as cognitive growth depend, are thus what Greenspan and Greenspan have termed "first feelings."[12]

According to some theorists, all of these tasks spring from an innate, genetically based timetable (the "nature" emphasis); according to others, development is spurred from experiences with people and things in the environment (the "nurture" emphasis). Today, most child development experts agree that there is considerable interaction between the varying abilities with which children are born and the basic environments in which they are played out. (For a more complete discussion, see Gamble and Zigler[11].)

Another reason for the depth of concern about the effects of child care on infants and toddlers is that, although older children also learn within an environment that is largely under the control of adults, infants and toddlers are less able to negotiate their social and physical surroundings and are thus presumed to be more vulnerable to negative effects. More than at any subsequent stage, the immediate environment and the adults in it are the small sphere in which all development must be accomplished. Older children have a larger sphere that includes school, teachers, and peers, as well as family. Psychological growth will proceed smoothly in that environment if the child has developed a sense of comfort and trust in the very first environments experienced in infancy.

An illustration of the infant's and toddler's reliance on the environment may be seen by contrasting the skills exhibited by very young as opposed to older children in areas such as toileting, feeding, and talking. A preschooler can tell a caregiver that she needs to use the bathroom and can get there under her own power; an infant must wait to be changed. A school-age child can explain that he missed lunch and then make his own sandwich, if necessary; an infant can only cry and wait until someone understands that he needs to be fed. Infants and toddlers are also more vulnerable to infection and certain types of injuries. They need adults to protect them through sound health and safety practices.

The centrality of adults to the physical survival of the infant and toddler has parallels in personality and intellectual development. If there is one major task of infancy, it is the development of close, secure ties to an adult, or small group of adults, who can be counted on to consistently supply the child's basic needs and to respond to him or her as an individual. This has obvious implications for social and emotional development, yet it should be considered in the area of cognitive development as well. For example, until sometime in the second half of the first year, infants do not know that a person who is out of sight has not disappeared entirely. When it becomes obvious from repeated experience that the caregiver the infant saw when she fell asleep is the same caregiver who appears when she wakes up and cries, the child establishes her first understanding of the permanence of physical objects (a cognitive issue) as well as a trusting relationship (a social-emotional issue). Language development, another cognitive task, is also encouraged by a sensitive caregiver who mimics infant babbling and recognizes and reinforces attempts to form words, all in the context of social interaction.

The Essentials of Infant/Toddler Care

All of these needs and changes highlight the most basic aspect of quality in any caregiving environment for the very young—the amount of individual attention the child receives. This is related both to the number of children per caregiver and to the number of children present. The latest revision of the FIDCR cited a ratio of one caregiver for every three infants or four toddlers as a minimum requirement. Having so few children to care for enables the caregiver to meet each child's needs promptly and allows her time to "tune in" to the child's individual personality. A maximum group size of six for infants and twelve for toddlers was also recommended. The rationale was that infants especially, with their wide variety of sleeping, waking, eating, and activity cycles, cannot contend with a large group of people without becoming withdrawn or irritable. Further, past research has indicated that controlling the size of the group can assist children to develop healthy relationships with caregivers (e.g., the 1979 National Day Care Study[18]). (However, some question about the significance of group size has been raised in more recent studies, as will be seen when Phillips, Howes, and Whitebook publish their complete findings. Whether or not this information will affect actual practice in child care centers is an issue that must be addressed in the future.)

The physical conditions of the environment, such as the type and amount of space, safety and sanitary conditions, and so forth, will have obvious effects on the child. Infants' cribs should not be too close together, for health and safety reasons and to allow undisturbed sleep when the child requires it. Infants and toddlers need floors with clean, comfortable surfaces so that they can have the means for creeping, crawling, walking, and other forms of physical exercise. Furniture should be child-sized, devoid of peeling toxic paint and with smooth, sanded edges. Toys should be washable and contain no small parts. Facilities for sanitary diaper changes should be provided, and sanitary food preparation practices should be observed. Physical conditions such as this are most commonly controlled by state and local regulations, although states vary from those that do not even specify that food handlers wash their hands before cooking or serving food, to those that require specific types of kitchen equipment and public health practices.[23]

Next, the daily program practiced in the child care facility should be developmentally appropriate and should be clearly outlined by caregivers and understood by parents. A "developmentally appropriate" program must be defined according to the individual needs of children at their particular stage of development. One four-month-old may delight in "standing" every time he is held on a shoulder or lap; another may resist placing feet on a surface and prefer to be nestled in one arm. A thirty-month-old may enjoy scribbling with crayons, while another may still be at the stage of eating crayons. Thus, an adequate infant/toddler program does not consist of anything resembling formal lessons. Instead, the "lessons" are initiated by the child, who indicates what he or she is ready to tackle.

A developmentally appropriate program for infants and toddlers must include such obvious elements as suitable toys, materials, and opportunities for experiences that foster the child's own growth patterns. The program should allow for the individual schedules of children as regards sleeping, exploratory activity, and feeding. Most important, it should also provide for the emergence and encouragement of the milestones of social-emotional development—the "first feelings" noted by Greenspan and Greenspan,[12] upon which future development in all phases is based. The "program" for infants and toddlers, then, should be considered as the creation of an atmosphere of interaction between children and caregivers, in which caregivers respond to individual children's behaviors appropriately.

Because each child is unique, there can be no exacting definition of a developmentally appropriate program. This may be one reason why 58% of the states do not mandate developmental programs of care for infants and toddlers.[24] Of those that do have specific regulations concerning the nature of the program, some are so minimal as to state that "infants and toddlers should be offered water at intervals. Infants shall not remain in cribs, baby beds or playpens all day."[24]

The necessity for a state to include the above statement mandating basically humane treatment of very young children underscores the most important element of quality of infant/toddler care: the number, qualifications, and training of staff. Ideally, the same caregiver should be responsible for the same group of children throughout the hours and days they are in care. Because child care providers control every aspect of the infant or toddler's developmental environment, proper training is absolutely essential. Appropriate training will help them understand infant/toddler development and become sensitive to individual differences and needs—both of children and of parents.

Contrary to popular belief, caring for the children of others on a daily basis is not exactly the same as raising one's own children. As we mentioned earlier, a unique kind of relationship develops between caregivers and children, which is not to be confused with the attachment between parents and their own children. A caregiver must form a relationship with a child that is mutual, loving, and respectful, as parents do. Yet caregivers must develop a sense of investment in the child's current welfare and future development, while understanding that they have little say in the portion of the child's environment that is centered in the family. They must be able to maintain that sense of investment and involvement, yet be willing to release children to the care of their families at the end of the day and at the end of months or years of caregiving with a minimum amount of strain on themselves, on their charges, or on parents. In short, caring for the children of others involves being able to engage intensely with children at the moment and to disengage gracefully and confidently at appropriate times.

We believe that good communication between parent and caregiver is one of the factors that helps to maintain the necessary climate for this type of caregiver involvement. Communication between home and caregiver is necessary in any child care setting, but it takes on special significance in the lives of infants and toddlers, who are least able to communicate their needs, feelings, and experiences verbally. Decisions about issues such as when and how to begin toilet training, how to determine feeding schedules, and how to handle the signs of minor illnesses, food allergies, and diaper rash must be arrived at by close observation of the child in the home and in the child care setting and by daily exchange of information between the child's caregivers and parents. Ultimately, however, parents make the final decisions about such issues—caregivers can only act as guides. In addition, many parents of infants are beset with guilt and worry over having to leave their babies in child care. These emotions can be allayed somewhat if the provider shares the events of the child's day with parents. New parents who are unsure of their own caregiving abilities could also learn from the provider if information is presented in a nonthreatening manner. Thus, a good caregiver nurtures not only the child but the family and is an integral part of the family support system.

An alliance between parents and caregivers is also very important to the child. When these significant adults share common methods and expectations, they promote continuity in the child's experiences between home and out-of-home care. When children are treated in a somewhat consistent manner, their development can proceed more smoothly than when they must continuously make adjustments to radically different environments. Continuity is such an important developmental nutrient, provided only through parent-caregiver communication, that parental involvement in child care settings was written into the FIDCR, and the National Association for the Education of Young Children included the principle in their accreditation program for child care centers. Indeed, the effort expended in a child care setting to promote a partnership between parents and caregivers is considered a subjective indicator of quality care.

Issues That Thwart Quality

Training for caregivers of infants and toddlers can take many forms, from two- or four-year programs in child development at the college level, to competency-based Child Development Associate credentials (Chapter 3), to state or privately run in-service training programs. Yet because of staff shortages and the high ratio of infants to caregivers needed, it is difficult for staff to be relieved from their duties long enough to participate in even a half-day workshop. For family day care providers, who may spend as much as 12 hours a day caring for their charges, attending training sessions outside of the home is even more difficult. Therefore, the attempt to upgrade training for child care providers, an essential element in any overall plan to improve infant/toddler care, is an uphill battle. Even if better training could be achieved, it would have to be linked to higher wages or there would be little incentive for caregivers to enroll.

This brings us to another barrier to the provision of quality infant care: economics. Because it is labor-intensive, infant/toddler care of adequate quality is the most expensive type of child care, costing as much as $150–200 per child per week in some areas of the country. It is no wonder that one of the primary reasons that parents choose one child care provider over another is cost, not qualifications. In spite of the high fees paid by parents, infant caregivers, like other child care workers, receive abysmally low wages considering the importance of the work they do. This fact largely explains why child care centers serving infants and toddlers have difficulty attracting even minimally trained and screened personnel and even more difficulty keeping them. According to Helen Ward of the Connecticut Association of Human Services, child care workers in Connecticut cite economic difficulties as the major factor in their decisions to leave the child care profession. This results in a high turnover in caregivers, creating a climate opposite to that required for infants and toddlers to form secure relationships with those who care for them.

The quality of infant and toddler care has been even more affected than that of preschool child care by the failure of licensing and regulation practices. Although the majority of working parents with children under preschool age choose family day care arrangements, several states do not deem it necessary to register these providers or to assist them in any way. Many states do attempt to license and regulate this type of child care, but the majority of family day care providers operate underground to escape the cost and inconvenience of monitoring and licensure. Where states do have requirements for both family day care homes and child care centers, many have few specific regulations for infant/toddler care. According to data drawn from a federal study done in 1982, several states had no regulations whatsoever concerning infant and toddler care, and only three states fulfilled the requirements set up under the 1980 FIDCR for staff-child ratio for both infant and toddler groups.[24]

In the absence of consistent national standards, parents are left on their own to evaluate caregiving environments for their infants and toddlers. Yet working parents probably have the least time to conduct investigations of this sort. A typical case is a parent who discovers she must return to the work force several weeks or months before she would like, and has only a short time in which to find suitable care for her infant. If there is an information and referral service in her community, she may receive a short list of licensed homes and centers, only to discover that they are all full. Frantic calls to friends and family may produce a few names of people who "might be interested" in taking on the daily care of an infant. Because of the shortage of providers for infant/toddler care, such parents may consider themselves lucky to find any facility with an opening and may hesitate to examine the providers and their references too closely. In short, out of desperation, they may decide that any place and any caregiver will do. As with other forms of child care, the key factors in the individual parent's decision are availability, accessibility, and affordability, not necessarily what is really best for their young child.

Parents, especially first-time parents of infants, need more support and information than they currently receive to choose wisely what will be a major environment for their children during their early development. They need a list of questions to consider about the setting in which they are placing their infants, and they need encouragement to speak to the provider about aspects of the center or home that trouble them, both at the time they first visit the facility and at any time during the period their children are enrolled there. Although some local resource and referral services and national groups offer checklists for evaluating a child care provider, few offer a list of factors to consider for the special care of infants and toddlers. One exception is a pamphlet by Laura Dittman, distributed by the National Association for the Education of Young Children and the National Center for Clinical Infant Programs, which explains in detail how to find and evaluate care for infants and toddlers.[7] There are also a number of useful books and magazine articles, but few parents know where to find them.

Yet even if the availability of such information were more widely known, the shortage of licensed settings would negate any benefits to families seeking safe and reliable child care. Knowing how to choose a child care environment is a moot point when environments that meet those specifications are unavailable.

Although we are not sure about the effects of good child care environments on infants and toddlers, it is clear that poor environments will interfere with healthy development and thus have consequences far beyond the lives of those babies and families experiencing the deficits. The quality of care that infants and toddlers receive will eventually affect the school, work place, community, and nation. The cost of insuring that adequate infant care is available is minute compared to the long-term and widespread cost of not providing it. To meet the crisis as a nation, we must realize that the needs of the society need not be in conflict with the needs of individual children and their families. Through appropriate systems of support, including infant care leaves, and an expanded child care service system, we can preserve the rights of each family to choose where, when, and how their infants and toddlers will be cared for. (See also Chapter 10.)

5

The Crisis of Infant Care: Meeting the Needs of Families

Decisions about placing an infant into child care are among the most anguishing ones ever made by a family. Before they can decide whether or not to entrust their child to a specific caregiving setting and at what age, each family must struggle with a series of personal questions that affect those choices. How long does the individual mother need, physically and psychologically, to recover from childbirth? How long do parents and infants need to develop secure attachments and regular routines and to adjust fully to the family dynamics that follow the addition of a new member of the household? And the most essential question is: How long can mothers (or fathers, in some cases) extend what little unpaid child-rearing leave they may have before they are required to return to work or lose jobs that represent a significant part, or perhaps all, of their family income?

In the ideal scenario, the decision that it is time for the child's main caregiver to return to the work place would be made by a family in consultation with a number of resources: the family physician or pediatrician, child care staff, the employer, and respected relatives and friends. It would be a decision that would reflect the family's and the child's personal needs as well as the needs of the work place. There would be ample government and private support, beginning with generous parental leave policies, to allow each family freedom to choose what is best for that child in that family. There would be sufficient time for the parents to weigh the pros and cons of their particular infant being in child care, and many alternative types of care would be available.

In reality, however, the decision to place their baby in care is usually made by parents under the combined siege of career pressures, financial pressures, and/or pressures from the employer. Thus, a family may be said to be in a personal crisis situation when the issue of placing an infant in child care arises before the parents and baby are fully adjusted to what is usually considered a happy, although moderately stressful, family situation—the addition of a new member by birth or adoption.

Yet a number of factors convert this personal crisis into a national and societal one. There is insufficient quality infant care for the families who need it. There is a paucity of reliable information about what constitutes adequate care, and there are not enough resources to enable providers to offer it or for families to pay for it. The lack of standard leaves from work for childbirth and neonatal care creates problems not only among families, but also among employers and the society as a whole. Employers suffer when parents settle too soon for too little, and then discover that they must miss workdays to care for a sick child, to cover for an irresponsible caregiver, or to search for a new child care arrangement. Society suffers when the future of a whole generation of citizens is ransomed for current work place needs and the immediate financial needs of families.

THE FAMILY'S NEEDS

The needs of any family at the time a new child is introduced into the household cannot be separated from the needs of the child discussed in Chapter 4. Like those of the newborn, family needs are emotional as well as physical and cognitive. Attachment and adaptation, as has been illustrated, are two-way processes. For parents to develop a comfortable and positive relationship with an infant, their own needs must be met. Otherwise, they will lack the resources and stamina to offer their best caregiving to their infants and their other children.

Mothers obviously need rest in the first months after a birth. Physical recovery from childbirth takes time as many bodily systems gradually return to their prepregnancy state. Fathers and adoptive parents also need extra rest to compensate for being awakened in the middle of the night for feedings or bouts of colic. Parents need periodic breaks from the 24-hour demands of an infant, especially one who is colicky or does not care to sleep much. All family members, not just nursing mothers, need to be adequately nourished to meet the physical demands placed upon them. And, of course, their financial needs are increased with the addition of a new family member.

Older children in a family need concrete information and reassurance about the newcomer's effect on their own lives. They need to participate, in ways suitable to their developmental levels, in the care of the newborn. They, like the parents, need to establish a mutually satisfying way of interacting with the new baby. Children's anxieties and sibling rivalry must be dealt with, and the everyday needs of their own developmental stages must be met at the same time. Given the importance of responsiveness to the newborn, caring for older children in the first weeks and months after birth represents a natural but enormous conflict for parents.

Parents of a new baby have their own emotional needs, which must be addressed if the family is to learn to function in its new structure. "Baby blues," or mild feelings of depression, are not uncommon in new mothers, although serious psychiatric conditions are rare.[18] Fathers living with new mothers who are feeling fatigued or melancholy will naturally have more demands placed upon them. Self-esteem, so important in the development of children, still must be nurtured in adults. In our society there is a dearth of parent training and parent support, which leaves many new mothers and fathers feeling unprepared for their new roles. Fearing they will be unable to meet the first-born infant's needs, to meet the needs of a handicapped or merely different infant, or to cope with the increasing demands on their resources occasioned by an additional child, parents of infants may be beset with feelings of inadequacy and potential failure. No real preparation for the physical and emotional reality of family life with an infant is available to most parents. Thus new parents have strong needs for the personal support of family, friends, and the society in which they live.

Like their infants, parents also have cognitive needs. Parenting itself is a "hands-on" learning experience, one that is largely unsupervised in American society today. Parents get to know each new baby by trial and error, by seeing what response works best with this child. They begin to recognize individual patterns of growth in addition to whatever general principles they have picked up from other adults, from reading, and from child development courses if they have been lucky enough to have them. Like the development of the child, parent development is ongoing. There is no one point in time, no particular day, when a parent becomes qualified.

Families with Special Needs

Of the 3.7 million babies born in the United States each year, 7% or about 250,000 of them are premature or low birthweight infants.[6]

These children may suffer from a variety of physical and neurological impairments. Between 100,000 and 150,000 others (3% to 5%) are born with congenital abnormalities that can lead to mental retardation, and an additional 1% to 2% have other identifiable disabilities. Far more common, but difficult to quantify, are the otherwise normal infants who suffer from colic or hypersensitivity.

In Chapter 7, the needs of these high-risk infants in child care environments will be discussed. Our focus here is on the families caring for such babies at home during the first weeks and months of life. Developmental or physical handicaps and chronic illnesses put increased stresses on parents in addition to the normal adjustments that must be made when a new child joins the family.

For example, tremendous challenge is created when a child must be hospitalized for weeks or months after the mother has been sent home following delivery. Medical professionals urge parents to assist in the day-to-day care of infants while they are in the hospital, and for good reason. Infants in intensive care need holding, feeding, and attention on a round-the-clock basis, and those who are lavished with such attention tend to gain weight faster and show greater improvement on a variety of health measures than do those who receive routine hospital care.[6] Also, while an infant is hospitalized, parents learn from nurses and other medical staff how to tend to the child's special physical needs, and begin the work of developing a close relationship with the child, work that under normal circumstances begins in the home.

Even after the newborn is physically stabilized and established at home, families may need to participate in special training or intervention programs to learn how to minimize the effects of physical or neurological impairment. They must also learn to interact socially with their special child. Preterm and handicapped infants are often more difficult partners in the attachment process than are other newborns. Their cues—crying and displaying readiness to learn and interact, for example—may be so obscure or different that parents must be specially trained to recognize them.[6]

Minor illnesses or variations in any child's development can interfere with parent-child communication and lengthen the time needed for a family's adjustment to the new baby. Common infant colic, or prolonged and inconsolable crying, is particularly frustrating to parents, as their best efforts to comfort the infant meet with little success. Given proper support and time to "ride out" the storm of colic or temporary illness, parents achieve a sense of mastery.[3] If, however, they have to cut short the time they need to deal with an infant who is ill, they may instead be overwhelmed with feelings of failure, and the relationship between parent and child will begin on a very shaky footing.

For reasons of family stability and cost, the special physical and emotional needs of a handicapped or ill infant are best met at home. If parents are forced by necessity to return to work, not only will the professional care required drain the family budget, but also the child and family may suffer untold damages to a relationship that never had a chance to develop fully. At such time as the child and the family are ready for a child care situation, the special needs of the child at home and in out-of-home care must be coordinated, as will be discussed in Chapter 7.

Society's Response

The basic, normal stresses and needs of families with new children have always existed and continue to exist, regardless of the social and demographic changes that have occurred in the institutions of family and work.[20] What is different today is that more women are likely to be working when they become pregnant than ever before, and more than half of them will return to work before their children are a year old. Many return within weeks of childbirth, long before they are physically and emotionally ready to do so.

Unfortunately, the amount of time father, mother, and child have to spend together is not determined by the extent of their needs, but by other factors. An overriding factor is the family's financial circumstances. Although parents report that they need the opportunity for one parent to stay home for a period of several months to care for the child,[4] many do not have that opportunity. The income of both parents may be necessary to provide for the family's well-being, and they may simply not be able to afford the time off or the risk of losing a job. In the case of a single mother, her income may provide the sole support for her family.

Other factors that determine the length of time parents spend at home with newborn and newly adopted children are policies established in the public and private sectors of the larger society. Policies set within the work place vary widely from one employer to another. Fathers may or may not be given a paid leave of one or two days when a child is born. Mothers may or may not have official paid medical leave for childbirth; in fact, only about 40% of all working women are eligible for maternity leave benefits that include partial wage replacement for the period of disability and a guarantee of a job when they return.[9]

Even when they do have such a leave, it is designed to cover only the average period of recovery from childbirth—six or seven weeks at most—not the six months or so that they need to adjust fully to the emotional and physical changes that are occurring in the family and to get to know their infants. And in cases of adoption, medical or disability leaves do not apply, even though the family has the same adjustments to make to the radical life changes introduced by a new member. Some parents are lucky enough to have employers who will make informal arrangements to accommodate family needs, but most cannot count on the good graces of their bosses to provide them with the income and the security they need as parents of small children.

The net result of such inadequate policies is that what ideally would be a private decision made by a family based on their own situation is really not the family's decision at all. Their fate is decided in the work place. In the recent past, state legislatures and the U.S. Congress have attempted to influence the decision, with minimal success. As a society we have by no means accepted that leaves from work for child-birth and child rearing are a public policy issue rather than private family problems to be solved by families as best they can.

As with child care, efforts to address the obvious need to guarantee parental leaves have met with resistance and adult-centered thinking. New Right thinkers argue that women *should* not be granted leaves for child rearing because they should not return to work anyway. Some representatives of private industry argue that companies cannot afford to grant child-rearing leaves to women because they *would* not return to work after the leave anyway. These arguments fly in the face of facts about women and work that have already been discussed: women's work patterns are increasingly resembling those of men. When women do not return from leaves as agreed, it is possible that they were expected back too soon and that they resigned as a means of extending their leave. The U.S. Census Bureau reports that in recent years (1981–1984) 71% of first-time mothers who received maternity benefits returned to work within six months of childbirth; only 43% of those who received no benefits returned by this time.[19]

We do know that over half of all mothers are working for someone within a year of childbirth. Whether a woman is working for her former employer or another may be related to a complex of perceptions and events beginning at the time she became pregnant. For example, a study conducted by the National Council of Jewish Women Center for the Child noted that when employers accommodate pregnancy-related needs women are more satisfied with their jobs and more willing to work later into pregnancy.[2] Whether or not childbearing leaves are long enough for women to perceive their employers as being flexible about family needs may determine their decisions about when—and if—they will return to a particular company.

The Role of Society in Family Life

American society's disregard of its responsibility to support and assist families with young children has been discussed in the preceding chapters and throughout the literature on American families. Today there is some evidence that this disregard may be eroding. Later in this chapter we will discuss efforts to create national parental leave policies; in Chapter 8 we will examine responses of the business sector to the needs of working families in general and specifically in the area of support for child care. However, we need to examine here one unworkable attitude our society perpetuates about the relationship of the society to the family: In spite of common rhetoric about the family being the central unit of the social structure, society's opinions and policies are based on the idea that citizens are *workers first, family members second.* The acceptance of these priorities results in stress in both the home and the work place and interferes with families finding their own ideal balance between these two major aspects of their lives.

The rapid increase in the number of mothers working has affected women and their children, of course. But fathers, too, have been forced to examine this question of work/family balance. In a family where the division of labor includes a father whose work is outside the home and a mother whose work is primarily within the home, men are able to compartmentalize work and family. As Betty Friedan points out in *The Second Stage,* the rapid increase of wives and mothers in the work force has resulted in much more than arguments over whose turn it is to do the dishes or to change the baby.[5] Both working men and working women today have been forced to reexamine the relationship of family to work. The responsibilities, successes, and failures inherent in each cannot be neatly divided into hours on or hours off the job. Family emergencies—an injured child, a school problem, an ill grandparent—spill into the work places of men as well as women. With increasing frequency, work emergencies—calls from the factory or office on weekends or in the middle of the night—intrude into the family lives of women as well as those of men.

At no time is the necessity for a work/family balance more keenly felt in the work place than at the time a working family is expecting a new child by birth or adoption. Pregnancy due dates are rarely precise enough for prospective parents and their employers to know exactly when and how work must be rescheduled or redistributed. Parents on adoption waiting lists, and the employers of those parents, have even less warning about when a child will arrive, and thus even less opportunity than birth parents to plan for time off to welcome the new child and to arrange for child care. Thus, many employers are already aware of the necessity to adapt the work place and its needs to accommodate the family and its needs around the time of childbirth or adoption.

However, this awareness needs to extend beyond the actual event of childbirth to encompass a sensitivity to the needs and responsibilities of workers who are developing relationships to their infant children. As a society, we need to adopt new attitudes about work and family if we take seriously the notion that we need to invest in human capital for the future as much as we need to produce financial capital in the present.

MODELS FROM OTHER NATIONS

Family leave policies in other industrialized nations have been shaped by goals related to maternal and child health, a sound economy, and the psychological well-being of present and future citizens.[8] Although the United States professes similar goals as a society, our nation remains completely out of step with the rest of the world when it comes to guaranteeing all workers the benefits they need to raise infants adequately. Germany, for example, began supplying unpaid leaves for childbirth in 1878, and paid leaves in 1937.[1] France's basic leave has existed since 1928, Sweden's since 1900. Both of these nations have considerably expanded their leave policies since then.[1] Today a total of 117 countries, including almost all industrialized nations and 81 developing countries, provide a maternity leave, that is, a leave covering the period of disability just before and after birth. Eighty-five countries around the world provide workers with paid sick leaves that cover both income protection and health care related to pregnancy and childbirth. Statutory maternity leave ranges from a minimum of six weeks in England to twelve weeks in Israel and the Netherlands.[8]

Leaves to provide for parenting of the newborn or newly adopted child are also covered under a variety of structures in many industrialized countries and some developing nations. They may be called supplementary maternity or parenting leaves, mother's wages, or child care grants. Although leaves for childbirth usually provide full or close to full wage replacement, supplementary parenting leaves—up to three years in some cases—typically are paid at a flat compensation rate or at some percentage of the average female salary.

Parental leave policies in three European countries serve to illustrate the backwardness of the United States in meeting the needs of families with infants. In Sweden, either parent can receive 90% of salary while caring for a baby for nine months. After that, the parent receives lesser compensation for three months. The parenting leave may be extended for an additional six months after the baby's first birthday on an unpaid basis if the family so desires. Or, an additional six months unpaid leave may be deferred and taken incrementally any time up to the child's eighth birthday.[1] Similarly, a French mother receives 90% of her salary as reimbursement for caring for her child for four months, with an unpaid leave including job security for up to two years after the birth. (Paid leaves in France, unlike those in Sweden, are restricted to mothers only, but either parent is eligible for the unpaid leave if they work for a company with more than 100 employees.) The Federal Republic of Germany (West Germany) provides biological mothers with a 100% salary reimbursement for the first three months after a birth and the U.S. equivalent of $285 per month for the next four months. No unpaid extensions are offered in West Germany.[1]

Sweden, France, and West Germany finance their maternity and parental leaves differently. Most of Sweden's salary reimbursements for new parents come from a payroll tax similar to our social security system, while the rest come from general revenues. The cost of France's parental leaves is raised through a general social security system. West Germans fund their parental leaves through a payroll tax paid directly into the employer's insurance fund, which is supplemented by direct payments from the employer.[1] Canada and Australia provide maternity leave benefits through unemployment insurance, and several other countries pay a flat family allowance to all families on the birth or adoption of children.[8] (An overview of maternity and parenting benefits throughout the world is provided in Zigler and Frank, *The Parental Leave Crisis*.[20])

If the United States is seriously interested in the welfare of working parents and their children, it would seem a simple matter to study and then adopt the various mechanisms by which other nations provide both leave time and funding for parents. Yet the United States is not Sweden, West Germany, or Canada. The benefits these nations provide are tied to unique networks of policies that cover the health and economic needs of workers and the unemployed as well as the needs of the economy. Leaves for childbirth and parenting are part of total benefit packages to which the citizens of those countries are entitled. In the same manner, any infant care leave policies proposed in this country will have to be integrated into already existing structures and policies. The movement during the 1980s to create a national leave policy through legislation illustrates an attempt to do so.

INFANT CARE LEAVES

Because of the questions raised in studies of out-of-home care of infants (see Chapter 4), and because of the needs of families to solidify and refine relationships with their babies within a materially and emotionally stable environment, part of the solution to the current crisis of infant child care must be to give families the means for caring for their own children during the first few months of life.

In November of 1985, a panel of experts who had studied and analyzed the problems faced by families of newborns concluded that we need national policies guaranteeing parents leave from their employment to care for their newborn or newly adopted children.[20] The panel, originally convened in 1983 as a special advisory committee to the Yale Bush Center in Child Development and Social Policy, consisted of representatives from the fields of child development, business, labor relations, and social policy. The overall goal of the Infant Care Leave Project, as the effort was named, was to explore "what had previously been only an intuition, that changes in the composition of the work force and the family were having an adverse effect on working families with infants."[20] Concluding from extensive research that this intuition was indeed true, the Advisory Committee of the Infant Care Leave Project recommended a six-month infant care leave for working parents, three months with partial wage compensation and three months unpaid.

Note that the term "infant care leave" extends the meaning of what was long called maternity leave to cover a broader range of needs experienced by families. Pregnancy or maternity leave applies to the period of what used to be called "confinement," that is, the period of time a woman is considered disabled due to physical challenges of the last stages of pregnancy, labor, and recovery. A maternity leave is designed solely to meet the physical needs of the mother. Parental or family leaves, on the other hand, encompass various kinds of leave that allow mothers or fathers to stay home with a newborn or newly adopted child and to deal with the adjustments of all family members. The Yale Bush Center's project directors and Advisory Committee chose to call this category infant care leave, because the greatest need of a family at this time is the suitable care of the infant by at least one parent. However, when we speak of infant care leaves, we intend to include leave time that meets the needs of the entire family at this stage in their lives. Recent efforts to insure these leaves to American parents have been complicated by their traditional association with maternity leaves—an area that has a long and confusing legal history.

Infant Care Leave and the Law

Historically, working women and working men have been treated differently under our nation's laws. Laws affecting the employment of married women have been based on the conventional notion that men and women have inherently different social roles, with men inhabiting the sphere of the work place and women that of the home. In spite of these notions, some women have always been employed in the out-of-home work force. Protective legislation in the 19th and 20th centuries was meant to shield working women from abuse and exploitation in the work place, but it also perpetuated the financial discrimination women suffered during those years[12] and deprived needy families of a mother's income.

For example, during the Great Depression in the 1930s, a number of states followed the recommendations of the Women's Bureau in the Department of Labor and passed laws prohibiting the employment of women during a fixed or vaguely specified period before and after childbirth. A woman could be dismissed from her job when her pregnancy became visible or otherwise evident to her employer. Terms such as "the confinement" covered a postpartum period which sometimes was construed as including the months mothers spent nursing their babies. Because of other laws passed to insure more jobs for men, new mothers were also excluded from unemployment benefits during the months they were at home.[12] Thus future and new mothers were categorically denied income and other benefits.

Some states passed temporary disability laws to provide at least partial wage replacement for workers who must be absent from work due to illness and injury. Yet pregnancy was specifically excluded or given only limited coverage under these laws. Overall, pregnancy existed in laws as a reason not to let women work.

The 1970s saw an increase in challenges to such practices as discriminatory under Title VII of the Civil Rights Act of 1964. The Equal Employment Opportunity Commission (EEOC) released guidelines clarifying this issue for employers: to exclude women from employment or from temporary disability benefits was indeed in violation of Title VII. Yet what women gained from winning cases based on the Civil Rights Act was the right to work up to the hour of labor and to return to work as soon as they were certified recovered by a physician. Women were not required to take a leave in most professions, but neither were employers required to pay them while they were on leave. Finally, many employers chose to ignore the EEOC guidelines, and different courts interpreted fine points of the law differently.

In 1978, Congress passed the Pregnancy Discrimination Act to amend Title VII of the Civil Rights Act. The new law specifically included pregnancy in the definition of sex discrimination practices. Employers were prohibited from denying disability benefits to pregnant workers if they provided them for other workers. Even then, most women were not much better off. Before and after birth, they could collect disability benefits only from those employers who offered them to all employees, and most did not. It is difficult to calculate the exact number, because even large corporations with generous benefit packages may not offer them to entry level or part-time workers, most of whom are women.

Legally, then, childbearing became a disability, not a natural event that happens in the majority of families. There is no room in arguments for or against disability leave to consider the needs of the infant or the family. Civil rights laws have also proven inadequate when applied to situations that affect families and children. Specifically, since family leaves are thought to benefit women more than men, arguments about special treatment versus equal treatment of women have surfaced. If infant care leaves are primarily taken by women, then they too are discriminatory under civil rights laws.

Feminists themselves have been divided about how to approach the problem of inadequate family leave policies because of the special versus equal treatment debate. One feminist group defended a California state statute that required all employers to offer maternity leaves even if they did not offer disability leaves for other purposes. They argued that special accommodation for infant care as well as pregnancy and childbirth is necessary to insure that women have equal rights with men both to have children and to participate in the work force. Another feminist group, however, challenged the California statute, claiming that unless disability leaves were extended to the entire working population of the state, the "special treatment" accorded to pregnant women would discourage employers from hiring women of childbearing age.[12] This would lead to further discrimination against women in the work force.

Special versus equal treatment is an argument that actually applies only to the period of physical disability around the time of birth, since only women give birth. Proposed leaves for family purposes, including infant care leaves, would be available to both men and women and to adoptive parents as well as birth parents, so they should be totally beyond the special versus equal treatment debate. Confusion in the public mind about the purposes of family leave, including infant care leave, is another example of our society treating child rearing and child care as women's issues rather than people's issues.

Proposed Federal Legislation

The mood in legislative circles has gradually shifted in recent years from a focus on women giving birth to the family obligations of working parents in general. This emphasis has spurred Congress to initiate draft legislation designed to supply working families with sufficient leave time to take care of pressing family matters, not only to care for an infant, but also to deal with the illness of a spouse, elderly parent, or child, educational problems, and other family crises. Since 1985, when the initial draft of the Parental Leave Act was introduced,[15] hearings have been held to determine the need for such legislation and to hammer out its specific content.

In their latest evolution, bills proposed in the 101st Congress include a provision for employed parents to take up to 10 weeks of unpaid, job-protected leave each year for "family leave." This would be time to meet obligations related to family matters, including but not limited to needs related to the birth or adoption of a child. In addition, both the House and Senate versions mandate a 12-week disability leave, which could be used by women for disability related to pregnancy and childbirth or by workers of either sex for any physical disability. Thus birth mothers could obtain up to 22 weeks of total leave time and fathers and adoptive parents could obtain up to 10 weeks as infant care leave.

Although the need for some kind of parental leave for infant care is recognized by legislators in both major political parties, the process of actually forging a bill to provide for it has been an uphill battle, involving numerous proposed amendments and revisions. As a result, the most recent versions of the bills have significant limitations. The most obvious is that employers would be required only to grant time for leave, not to compensate parents for lost income. Because most people work to support their families, only those who can afford to forgo the income of one spouse during the leave period will benefit from the legislation. Consequently, some observers have dubbed the Parental Leave Act, or Family and Medical Leave Act as it is now called, a "Yuppie" bill, applicable only to two-wage-earner families in the upper and upper-middle income brackets. Such critics have a point, but they ignore the basic features of the bill that are most important to the working poor: job guarantees and continuation of medical benefits for the worker and the family.

Nor would those who work for firms that employ fewer than 50 workers be covered by the proposed law, although late revisions would reduce that ceiling to 35 workers after the law has been in effect for three years. Further exemptions would be granted to employers who can demonstrate that significant financial losses would result should so-called "key employees" be absent for family leaves. The bill does give parents the right to take the full 10 weeks in segments if they wish, and they may take the leave in partial days. But it also allows employers to deny such incremental leave to certain employees, such as teachers, whose labors are needed during a specific time schedule. This would prove particularly difficult for parents who wish to work part time when their children are small or who wish to take turns caring for a sick child. It would also eliminate the broader purpose of the leave—to handle any family emergency when the need arises. In short, the bill as written will not guarantee a family leave to every working parent in the United States. For this as well as for political reasons, the Family and Medical Leave Act still awaits final compromise from both houses of Congress. Lawmakers' willingness to compromise may be hindered by President Bush's promise to veto the bill.

The current stage of the family leave legislation is at least an initial step toward easing the emotional and economic stress on working families during certain times of personal need. For one thing, it would provide infant care leaves for at least some parents who are not now eligible for them. For another, it would encourage the states to continue to develop their own programs to supplement the benefits to infants and their families outlined in federal legislation. In fact, in the absence of a national policy, several states have taken their own initiatives to assure family leaves for their residents. Among the most sweeping leave policies is that of Connecticut, where several failed attempts were followed by a law guaranteeing leaves to state employees. In 1989, a state-wide bill sponsored by the state senate's President Pro Tempore, John Larson, was finally enacted. After a phase-in period, employers with 75 or more workers will have to provide 16 weeks of family leave to care for an infant, child, or other relative. The Connecticut experience shows the slow process of making family leaves a reality. Most important, however, the family leave proposals in this and other states as well as on Capitol Hill represent a first glimpse of a major change in the relationship of society to the very youngest of its members—infants—who will become the citizenry in future generations.

Stumbling Blocks

As the years of heated debates in Congress show, there are many barriers to the creation of a comprehensive national family leave policy. Perhaps the most formidable concerns historical attitudes about work and family. Some members of the society are still worrying about whether or not government should be in the business of encouraging or discouraging people from becoming parents. Others worry that government, by establishing national policies to provide maternity and infant care leaves, is fostering the entrance of mothers into the work force. We must face the fact that women are having children—albeit statistically fewer than they did in past generations—and that they are also working. They will continue to work as long as their families and the society need their labor. We must cease complaining about this necessary state of affairs and instead insure that all parents in the society have ample leave to care for their own and their families' needs before they resume their role in the economy.

We must also discard the notion that society and government are intervening in the private lives of citizens by setting policies that support families in their normal functions. An infant care leave policy, like child care, is not an intervention in any definition of the term. It is a minimal support structure that allows workers to choose whether or not to have children and when, to gain some personal control over their work/family balance, and to participate fully in the life of the society. As for the children's rights, laws to protect and provide for dependent citizens have a long history in America. Instead of intervening in the role of the family, leave policies will enable us further to insure that the needs of children and of those who care for them are met.

Another imposing barrier to a comprehensive infant care leave policy concerns how to insure benefit and possible salary continuation so the leave is an option for parents of all economic levels. Even those fathers and mothers who can afford to take an unpaid leave of absence to care for a newborn or newly adopted child may not be able to do so if their medical insurance will be withdrawn. And those in the lower income brackets will require some kind of financial assistance during the infant care leave period. Recognizing that it would be unrealistic in today's economy to supply income replacement for as much as six months, the Yale Bush Center Advisory Committee recommended a 75% salary reimbursement for three months after a birth or adoption. Yet even if Congress only manages to guarantee American workers an unpaid leave with job and benefit protection, whatever the length, the framework of a more comprehensive policy will be in place.

There are a number of mechanisms consistent with our society and government through which partial income replacement could be offered to families while one parent stays home with an infant. There could be a federally managed insurance fund, modeled on social security or on the short-term disability funds operated by the states of New York and New Jersey. An alternative would be to have the states manage such insurance funds. A third possibility is to follow the State of Hawaii's lead and to require employers to purchase private disability coverage. Whatever mechanism we choose, it should be one that distributes the cost of supporting families who have children among all of us, not one that lays the entire bill at the feet of employers or workers or the federal government. (See also Chapter 10.)

COMMUNITY SUPPORT FOR WORKING FAMILIES WITH INFANTS

A national policy to provide family leaves will address some but certainly not all of the needs of parents of infants. The other essential part of the solution to the crisis in infant care is a host of societal supports for working families. Some of these supports need to come from the work place, and others from the communities in which parents live and work. For example, the months during which one parent is at home caring for the infant are the opportune time to offer assistance with the arduous process of visiting and evaluating child care sites for the day when the infant care leave is over. Information and referral services, as described in Chapter 1, do not necessarily provide parents with sufficient information and strategies for assessing the critical environments in which they will place their infants. Family support approaches are advocated by those who recognize that all parents, not just those in the high-risk groups, may need advice and support beyond the lists of licensed facilities typically provided by resource and referral (R&R) services. Some parents may need help in learning how to interview potential infant caregivers or how to cope with the period of separation they encounter daily once an infant is enrolled in child care. Others may want more concrete assistance, such as someone to go with them to interview the caregiver or help in applying for financial aid. Preserving the autonomy of the family in making child care decisions while providing appropriate supports for making those decisions is a goal of many local programs in the nationwide family support movement (see Kagan, Powell, Weissbourd, and Zigler[7]).

Unfortunately, some of the families who most need it are the least likely to find and benefit from resource and referral services. Powell points out that well-functioning families with adequate sources of informal support—close ties with extended family, neighborhood and church groups, and co-workers—are inclined to use R&R services only at the end of their search for child care, after they have exhausted all other sources of information.[13] R&R services are also an excellent resource for families who have had close ties with the community in the past, but have moved to a new town or neighborhood. Yet research in family support programs in general (see Wandersman[17]) indicates that parents in high-risk groups—teenage mothers, single parents, and those who for whatever reason are isolated from sources of informal support—have difficulty reaching out for and making use of formal family support programs as well. If they do ask for assistance finding child care, therefore, it is likely that they will seek it within an agency that has succeeded in gaining their trust and has provided other services in an atmosphere of mutual respect (see Moroney[10]). For this reason, some of the most successful child care resource and referral programs, such as that operated by Bananas in Oakland, California,[14] have begun not as child care listings but as part of multiple services including child development information and provider training.

As mentioned in Chapter 1, agencies that provide resource and referral services can also stimulate the development of child care facilities in a community. Networks of family day care homes also provide the impetus for more child care, especially the provision of infant care, and improve its quality. The Edith B. Jackson Program in New Haven, Connecticut and the Jewish Family Day Care Network in New York City are examples of family day care networks that reduce the isolation of children and caregivers and expand developmental opportunities for children.[14] Based on these models, networks that focus specifically on the provision of care for infants and toddlers would help parents find available care of good quality.

When an infant or toddler has entered child care, families continue to need the support of their communities in adjusting to the day-to-day realities of working and raising young children. The Child Care Council of Westport-Weston, Inc. and the Ute Mountain Ute Family Resource and Day Care Center are examples of two different kinds of community support services for families with children in child care.[14] The Westport-Weston group provides the working middle-class families of Fairfield County, Connecticut with weekly parent discussion groups, parenting workshops, and parent-child activities, all scheduled at times of day that permit working parents to participate. The Ute Family Resource Center is linked with a child care center on an Indian reservation and serves a population that suffers from high rates of unemployment, alcohol abuse, and foster home placement. Whole child and family support services include course offerings for parents in first aid, child development, and also in subjects leading to the high school equivalency diploma.

Family support for infants and toddlers with special needs is offered by some communities through health agencies and local and state public education departments. State departments of education, for example, can assist parents of handicapped infants and toddlers to find the specialized care their infants need to facilitate eventual entry into school (see Chapter 7). An example is the Colorado state education department's Interagency Coordinating Council. With the aid of a federal grant, the Council is assembling a computerized resource bank of individuals and organizations across the state who provide child care and other services for special needs infants and toddlers. The resource bank is being monitored by a statewide task force called "First Impressions," under the personal eye of the state's first lady, Bea Romer. The task force's many goals include improving child care for all the children in the state under five years old. As illustrated by these examples, the crisis of infant care can be ameliorated by services to entire families, services that emanate from the community that comprises those families.

Support from the Work Place

Employers are a major part of any community and thus have their own support to offer families. Indeed, a variety of employer policies designed to assist families in achieving both a productive work life and a productive family life have begun to appear in work places nation-wide. Some of these will be discussed in Chapter 8. Particularly applicable to this discussion are policies that specifically affect the infant-parent relationship when the parent is also an employee. Each of these policies demonstrates the beginning of a shift in thinking that allows us to view family and work as equal endeavors in the building of a well-balanced nation for the 21st century.

One important support for parents of infants is group medical insurance that includes prenatal care, childbirth, and postnatal follow-up for employees and their spouses. Yet, with the average cost of prenatal care and delivery now at about $3,000, nearly 15 million American women of childbearing age are without public or private medical insurance. Annually, about half a million women give birth without medical protection for themselves or their infants.[15] There is also a need for medical insurance to cover employees' dependent children from the time of birth. A newborn's hospital bill is likely to exceed that of the mother, and costs skyrocket if there is a birth-related problem or defect. One wonders how many new mothers return to work as soon as they can because they need the money to pay their medical expenses.

Although there is no nationally mandated infant care leave policy, some employers do provide this time as an employee benefit. An actual infant care leave is rare in America, and it is usually offered on an unpaid basis or with a greatly reduced percentage of wages. More common is short-term disability coverage that can be applied to maternity leave or pregnancy-related absences from work. Although few employers offer a specifically designated paternity leave, more grant a general personal leave that fathers may use to attend the birth of a child and to care for other children while the infant and mother are hospitalized and when they return home. Employees with vacation time that they can take at their discretion (rather than at specific seasons of the year) can use this time to apply to the needs of the family when an infant is born or adopted. This simple policy allows families precious time together without the loss of income.

Other aspects of employer support for parents and infants are policies that permit flexible hours or work schedules, job sharing, and temporary part-time employment. The opportunity to return gradually to full-time employment assists both parents and older infants in making the transition to a schedule that includes parent work outside the home. Inevitable problems that will arise, such as time to deal with the failure of a child care situation or to take a child to medical appointments, can also be met with employer flexibility.

Finally, family-oriented employers can help parents locate suitable child care by purchasing the services of a resource and referral agency. They might also sponsor child care centers on or near the work site and/or provide child care vouchers. Such programs will be discussed more fully in Chapter 8.

Why Should Employers Offer Family Benefits?

Some of the measures to aid families with infants mentioned above are seen by business as extremely costly. One would assume that a large corporation would be able to afford the maximum in family support at the time of birth or adoption, while a small business would be able to afford few benefits to support the family. Yet fewer than half of mid-sized to large corporations in the United States offer medical maternity leaves to their employees,[8] one of the minimum options for family support. Only a handful of employers offer all the family benefits discussed above, and many offer none. This is evidence that the importance of supporting families with infants, although discussed widely, has still not been established as a general priority of the American work place.

A common argument against benefits for families with infants is that they are not the responsibility of the employer, because work and family are separate spheres. Although what happens to an employee while at work—such as a job-related injury—is generally accepted as part of the cost of doing business and thus the employer's responsibility, what an employee experiences in his or her private life—such as having a child—is believed to have no direct effect on business and thus is the employee's problem. In fact, many aspects of an employee's supposedly private life do affect business. In realization of this, enlightened employers have instituted programs to address some of the more dramatic ways in which an employee's personal life affects performance in the work place, such as drug and alcohol abuse, and some less dramatic health issues such as smoking.

Childbirth and child rearing, of course, cannot be equated with drug and alcohol abuse, as childbirth and child rearing are considered normal aspects of adult life. Raising children is not considered a "problem" on the job, and it should not have to be if appropriate supports for working parents of infants are in place. Yet employers who can argue that they need not assist employees in child rearing because it is part of their personal lives, while still supporting exercise and smoking cessation programs, fail to see the irony of their position.

Another reason that many employers do not support family needs is that it is difficult to assess objectively the cost of policies that support workers with infants as opposed to the cost of not supporting them. It may seem more efficient to allow staff as little family-related leave as possible, so as to keep the maximum number of employees on the job at all times. This may appear to be cost effective in the short term, but forward thinking corporate executives examine the long-term effects on their businesses as well as the short-term effects on quarterly reports. Workers in businesses with family-friendly policies are likely to be more productive and loyal, have lower absentee rates, and stay with the company longer than those in more typical employment situations. (See Chapter 8 for a discussion of the evidence of effects of child care policy on employee behavior.)

Another argument against federally mandated employer support of the family at the time of the birth or adoption of a child concerns the uneven distribution of public and private responsibility. Some employers argue that they already pay for social programs with income and corporate taxes collected by state and federal governments. "We pay taxes for such things [as parental leaves]," argued a Connecticut businessman in a radio call-in show recently.[11] "Why can't state and federal government bear the entire cost?" In other words, some employers believe that federally mandated infant care leave policies are fine, as long as they are also backed by federal funds. Others, like the United States Chamber of Commerce, have argued that the federal government already has too much control over what should be private negotiations between companies and their employees concerning benefits.[16] Although they support the notion of parental leave, the Chamber opposed the Family and Medical Leave Act in 1989. Part of their argument was on the grounds that leave policies should be neither federally mandated nor federally funded, but should be strictly a private sector decision. Yet because the private sector has barely moved in this direction, many bipartisan groups within government as well as children's and women's advocacy groups continue to urge the federal government to take an active role in standardizing the benefits American workers receive at the time of the birth or adoption of a child.

While the debate rages about whether or not national legislation for a comprehensive family leave policy is appropriate, employers can institute those policies mentioned above that are consistent with the needs of families of infants and those of the work place. Some of these policies, such as flexibility, need not be terribly expensive. Regardless of whether the legislation passes, employers must still recognize that infant care leave issues do not disappear when infants enter child care and parents return to work. The balance between work and family needs and the relationship between parent and child continue to be issues that must be dealt with throughout the child's development. And how society handles infant care leave and later family needs establishes our relationships not only with today's workers, but also with tomorrow's.

6

School-Age Child Care

Whenever the subject of the child care crisis is raised, most of the concern seems to center on infants, toddlers, and preschoolers. Yet around two-thirds of children who need care are of school age. Not only are those between the ages of about five and twelve a much larger group than infants and toddlers, but more mothers seek employment once their children enter school. Unfortunately, just as the preschooler is often ignored when communities plan for public education, the school-age child is often overlooked in planning for the supply and quality of child care.

The course of finding appropriate and affordable care for a child of any age rarely runs smoothly, as we discussed in Chapter 1. By the time a child is three or four years old, parents are likely to be quite weary of the child care hassle and may look forward to school entrance as the end of their dilemma. Yet when a child reaches kindergarten age, families discover that there is a new set of hurdles to overcome. Perhaps the center or family day care home they have been using limits enrollment to preschoolers. Or the facility may not accept children for half days, meaning that a new search must be launched for care before and after the standard two and one-half hour kindergarten session. Perhaps there is no transportation between school and the child care facility. Or, if there is a convenient after-school program in place, there may be no one to watch the child between the time parents leave for work in the morning and the time school opens. Parents soon learn that there is a sharp division between the business of the school—formal education—and the business of the mixed system of child care. In the case of school-age children, this system is more varied and less satisfactory than they had ever imagined.

One response to the child care needs of children just entering public school has been the rapid development of extended-day kindergartens, now serving almost half of all five-year-olds in the United States.[18]

While the supposed educational benefits of sending such young children to school for a full day are being seriously questioned,[11] school systems that provide these programs believe that at the least they are serving parents by reducing their child care burdens. Yet, as Olsen and Zigler point out, an "extended" day generally means that kindergarteners attend school for six hours rather than for two and one-half.[18] This still leaves parents who work outside the home with the problem of finding care for their children before school and between the close of school and the end of their workday—often an additional two to three hours. The extended-day kindergarten is thus not much of a solution to the child care dilemma for five-year-olds.

The hassle of finding someone willing to provide part-time care and perhaps transportation for a school-age child leads to a tempting solution: leaving the child home alone. Sometime in the middle of grammar school, children enter new stages, blossoming socially as well as intellectually. They begin to develop independent interests such as hobbies, friends, sports, and organized clubs. As leisure time decreases in proportion to increased amounts of homework, children begin to need and demand more freedom in how they organize that leisure time. They begin to express more dissatisfaction with encroachments on their fledgling attempts at self-direction, both in and out of school. Not surprisingly, sometime between about the fourth and the sixth grade children may start to complain that their child care arrangements are "boring" or "babyish" and may ask to be left on their own before and after school. Parents, faced with the continued expense and inconvenience of arranging child care, may wonder whether or not it is even necessary after the child reaches age nine or ten. Some may even begin to consider the questionable practice of leaving a child that age in charge of younger siblings.

Just as the issue of when a child is ready to begin child care is somewhat ambiguous, the answer to when children are ready for self-care is not at all clear-cut. Our position is that all children need adult supervision during nonschool hours through grade six, and that most need supervision of some kind through junior high or middle school. Some may even require it into the high school years, depending on individual circumstances. Our discussion of school-age child care will focus on children through age 14, since we consider virtually all of them in need of adult-supervised care. However, the nature of that care is radically different from that required by an infant or preschooler, because the needs of grade school and middle school children are so different. Appropriate child care for a fifth grader is also quite different from that for a first grader. In this chapter, we will explore the developmental needs of children of school age and discuss what we believe are typical after-school experiences—both good and bad. We will also look at some of the alternatives that have been developed by communities in their search for appropriate supervision for school-age children.

THE LATCHKEY CHILD

Although there is some disagreement in the field about the definition of latchkey children, we will define them here as those who routinely care for themselves during nonschool hours while parents are away from home. They were originally dubbed "latchkey" because teachers and others noticed that they were coming to school with their house keys on a string around their necks, so that they would not lose them. Latchkey children are often cautioned to keep their keys hidden beneath their clothing so that strangers or aggressive older children will not be aware that they are without adult supervision and thus vulnerable.

The number of children left to care for themselves is very difficult to estimate. Parents surveyed about child care arrangements may be reluctant to admit that their young children are staying home alone for many hours each day. Those parents who believe that self-care is appropriate during the grammar school years may say that they have no children of child care age. If the child is in charge of younger siblings, parents may report that their children receive care from a babysitter.

A national survey conducted in 1984 by the U.S. Bureau of the Census reported that 2.1 million children between the ages of five and thirteen are unsupervised after school, and one-half million are alone before school.[32] The majority of both groups had mothers who were employed full time. These figures seem incredibly low. For example, the report indicated that in 58% of the households in which the mother worked full time, the children were cared for by a parent. Certainly some fathers work night shifts and do care for their children after school, or the mothers work nights or are engaged in cottage industries. But such arrangements are rare and certainly do not hold in 58% of households in which parents work full time. The Census Bureau defended the validity of this statistic, citing evidence that many parents work different shifts, at home, only during school hours, or are able to bring their children to the work place. The Bureau did raise the possibility that some parents deliberately misreported their child care arrangements "because of a perceived illegality of leaving children unattended (child neglect),"[32] or because of the fear they might be putting their child in jeopardy by telling a stranger the child was alone.

Earlier estimates of 2 to 7 million latchkey children nationwide[24] do not help much either, since such a broad range does not tell us if this is a major or minor problem. The Wellesley School-Age Child Care Project reported that there may be 10 million or more latchkey children in the United States, basing their estimate on local surveys.[26] We believe this figure is closer to the actual prevalence.

There are some other indicators of the extent of the latchkey problem in the form of local surveys conducted by community organizations. A Los Angeles United Way survey reported that nearly one-fourth of children ages seven to nine in that city had no adult supervision after school, and that three-fourths of children ages ten to thirteen were unsupervised.[25] In Madison, Wisconsin, a survey conducted by a community agency revealed that 26% of elementary school children were unattended or cared for by a sibling.[7] Of 807 parents queried in the District of Columbia area, 15% of the respondents with children eight to thirteen years old left them in self-care on a regular basis; even some six- and seven-year-olds had no adult supervision before and after school.[6] Surveys such as these by local groups and schools probably give a more accurate picture within a given community than do official census reports, because parents are likely to view these organizations as less threatening than government agencies. The local survey is also perceived favorably because it is seen as the community's attempt to develop solutions to child care problems.

What Children in Self-care Actually Do

Children in self-care cannot really be observed, so our knowledge of their activities only comes from self-reports and adult speculations. Such children may arrive home to an environment their parents have attempted to structure in advance or to a totally unstructured time space. They may have long lists of verbal or even written rules and instructions: "Lock the door behind you; don't go out; don't let anyone in; call Mom at work; do your homework; start dinner; don't turn on the stove." Conversely, they may have little or no direction from parents about what to do and what not to do.

Both situations can have their good and bad points. When guidelines are minimal, for example, children may be more likely to place themselves in dangerous situations. Even if they "know better," they may be at a loss as to what to do with themselves or feel that no one cares about them. On the other hand, directions that are highly restrictive may induce fear and create feelings that the world is a dangerous place filled with evil people and things that can bring harm. Very young children may become confused by what to them are conflicting parental instructions. They may know to dial 911 or a neighbor in event of a fire or other emergency, then be afraid to unlock the door to fire fighters, police, or even familiar neighbors.

In many areas, having a nearby adult to call upon is a luxury. With the increasing number of women joining the work force, many children arrive after school to empty neighborhoods as well as empty homes. They have no one with whom to share the events of their day, such as delight over a passing test grade or upset over a social conflict. Children at home alone in the afternoons tend to watch more television and to snack more. Often, they cannot participate in after-school activities for which transportation is necessary. Many cannot engage in informal play with neighborhood children, who may be closeted in their own houses. Although they may be instructed to do their homework, there is no one to consult if they have a question.

In some instances, unsupervised children as young as seven or eight years old may be in charge of younger brothers or sisters or neighbors' children for hours each day. This "babysitter" role may make them feel competent, as some adults assert, or it may frighten them. We believe strongly that children of grammar school age are not yet capable of caring for themselves for extended periods and on a daily basis, let alone caring for younger children. In many states the law supports this assertion, defining child neglect and risk of injury to a minor as leaving unattended a child who is younger than the middle school or teen years. Such statutes are rarely enforced, however, until an accident or other tragedy calls the latchkey situation to the attention of officials.

Although children left in self-care may initially feel competent and "grown up," indications are that these attitudes soon wear thin. Latchkey children who are given the opportunity to describe their activities and feelings communicate a void in their lives caused by the lack of adult involvement. In testimony before the Select Committee on Children, Youth and Families in the U.S. House of Representatives, one sixth-grade boy who had spent the last three years caring for himself after school described his afternoons as follows:

When I'm alone, I do what I have to do first; then I watch TV, talk on the phone, or listen to the radio or records. Sometimes I get lonely when there is nothing to do or it is raining. I get scared when our neighbor's [burglar] alarm goes off because I'm afraid that there is a robber nearby . . . . One day my friend and I were making something to eat and he cut his finger. . . . If a grownup had been around it would have been OK.[24]

Although this boy did manage to remember his first aid and his friend's cut was not severe enough to require stitches, other children are not so lucky. According to the National Safety Council, over 4,100 children aged 5–14 years die as a result of accidental injuries each year, about 460 of them in fires and 250 of them from gunshot wounds.[16] No statistics are available concerning how many of these victims were unattended at the time of their injuries, but 800 died from injuries incurred at home. The accident rate for injuries requiring hospitalization in this age group is 9.2 per 1,000, according to the World Health Organization.[16] Although injury rates in general peak during the ages 15–24, there are some injuries to which school-age children are particularly vulnerable. Deaths from burns and other fire-related injuries peak at the age of five years (27.5 per million), remain high through the age of eleven (10.7 per million), and decline thereafter. Fireworks injuries requiring emergency room treatment are about the same for children 5–14 (3,757 per year) as they are for youths 15–24 (3,779). Males are involved in over 70% of these injuries.[16]

Although physical injury represents a certain risk to children left on their own, they may also suffer emotional pain. A 10-year-old girl described her feelings to the Select Committee this way: "Some things scare me when I'm alone, like the wind, the door creaking and the sky getting dark fast. This may not seem scary to you, but it is to young people who are alone."[24] These words certainly convey that this child is not yet ready to assume responsibility for herself in a world she does not quite understand.

Thus it is not simply the real possibility of accidental injury or victimization of children who are alone that most concerns those who advocate more appropriate school-age child care. There are psychological undertones that may hamper social and emotional development. What we are seeing in this decade is an erosion of a portion of the school-age child's environment, a drop below the threshold of environmental quality that sustains optimal growth of all systems of development. Unlike children with the supervision of a parent, children in self-care do not learn gradually to organize their own time, to become independent, and to understand the world in which they live. Instead, adult responsibilities are suddenly thrust upon them before their growing experiences and abilities have prepared them for such a role. The tragedy of this premature assumption of adult roles is described by Elkind[5] and Winn.[34] Whatever the immediate dangers or long-term consequences, this situation is inconsistent with a child's developmental needs in the grammar and middle school years.

Consequences of Self-Care

The potential effects of self-care are largely negative. As suggested above, they range from physical danger—vulnerability to crime, fire, and injury, for example—to psychological damage. Results of much of the research in this area have been suggestive and informative rather than clear-cut. As we have seen, this situation is similar to that of any research in the child care field, because we are searching for consistent effects of a mixed system that is full of variables and inconsistencies. The question of what effects to search for is also in evidence. Researchers may explore how self-care affects school performance or social behavior, but may find that effects on the quality of the child's life are difficult to define and to quantify.

Some studies of latchkey children report negative consequences. Merilyn Woods studied supervised and unsupervised black fifth graders in an urban ghetto.[35] She found that more girls than boys were left unsupervised after school, and that they were more apt to exhibit lower academic achievement and more personal and social difficulties than were supervised girls. Two of the best-known writers on the latchkey problem are Lynette and Thomas Long, whose numerous studies suggest that unsupervised children are bored, lonely, isolated, and that they are sometimes terrified, prematurely sexually active, and subject to nightmares.[14,15] Most of the Longs' data were obtained through subject interviews and are considered valuable as anecdotal evidence rather than evidence based on standardized measures.

Ambiguous results were obtained by Galambos and Garbarino, who found no differences in academic achievement between supervised and self-care fifth and seventh graders in a rural community.[10] Girls in self-care, however, tended to be more fearful in their situation than did boys. Laurence Steinberg found that among adolescents in grades five to nine, there were few differences between those who returned home after school to a parent-present or parent-absent setting.[29] The study did show, however, that those unsupervised students who spent their after-school hours at a friend's house or roaming the streets rather than at home were more susceptible to peer pressure and more likely to engage in antisocial activities.

Some studies seem on the surface to indicate that no harm necessarily ensues if a child is unsupervised after school. A study conducted in a school district in North Carolina reported no differences between latch-key and supervised children in grades four through seven on measures of social and psychological functioning.[22] Nor were differences found between mother care and self-care in suburban Dallas by Vandell and Corasaniti.[33] Children of comparable age in both groups were similar in peer assessments, academic grades, standardized test scores, and parent/teacher ratings.

Looking at older children and consequences other than social and academic ones, Richardson, Dwyer, McGuigan, and six other medical researchers reported strong differences between supervised and unsupervised young adolescents.[21] These investigators studied substance use in over 4,900 eighth graders in the Los Angeles and San Diego metropolitan areas. They found that children who cared for themselves 11 or more hours per week were twice as likely as those who had constant supervision to use alcohol, tobacco, and/or marijuana. The authors took into account other factors known to affect substance use and found that the risk persisted regardless of whether the child was from a high- or low-income family, a single- or dual-parent home, had parents who did or did not smoke, was white or minority, received good or poor school grades, engaged in extracurricular activities or not, reported high or low stress levels, or said that their parents or peers were their greatest source of influence. In other words, self-care was the only life circumstance studied that related to the child's use of addictive substances. In a rather cautious interpretation of these striking results, the authors suggested that parenting styles or strategies of self-care, rather than self-care per se, might increase or reduce the risk, particularly the amount of parental guidance over the hours spent alone (clear rules, lists of chores, calling in, etc.). Nonetheless, they called for alternatives to self-care for children of this age.

Another study by Long and Long of teenagers in grades seven to ten revealed that some used their unsupervised after-school hours to experiment with sex.[7] Fifteen percent of these parochial school students from two-adult homes and 40% of those from single-parent families reported engaging in intercourse, petting, and nudity, most commonly in the girls' homes. Thomas Long told the press, "Teenagers these days don't get pregnant in motels and cars at 10 at night. Sex happens at home at three in the afternoon while mom and dad are at work."[19]

Crime is another risk to unsupervised children. In several of the studies cited above, children living in urban as opposed to more rural areas exhibited more fear, anxiety, and other negative psychological effects from being by themselves each day, and with good reason. Crime is more prevalent in cities, and so the children's day-to-day experiences are likely to be more fear inducing. Although children in cities may indeed be more likely to be the victims of crime, those in rural areas may be victimized because of their greater isolation. Children whose mothers work also suffer more sexual abuse according to four studies, although no relation was found in a fifth.[9] As drug-related crimes have increased in both urban and suburban areas during the 1980s, the potential risks to unsupervised children have certainly grown.

Children in self-care may become not only the victims but also the perpetrators of crime. Note that in the Steinberg study, children roaming the streets with nothing to do after school were more likely to engage in antisocial activities.[29] This kind of finding comes as no surprise to local police and fire departments or to shopkeepers, who have begun to realize serious losses from juvenile shoplifters. According to local fire officials in many cities, unsupervised children account for a larger portion of fires and are more likely to be injured in a fire than those who have an adult present. An investigator in Detroit, Michigan found that as many as one out of six fires in that city involve an unattended school-age child.[28] In school districts across the nation, a common justification cited by advocates of school-age child care programs is the perceived reduction in vandalism to schools, virtually all of which occurs during after-school hours.

In sum, children in self-care may be a risk both to themselves and to their communities. Their situation was succinctly stated by Coolsen, Seligson, and Garbarino, who listed four types of risk associated with being a latchkey child.[4] First, children who are home alone each day may feel bad, eventually developing a sense of rejection or alienation. Second, they may be treated badly by others or by the environment, becoming the victims of crime or accidents. Third, they may develop badly, displaying such symptoms as poor school performance and failure to take on appropriate responsibilities as time goes on. Fourth, they may act badly, participating in acts of delinquency or vandalism. Even in the absence of accurate statistics, it is no wonder that parents, teachers, community leaders, and researchers themselves continue to deplore the prevalence of self-care. In virtually every state, they are working to create appropriate programs for the before- and after-school care of children who might otherwise be left alone.

A CONTINUUM OF SCHOOL-AGE CHILD CARE
ARRANGEMENTS

There is a wide range of possible arrangements for the supervision of children of school age. The choice of each is dependent upon individual family circumstances—what degree of care is perceived as needed, and what is available, affordable, and practical. Yet children's behavior in a variety of child care settings suggests they have fairly universal needs for age-appropriate activities and supervision outside of school hours. We begin by discussing what is generally considered the model for school-aged child care programs—the activities of children whose parents are home when they are.

Supervision by a Parent

In the brief history of American child care presented in Chapter 2, we saw that there has not been in this century a "golden age" in which all children had one parent at home to care for them. Yet we also saw that there have been times, such as the immediate post-World War II years, when a majority of mothers remained at home until they believed their children were old enough to care for themselves. Thus, many of today's parents remember a time when their own mothers were home to welcome them after school and to supervise their activities. These memories are eloquently described by Dale Fink, a research associate at Wellesley's Center for Research on Women:

> [My mother] made sure my brother and I got a snack at the
> end of the school day and she looked at any work we brought
> home and asked us about our day. . . . She was always there
> if we needed first aid or we couldn't find the spinner for one of
> our board games . . . . [But] Much of the time, we were at the
> corner lot on 55th street, playing baseball. Or over on Carl
> Johnson's driveway . . . trading baseball cards . . . immersed
> in a book or in my chemistry set . . . sitting in Jimmy Ferguson's
> treehouse . . . [taking] piano lessons . . . . But most of the time
> we were out doing things. Or inside each other's and our own
> houses doing things—[with a parent nearby but] without an
> adult hanging over us.[8]

With the numbers of mothers in the work force today, a minority of children enjoy such a relaxed and active situation. Although the goals of child care programs are more complex than simply providing freshly baked cookies and watchful peeks out the window, at-home care does provide a familiar model through which we can understand the school-age child's activities and developmental needs.

Children whose parents are able to arrange their schedules so that someone is at home after school do not engage in uniform behaviors, but they follow certain predictable patterns. Children routinely arrive home from school, speak briefly with the parent—perhaps about their school day and their plans for the afternoon—have a snack, and then wander off to pursue a variety of individual activities. These may include informal play with friends in the neighborhood, sports, club or scout meetings, music or gymnastic lessons, homework, hobbies, religious youth groups, and other personal interests. They may simply watch television, play video games, or read, depending on what their parents permit.

There is tremendous heterogeneity in the type of interaction between children and their parents after school, as there is at all times of the day, depending on the child's maturity level and the adult's parenting style. However, the general pattern is for children in the early grammar school years to engage in a relatively greater proportion of activities with or close by a parent. As each year passes, they become less reliant on direct adult interaction and engage in more independent play. Families also vary a great deal, depending on the neighborhoods in which they live and their own standards, about how far the child may range away from home. However, one common characteristic of children in the intermediate grades (grade four and up) is that they spend little time directly involved with the parent after their initial contact. They tend to use the parent as a base—a person to check in with as often as needed or instructed. As children grow, parents may even leave the house for a brief period to run an errand or transport a sibling, allowing the child to experience gradually longer periods of self-care. Some 11- and 12-year-olds are even mature enough to do occasional babysitting, as long as a parent is not far away if they need help. Thus school-age children who have a parent at home are given by degrees the freedom to choose their own activities and to organize their own time, with parents nearby to set appropriate limits and to intervene in emergencies.

Supervision by a Neighbor

Fink's description of mother care cited above includes more than being cared for by a single adult. In many areas only a few decades ago, the neighborhood itself provided for the total environment of a child after school. Children were free to roam from their homes to play with friends, and their mothers' supervision did not need to be relentless. Nearly every child had a parent at home, and—always with a few exceptions—parents tended to agree on the basic limits for their children. One or two children whose mothers could not be home could be absorbed into a cohesive suburban or urban neighborhood. Today, with so many mothers of school-age children working, such neighborhoods are few and far between.

A modern form of neighborhood care is emerging that lies somewhere between the extremes of self-care and parental supervision. On some blocks throughout America a few parents are at home, because they can afford not to work, because the area suffers high unemployment, o. because they work evening shifts. Children reported to be in self-care in this type of neighborhood may actually be cared for to a limited extent by another adult or group of adults on an informal basis.

In fact, a disadvantage of being a parent who stays at home these days is that one tends to be designated what Larry, one father with a home office, calls "the neighborhood den mother." Similar to the leader of a group of Cub Scouts, the neighborhood den mother suddenly finds him- or herself responsible for the safety and entertainment of area children who have no parent at home from about three o'clock to five or six. As opposed to the family day care provider, den mothers are not offered payment. They may or may not be formally asked by neighbors to watch the children after school. Sometimes working parents assume that other adults at home in the neighborhood will feel responsible to look out for their children. At times this assumption is justified and the relationship is reciprocal; at other times, it causes resentment among neighbors or potential danger for the children when the den mother goes out. Sometimes lonesome children are simply attracted to the home where there is a friendly adult and visit on their own.

School-age children who are cared for informally by neighbors often check in with the den mother soon after arriving home. They may pursue their own activities independently, using the den mother as a base, just as children cared for by their own parents will do. Or, they may develop patterns similar to those of unsupervised children, remaining in their own homes to snack and watch television, only consulting the den mother in emergencies or when they have lost their house keys.

Whether or not informal neighborhood supervision is a viable form of care for a particular school-age child is largely a function of the cohesiveness of the neighborhood and the relationship between the family and the neighbors. In some areas this type of care works smoothly and is the next best thing to a parent at home. In other places where there are few or no adults at home within a reasonable distance, this type of child care is not an alternative for area school children.

School-Age Children Integrated into Other Programs

In the absence of formal school-age child care programs in many communities, parents who live in "empty neighborhoods" must seek out other methods of after-school supervision. Families with younger children, those who live in high-crime districts, or those whose children are immature or have behavior problems are most likely to reject self-care and become inventive in their search for alternatives. As with other types of child care, their choices are restricted by their financial circumstances, but also by the willingness of the mixed system to incorporate their needs.

In-Home Caregivers. An ideal arrangement for families who have a child in school and others who are younger is to hire an in-home caregiver. Interestingly, a person hired as a housekeeper who happens to be at the home when children return from school is considered to provide child care under Internal Revenue Service codes. A portion of her annual salary may be used as an income tax credit, or up to $5,000 of her salary can be deducted from parents' pretax income under flexible benefit plans (Chapter 8), regardless of whether or not such a person is actually supervising children. When all the children in a family attend school, parents may hire a high school student or a retired woman to provide child care after school and on days schools are not in session. Depending upon the flexibility and interests of the caregiver, the school-age children cared for by another person in the home may be allowed to come and go to pursue their own interests, as they would if cared for by their own parents. Or they may be locked into a schedule and into activities geared toward the younger children in the family.

Family Day Care Homes. Some family day care providers accept children for after-school care. As we discussed in Chapter 1, the vast majority of family day care homes are unlicensed. We have as little knowledge of the day-to-day experiences of school-age children in these unlicensed homes as we have of those of younger children. However, the activity patterns of school-age children in general would indicate that they may behave in similar ways with the family day care provider as they do with their own parents, engaging in direct contact with the caregiver while they are in the primary grades and gradually seeking autonomy as they grow older. A sensitive caregiver may be willing to share the events of the child's day and offer a secure base from which the children can pursue their own interests and work on homework. In some family day care homes, however, children may spend the majority of their time after school snacking and watching television. They may play with the younger children present, or compete with them for the caregiver's attention. Thus family day care for school-age children, like that for younger children, can meet their needs very well or very poorly. Later in this chapter, we will discuss some unique efforts to improve the quality of family day care arrangements for school-age children.

Informal After-School Interest Programs. Libraries, park and recreation departments, school districts, and other organizations that provide recreational opportunities for children sometimes offer after-school activities on an irregular or seasonal basis: sports, arts and crafts, educational films, music lessons, ecology projects, and the like. Typically, activities are not offered daily and are optional. Parental permission and registration may be required to participate in some of these activities, or they may be offered on a drop-in basis. Fees can vary from nominal to several hundred dollars. Transportation is rarely offered, so this can pose a problem to children whose parents work.

Like self-care, this form of after-school experience cannot be labeled child care. The purpose of such activities is recreation for children who share a common interest, not to provide supervision for children during after-school hours. Yet recreational and library staff in many communities are discovering that after-school interest programs have become a haven for children who have no interest in the activity being offered but who have nowhere else to go. "It's a difficult situation," said Penny Markey, coordinator of children's services for the Los Angeles county public library system. "These children are coming in after they've been in school all day, they're full of energy, and [it's difficult] for them to behave under those circumstances."[17] So great is the concern nationally about children being left unattended in libraries, whether or not an activity is scheduled, that the *New York Times* devoted a front page story to the problem.[17] The *Times* reported that libraries in cities in Arizona, Texas, Georgia, and Maryland have put into place or are considering policies barring unsupervised children, ranging from posted prohibitions to threats of criminal prosecution of parents for child neglect. Innovative solutions to this problem will be noted when we discuss models for school-age child care.

Formal After-School Programs

Through the auspices of a variety of for-profit and nonprofit organizations, sometimes in combination, many communities offer some form of regular, after-school program, either in a public school or in a youth or child care facility. The YMCA-YWCA programs are among the best known. Models for these programs will be described later in this chapter. If the program is not located in the children's school, they may be transported by bus or van to the facility where they will be supervised.

Children in latchkey care programs, like children in any form of child care, have a variety of experiences, depending on the quality of the programs and the sensitivity of their caregivers to their needs. Some programs in child care centers that routinely serve younger children may actually be as "babyish" and "boring" as the school-age children report that they are. Even if a separate age-appropriate program is offered, being picked up in a child care center van and transported to a place where younger children are cared for may be humiliating to the older grammar school student and would definitely be considered out of the question by the seventh or eighth grader. In fact, Vandell and Corasaniti found that children who attended day care centers after school were correct in assuming that their peers considered this an inappropriate form of care.[33] The center children received more negative peer evaluations than did those who were cared for by parents or cared for themselves. They also had lower grades and lower standardized test scores.

Good after-school programs offer the type of activities that children might participate in on their own when they can choose how to spend their time: sports, arts and crafts, homework help, cooking, and the like. The range of activity options should include both teacher-led activities and child-initiated experiences.[1] A fifth-grade girl whose passion is to build tableaux of historical events from found materials should not be expected to spend her entire afternoon making brownies because that is what is on the caregiver's agenda. A fourth-grade boy who runs out of the classroom door bursting with pent-up physical energy should not be saddled with an afternoon schedule that begins with homework and progresses to a trip to the library. Yet the library trip should be an available option for the child who needs to use the encyclopedia or whose idea of fun is to read all the books on hockey or all the novels by a single author. The program must be organized around the individual interests of the children served and capitalize on the special talents and interests of the staff members.

Like their peers who are supervised at home, school-age children in latchkey care programs need an adult interested in them. They need to have someone who will give them a snack, listen to them talk about their day and their plans, then let them go about their own agendas, offering help when needed. Although the schedule can and should be open-ended and spontaneous, staff and children should have a clear sense of what the rules are. As school-age children experiment with their growing independence, it is most important that behavioral expectations and limits be clearly communicated.[1]

As noted in Chapter 3, the National Association for the Education of Young Children (NAEYC) has developed criteria to assess quality in child care and early childhood programs.[2] These criteria apply equally to programs serving older children. The NAEYC recommends that quality programs include the following: a qualified staff who have opportunities for professional development, efficient administration, enough staff to serve the children in care, a physical environment and program designed to promote growth and development, health and safety features, and interaction between parents and staff. More specifically applicable to programs serving school-age children are additional quality components proposed by the Wellesley School-Age Child Care Project.[26] These include an atmosphere of informal learning that allows children to make choices, expand their cultural horizons, achieve a gradual sense of independence as they grow, and participate in peer culture. Thus, a quality after-school program that meets the children's needs for that portion of the day provides the type of experiences they would encounter in parent care.

MODELS OF SERVICES FOR SCHOOL-AGE CHILDREN

When there are too many school-age children who are not appropriately served after school, communities can take two approaches. One is to organize more school-age child care programs. Another is to accept as inevitable the large numbers of latchkey children roaming the streets or locked into their homes and to provide some kind of services to ameliorate the perceived negative effects. This second approach is extremely limited in scope and effectiveness, and cannot be considered child care in any sense of the word. It is intervention with at-risk children who are outside the mixed child care system. Yet many communities have found it necessary to institute latchkey assistance as a needed social service.

Latchkey Assistance

Whereas formal school-age child care programs provide direct adult supervision for children, latchkey assistance programs provide some kind of service to children while they are in self-care. These services include courses or seminars for parents and/or children on self-care, books and pamphlets explaining how to set rules for self-care and how children should respond to emergencies, and "warm lines"—telephone numbers children alone can call when they are frightened or lonely.

Coolsen et al.'s descriptions of the four types of risk to latchkey children—that they may feel bad, behave badly, develop badly, or be treated badly—point up the severe limitations of latchkey assistance projects. Whereas appropriate school-age child care addresses all of these risks to some extent, most latchkey projects only address one or two of these risks.

For example, a warm line service called PhoneFriend is operated by the local branch of the American Association of University Women in State College, Pennsylvania.[4] Similar community help lines for latchkey children exist in towns and cities across the country. Warm lines provide a number that children can call if they are bored, lonesome, or frightened, which addresses at least partially the problem of children feeling bad while they are alone. The warm line counselor is also there in case the child needs emergency advice or when police or fire departments need to be called, offering a small buffer against the problem of victimization of children alone. Some warm lines also offer homework help.

In spite of the good they do, especially for children whose parents cannot be contacted at work, it would be a mistake to assume that having a warm line service in a community will safeguard latchkey children against crime, injury, and school failure. A voice at the end of the phone will not protect children if someone breaks into the house or if they have been playing with matches and are already burned. Nor can warm lines totally assuage children's feelings of abandonment, depression, and loneliness induced by the latchkey situation. The advantage of the warm line is that such feelings might be picked up by a trained warm line volunteer and appropriate referral made if the child is seriously depressed.

Several books have been published to train latchkey children in advance how to handle self-care and any emergency that might come up. These include Helen Swan and Victoria Houston's *Alone After School: A Self-care Guide for Latchkey Children and Their Parents*[30];

Kathy Kyte's *In Charge: A Complete Handbook for Kids with Working Parents*[12]; and Lynette Long's *On My Own: The Kid's Self-care Book.*[13] The authors and sponsors of such books recognize their limited usefulness, especially for children in primary grades, and many include admonitions that the best place for children after school is in the care of an adult.

The advice in books for latchkey children and their parents generally includes training children to dial emergency numbers, discussing house rules with them, and practicing scenarios involving typical emergency situations. All of this is good advice, yet the reason children in grammar school need an adult around is that they have not yet reached the level of reasoning where they can consistently apply generalized facts to decisions about how to behave in novel situations. In an emergency, they may follow a set of guidelines that do not apply to the circumstances, or they may panic and forget what they have been taught. Although all children may find themselves alone at some time and should be instructed what to do if they are approached by a stranger or if their clothing catches fire, parents cannot assume that any child knows what to do if sexual advances are made by a family friend or if the fire is next to the telephone they are supposed to use to call.

Seminars and courses for latchkey children are offered by a variety of groups, including schools, civic organizations, and some businesses as part of family-oriented programs. The American Red Cross presents Basic Aid Training (BAT), a first aid and safety awareness course for fourth through sixth graders. The Kansas Committee for Prevention of Child Abuse offers a program for upper grammar school children and their parents that fosters communication between parents and children and assists them in making the decision about when self-care is appropriate. "I Can Do It," sponsored by National Campfire, Inc., is a course for second and third graders on self-help skills, home safety, and family responsibility.[4] Such courses are most useful for children as preparation for the transition to self-care as they approach high school age; they cannot change a younger child's developmental level nor teach children to behave in an adult-like manner. Both seminars and advice books may give parents a false sense of security—their children are now trained and they need not worry about what they are doing at home in the afternoon and what dangers they may be facing.

None of these programs really addresses the problems of children behaving badly or developing badly. Children who are left alone are free to break every parental rule until they are finally caught in a serious crime or dangerous violation of safety precautions resulting in injury. Although all children will break rules from time to time, no matter how carefully monitored, the child in the care of an attentive adult will have misbehavior noticed sooner, and corrective action can be taken immediately.

Given the limitations of latchkey assistance projects, many communities are pressed by parents, teachers, and other adults to increase the availability of child care before and after school hours. Some promising models have been devised across the nation involving a variety of settings and a variety of forms of sponsorship.

The Family Day Care Network Model: Checking In

Licensed family day care homes, if adapted to the needs of school-age children, can be ideal sites for before- and after-school care. Because older children tend to use the neighborhood rather than the home as the setting for their activities, familiarity with the neighborhood is a distinct advantage for the family day care provider attempting to supervise school-age children appropriately. Family day care is also a local business and is more likely than other child care facilities to be within walking distance of the school or near the children's regular bus stop. This eliminates transportation problems and prevents children from being isolated from their regular friendship groups.

In many areas bureaucratic problems prevent family day care providers from accepting children for before- and after-school care. Policies in many school districts prohibit transportation of children to any site other than their own homes. Enlightened school boards can change these policies and rewrite contracts with their bus and insurance companies to accommodate the transportation needs of children whose parents are at work. Another deterrent is state laws that restrict the number of children in a family day care home. Since school-age children do not require the intense care that infants and toddlers need, these laws might be relaxed for the short time period before and after school (provided, of course, that the caregiver feels she can still attend to the needs of the younger children). In Connecticut, for example, capacity laws for family day care were changed to allow up to three additional children in the early morning and after-school hours only. This change was opposed by a number of groups under the auspices of the Connecticut Association of Human Services, which argued that none of the children could receive appropriate care in such a large and mixed age group. Perhaps the admission of school-age children into the family day care home works best if they arrive before some of the younger children, and return when some of them are napping or have already gone home.

Adapting a neighborhood family day care home into a nurturing environment for school-age children can be accomplished by parent and provider, especially when assisted with program development by a family day care network (see Chapter 1). Parents of middle school children, who are in the stage of transition between closely supervised care and appropriate self-care, can give the provider a list of preapproved places the children may go and activities they may pursue. Thus the children can use the family day care home as a base, checking in at previously arranged intervals, just as they would with their parents.

The Family Satellite Program in Reston, Virginia is an innovative approach to family day care after-school programs.[31] There the Reston Children's Center (RCC) operates a network of family day care homes in conjunction with its center-based preschool and school-age services. The family caregivers become employees of RCC and receive benefits including paid holidays and sick time. They are also given program support in the form of field trip planning, materials and supplies, and activity plans. This assures that children will have something interesting to do after school and will be active rather than sitting for hours in front of the television. After the age of nine or ten, children and their parents may opt instead for a check-in program, as discussed above. In the RCC Check-In model, which was designed with the help of a federal grant, a written contract lists specific places the child has permission to go, including his or her own home. This model provides an appropriate transition for the child too old for many of the activities offered in the day care home and too young for self-care.

Integrating School-Age Children into Center Programs

There are no national data on how many child care centers have expanded to include part-time care for school-age children. Since many mothers seek employment once their children are in school, indications are that center operators are moving to supply this ready market. Many nursery school and preschool child care programs have instituted half-day sessions for kindergarteners only. Their staff may be certified only in early childhood education, and the play materials and standard activities would not have to be changed much to integrate these slightly older children. Other centers, however, are opening their doors to all children of grade school age. Kinder-Care, for example, provides school-age services in many of its preschool centers nationwide, and has instituted a "Klubmates" program which serves 20,000 school children during the summer.

For younger school-age children, after-school programs at child care centers can provide a link between the familiar activities of their pre-school days and the less familiar expectations of school and nonparental care. Yet centers that serve predominantly younger children must pay particular attention to the programs developed for school-agers, allowing them to pursue a range of activities and interests that varies from age level to age level. Those who develop such programs must also be aware of the stigma older children attach to attendance at a day care center, even if the name of the program and the activities involved are geared to their level. Even when such care is taken, after-school programs in child care centers are likely to be more attractive to children in the lower grades (to about third grade) and less so to children in the upper grades.

Considering the relatively few hours that school-age children need care and the variety of materials and staff skills needed, for-profit centers may discover that after-school programs are not very profitable. Staffing can be a particular problem. For example, some states make a clear distinction between training in early childhood education and training for work with school-age youngsters. Thus the center cannot simply divert caregivers from groups of preschoolers in full-day care as older children arrive from school. Part-time staff must be hired at additional cost. Yet, some for-profit centers are willing to provide after-school care in order to attract the business of families with children in different age groups.

Transforming Recreation Programs to Child Care Services

Because of the increasing numbers of latchkey children gravitating toward youth recreation programs, playgrounds, and libraries, many communities have developed more organized after-school child care within agencies that formerly provided drop-in events and activities. Programs may be operated by youth organizations, libraries, park and recreation departments, or by coalitions of these groups. For example, San Francisco funds after-school and weekend supervision programs at school playgrounds and gymnasiums in the city.[23] These programs are administered under the guidance of a task force composed of community leaders, the Parent Teacher Association, the library trustees, police officials, and the parks and recreation department. Indiana allocates part of its cigarette tax for school-age child care programs. The money is given to schools, who either develop their own programs or work with nonprofit groups such as the Y to establish new or support existing programs.

The public library association in New London, Connecticut is one of many library groups that have cooperated in the development of programs to supervise children after school. According to Jane Glover, children's librarian, the library there was formerly besieged by grammar school students who had nowhere to go after school, some of them staying until well after 6 P.M. when the building closed. Now the local YWCA provides staffing for an after-school program at the library, and the children's librarian supplements the program with films and reading materials.

Private youth service agencies such as the YMCA and Boys' and Girls' Clubs have made the switch from drop-in programs to formal school-age child care in many communities. The YMCA reported in 1987 that 962 of its 2,200 branches operate school-age child care programs, and 54 of the 400 YWCAs do so. A 1987 survey revealed that half of the 112 Girls Club of America branches provide regular programs after school each day, and the Boys Club reports that many of its 1,100 clubs have changed from drop-in to school-age child care programs.[26]

As in the case of park and recreation departments, private youth service agencies may operate programs entirely on their own or in coalition with other community agencies. In Hudson, Massachusetts, the school board and various youth organizations jointly administer an after-school program, which uses space in a public school building as well as in member youth facilities.[26] In this case, the park and recreation department provides transportation among the schools and facilities taking part in the program. This certainly allows for the wide range of individual interests school children exhibit.

In some areas, organizations which traditionally have little to do with children have begun to address the problem of after-school care. Many public housing agencies serving low- to moderate-income families have become acutely concerned about the numbers of latchkey children at risk in crime and drug infested public housing developments. Communities such as Dover, Delaware have instituted child care within housing projects, with space donated by the housing authority and with combined funding from parent fees, Title XX funds, and state or federal work incentive subsidies. The Glendale Child Development Center, located in a housing project in Minneapolis, was initially designed to serve preschoolers. Now a staff person is stationed there to meet children after school and to escort them to community programs run by the YMCA, the arts council, and other community agencies.[20]

SCHOOL-BASED CHILD CARE PROGRAMS

As can be seen from some of the coalition approaches to school-age child care mentioned above, not all communities still believe that schools are only useful as sites for formal education and that their business with children ends at three o'clock. They are beginning to see schools as one of a variety of community resources that can be adapted to the total needs of the children they serve daily. There are many advantages to parents, children, and the community to using the public schools as either the primary site or the base for a variety of child care programs. For school-age children, the school is already the center of much of their daily lives, and is second only to the family in providing for their developmental needs. Schools also have facilities that support educational and recreational activities for children: gymnasiums and athletic equipment, playgrounds, libraries, bathrooms, cafeterias, child-sized furniture, and health and safety features and practices, such as fire drills. These facilities and the familiar activities offered in them combine to make schools in general safe, comfortable, and welcoming places for children. Many schools also welcome adults in the community, whose taxes support them. Many offer a central place in which to hold community events and adult education courses.

One of the most practical advantages of using the public schools as sites for school-age child care is that the children are already there. They do not have to be transported, except on days they might travel to special resources or programs elsewhere. Recent patterns of declining and shifting enrollment mean that some public schools are seriously overcrowded, while others have unused or underutilized classrooms. Most do not employ their public spaces—gymnasiums, playgrounds, and cafeterias—at all immediately after school. Even in towns experiencing population increases, the school buildings are only fully utilized for about six hours a day. Providing school-age child care space can maximize the efficient use of the schools and provide a sound argument for not closing a school in which enrollment is declining.

Practical Issues in Setting Up School-Based Child Care

School boards who resist the use of school buildings for child care raise a number of specific objections or anticipated problems. These generally revolve around issues of authority and staff utilization, liability and legality, and particularly cost and funding.

When parents or community organizations ask to use a school building and grounds as the site of a latchkey care program, school administrators appropriately seek reassurance that they will maintain authority over facilities and school property, and that the needs of the regular school staff will not be displaced. For example, requests to use classrooms after hours may not be granted. Teachers may not want equipment, teaching aids, or student work disturbed, or they may use their classrooms for an hour or two after school for lesson planning and extra help for their students. Although child care programs generally supply their own staff, agreements may have to be made to pay overtime to custodians remaining after hours. Arrangements about the use of school equipment and supplies must also be made. Clearly, the activities of children after school should not interfere with the smooth running of the regular educational program.

Issues of legality and liability are best handled by careful research and planning by all parties involved, including legal counsel for the school district. The first question that must be answered before a school-age child care program is approved is whether or not the school system is legally empowered to undertake the responsibility for child care during nonschool hours. With widespread community support, most state statutes will be interpreted by the courts to enable schools to provide child care services.[3] Nonetheless, state and local legislation governing approved uses of school buildings must be studied to insure that such a program falls within regulations. Liability and insurance questions need to be approached with the same thoroughness. Even if the school is insured for after-school activities, school-based child care programs may need their own insurance. Finally, most local school districts operate on very tight budgets that represent the major expenditure of tax revenues. Explicit agreements must be made as to who will be responsible for the cost of equipment, utilities, and consumable materials.

Because the planning for school-age child care is complex, it can be helpful to designate a broker—an individual or department within the local government who is responsible for advocating development of school-age child care and for coordination among the private and public sector agencies who sponsor it. The broker can also assist in drawing up contracts between sponsors and schools, coordinating transportation to and from other community facilities, and collecting parent fees. Since child care is a new experience for most schools, a broker can do most of the homework and legwork to make such a program possible.

Investment in School-Age Child Care

A 1988 survey done by the Wellesley School-Age Child Care Project revealed that the average salary of senior school-age child care providers was $6.30 per hour, with assistants receiving less.[27] The average parent fee for after-school child care was about $26 per week. Involvement and financial investment by a range of local public and private sector agencies help keep parent fees down. When school buildings are used for after-school care, the space and upkeep are already being paid for by tax dollars and represent the community's contribution to caring for children. Compared to the ranges previously reported for infant/toddler care, school-age child care is relatively cheap and can be made attractive to parents who might otherwise choose self-care. Yet even such a small fee can be too high for many families, especially if they have more than one child requiring care. School-age child care programs are often instigated and supported by middle-class families, while low-income families are left to compete for the limited number of spaces for which scholarships or sliding fees are available.

No matter who pays what part of the tab, it is school-age children, not their parents, who are the actual consumers of latchkey care programs. If the program is perceived as just an extension of the school day and does not provide for their other developmental needs, they may "vote with their feet" and refuse to attend. Then we can not be sure whether their environments will fall above or below the quality threshold sufficient to support their development.

By the early years of this century, communities across the nation had decided that American children belong in school, not in factories. Now our communities must decide where school-age children belong during those hours their parents are not at home and school is not in session. A wide variety of models is available to choose from, and within each community, families should have the chance to choose the form of adult supervision their children need at a particular stage. They should not be forced to choose inappropriate self-care, in which children are sitting at home in front of the television jumping every time the wind blows, the door creaks, or the neighbor's burglar alarm goes off.

7

---◆◆---

The Challenge of Providing Child Care for Children with Special Needs

As we have noted in the preceding chapters, all but the luckiest of families may have difficulty finding child care at one time or another. And even these lucky ones will have to struggle with arrangements on the inevitable days when their children wake up with a fever or sore throat. For families whose children have special needs, however, the struggle to obtain appropriate child care is a constant dilemma. These are children who are physically or mentally handicapped, chronically ill, bilingual, from migrant families, and/or emotionally disturbed. Their parents are often under great financial strain, either because they have a low income or because they bear the costly burden of therapeutic services and supplies. For them, employment is necessary to provide income or insurance. Yet the child care that would enable them to work is likely to be nonexistent or inaccessible.

Like many families, those with special needs children confront the common problems of finding available, affordable, appropriate care, but these problems are greatly magnified. And on top of these difficulties, there are other imposing barriers to having special child care needs met. There is a lack of understanding about the real nature of these children, common prejudices and fears about those who are in any way different, a dearth of caregivers with specialty training, and a host of physical, geographic, and administrative obstacles that make good child care an impossible dream. Each of the special populations feels the weight of these burdens in different degrees. Transportation poses one problem to a parent whose child is in a wheelchair and who cannot find a day care center with access ramps; it poses another kind of problem to a parent who cannot afford a car. Language barriers mean one thing for a speech-impaired child and something quite different for a child who speaks a language other than English.

In this chapter we will examine the child care needs of these special groups and underscore the attitudinal and other barriers to the provision of services for them. We will also discuss some theoretical issues involved in determining what type of care is appropriate for these children, and how to coordinate their child care experience with other social service and medical programs. Finally, we will look at existing efforts to ease the child care burdens of their families. These scattered and typically small programs can suggest some promising solutions to what is a most difficult aspect of the American child care crisis.

ATTITUDINAL BARRIERS TO MEETING THE NEEDS OF SELECTED POPULATIONS

All children need loving, predictable, and developmentally appropriate care throughout their growing years. Continuity of care is especially important for young children, but for those with special needs it is imperative. All types of intervention—whether physical therapy or teaching the names of colors and numbers in two languages—must be delivered continuously to be effective. This can best be accomplished by a nurturing and skilled caregiver who will stay on the job long enough to be aware of and reinforce the child's progress. Care that is appropriate to a child's developmental level takes on special meaning for children with or at risk of developmental problems; to ascertain and deliver appropriate care, the caregiver must provide a high degree of individual attention. Finally, like other children, those who have special problems also need peer contact to develop socially, cognitively, and physically.

Many families have difficulty obtaining quality child care that includes a knowledgeable, consistent caregiver and an individually tailored program. For those who share the universal needs and have special needs as well, quality care can be even more elusive. To better understand their child care dilemmas, we will examine the actual needs of selected populations and probe some of the conceptions and misconceptions about them.

Handicapped Children

The term "handicapped" encompasses a wide variety of disabilities, ranging in form and severity from speech, hearing, or visual impairments to orthopedic problems, emotional disorders, and mental retardation. Families with handicapped children suffer many adjustment difficulties. These include elevated levels of stress and anxiety, guilt, financial problems, social isolation, marital discord, sibling adaptation problems, restrictions on family activities, and household disorganization.[15,22] In other words, the birth of a handicapped child can shatter familiar lifestyles and disrupt relationships with family and friends. Affordable and appropriate child care can alleviate some of these problems by complementing the family's functions and offering parents a respite from the intensive care their child may require.

Optimal child care for a handicapped child must not only be nurturing but oriented to intervention as well. Deaf children must learn to communicate their needs, blind and wheelchair-bound children must learn to negotiate their surroundings, and retarded children need specific types of intellectual stimulation. Constant positive reinforcement of these activities can facilitate desired results. All of this might seem to imply the need for caregivers who are special educators or therapists. Remember, however, that parents are the primary caregivers and are commonly taught how to provide any special care their child requires. A child care provider could be taught just as easily, perhaps by the parents themselves.

Nonetheless, the vast majority of child care facilities will not admit a handicapped child. In a survey conducted by the School-Age Child Care Project, 25% of parents of disabled five- to seven-year-old children had been denied admission or been discouraged from applying to a child care program since their children entered school.[6] Of children 12 to 16 years old, nearly half had been refused during their longer years in school. This School-Age/Special Needs Study was not a scientific sampling, but rather was meant to provide "a series of snapshots" of child care problems. However, these numbers suggest a serious problem, since many of the parents surveyed had never attempted to enroll their children in child care. If admission to child care was denied to 25% of the parents of children just entering school, including those who did not apply, the percentage who wanted it but could not obtain it is much higher than this statistic indicates. Even programs that ostensibly provide services to disabled children have requirements that for all practical purposes exclude them. For example, in 1982, 58% of the centers in the metropolitan Washington, D.C. area stated that they were willing to accept handicapped children, but many of them required that the child be mobile and toilet trained.[3] One mother who responded to the School-Age/Special Needs Study reported that "day care did not want a handicapped child with anything more serious than eyeglasses."[6]

Proposed legislation, the Americans with Disabilities Act, would ban the denial of services (and employment) to those with disabilities. The latest revisions of the Act specifically mention child care centers as a sector that must make efforts to serve disabled children. The version passed by the Senate in 1989 (S. 933) would exempt family day care homes. If the Act becomes law, it remains to be seen if it effectively increases the availability of child care for disabled children. It is mentioned here because debates in Congress may at least heighten the sensitivity of caregivers to the unmet need for supplementary care that exists in this population.

There are a number of common sentiments that hinder the provision of child care services for handicapped children. One is the mistaken belief that they are "being taken care of" by various laws that mandate appropriate treatments and make these children the responsibility of public human services departments. In reality, most of these laws pertain primarily to formal public education and physical access to buildings supported by public funds. In addition, common irrational fears concerning individuals who are in any way disabled create a resistance to making accommodations for them in child care programs attended by "normal" children. Finally, most day care facilities are beset with problems ranging from compliance with complex regulations to the inability to attract and retain competent staff. Directors may fear that the addition of a handicapped client will only add to their hardships. Besides, many facilities have long waiting lists of children who are easier to care for, giving the handicapped child even less hope of admission.

Bilingual Children

The majority of bilingual American children are of Hispanic origin. Many others live in ethnic communities throughout the country where the predominant language is Cambodian, Thai, French, or Russian, for example. Most of these families are immigrants who are trying to establish a new home and place in American society. Employment is their only key to success in achieving these goals. The majority have few skills adaptable to the American work place, so they are relegated to entry-level, low-paying jobs. Many of the adults speak little English, so they do not know about available community resources. Thus they have even more difficulty than most families in finding child care and in paying for it.

The type of child care appropriate for bilingual children is a matter of controversy. On the one hand, their families are attempting to become "Americanized," so their children should be exposed to the mainstream language and practices. On the other, child care services that are not linguistically and culturally relevant may result in children's rejection of their heritage. This could possibly hinder their psychological and social development. The conflict over whether and how much to mainstream bilingual child care services is part of the larger controversy concerning bilingual education, which to date remains unresolved.

A more formidable hindrance is the racial and ethnic prejudice which continues to pervade our so-called "melting pot" society. The presence of a Vietnamese or Hispanic child in a white, middle-class day care setting is still likely to be met with opposition by some parents. Another problem is in finding bilingual caregivers sensitive to the cultural needs and values of these children. Many states require caregivers to have at least a high school diploma, but the higher dropout rate of minorities (particularly among those who are poor and live in urban areas) means that more whites will fulfill this requirement.[4] The low pay offered most caregivers would not readily attract an applicant fluent in two languages, since this skill would enable her to obtain a higher paying job in other occupations. Finally, the lack of affordable child care (bilingual or otherwise) is an acute problem for non-English speaking families, many of whom have incomes below the poverty level.[7]

Children of Migrant Families

A "migrant farm worker" is defined as a person whose principal employment is in agriculture on a seasonal basis, and who establishes a temporary abode for the purposes of such employment.[16] Many of these workers are ethnic minorities and/or illegal aliens. They work very long hours, often seven days a week, and are paid extremely low wages. In most cases, all adults in the household and all but the youngest children must labor in the fields to obtain income for the barest essentials. Constant changes in residence make it terribly difficult for these families to find necessary services for themselves and their children.

The children's needs for child care are no different from those of all children, except that continuity of care may be an even more crucial element. Constant, unpredictable change is often a condition of daily life for the children of migrant workers. Predictability in their daily activities—with the same basic routines, toys, bed, and caregivers—would help stabilize their world and allow them to make sense of their experiences. Unfortunately, this constancy can be all but impossible to achieve. Since their families are rarely in residence for more than seven months, due to seasonal changes in crop harvesting, it may be difficult to find facilities willing to accept them. When child care is found, the ethnic (and often linguistic) dissimilarity between the host community and the migrant family can alienate the children from staff and can inhibit the formation of solid adult-child relationships so essential for optimal child development. Added to the child care problems associated with frequent moves is the family's genuine inability to pay. The result is an entire population of children who are at risk due to lack of access to child care.

The consequences of this lack of care for the children of migrant workers are devastating. In California alone, there were about 287,000 migrant children eligible for subsidized child care services in 1984. Only 2,800 children actually received subsidized center-based care. Another 95,000 were left alone or were cared for by other young children for an average of 43 hours per week.[17] It is estimated that 2,600 children under three years of age are "left alone in cars, boxes at the ends of rows in the fields, or nearby tents; and one-fourth of the deaths of children under 14 are caused by drowning in irrigation ditches and canals."[17]

There are myriad obstacles that undermine the provision of child care for migrant families. While some farm employers make an effort to meet the needs of their workers' children, many simply cannot afford to do so. Others hire and exploit illegal aliens without regard to the consequences for the children. In addition, the barriers created by prejudice, noted in the above discussion of bilingual children, also hurt migrant families. They are likely to be discriminated against because of ethnic, linguistic, and/or social class differences. Further, the host community may feel it has no obligations to these children because they are not permanent residents.

The federal government does supply some child care services for migrant children, specifically the Federal Migrant Child Care Programs. Head Start also has a division for migrant workers' (and Indian) children, and some of these local programs are open long hours to accommodate child care needs. As with many federal programs, however, there are not enough funds for either of these services to provide care for all of the eligible children. Those migrant workers who are in this country illegally would probably avoid Head Start or other public child care programs anyway for fear of discovery and deportation.

Ill Children

In the context of child care services, the general phrase "ill children" refers to two distinct groups. One consists of children suffering from acute infectious illnesses such as flu, ear infections, or chicken pox, who are in need of short-term care in isolation from their healthy peers. The other consists of children suffering from chronic noninfectious illnesses who require long-term special care.

Care for children suffering from the common diseases of childhood poses a variety of problems. Need for such care is obviously unpredictable. Imagine the following scenario. A working mother rouses the family to begin the morning rush to get everyone ready. Her young son complains of not feeling well and promptly vomits. The day care center will not admit an ill child, the teenager who sometimes babysits on weekends is, of course, in school, and all of the "at home" mothers in the neighborhood would not want to expose their own children to the boy's illness. The parent will not be paid if she misses work, however, and the day care center will still require the full weekly fee even though her son was absent.

This parent's dilemma is overshadowed by the ill child's needs. If the child could be cared for in his regular center, at least he would be in familiar surroundings with known caregivers. This is, of course, not possible when children have illnesses that pose too great an infectious risk for others. Furthermore, children in the midst of an acute sickness are not well enough to travel. Their immediate need is for the comfort of their own beds and homes, and the loving care that only parents can provide. This is not an option open to many working parents, however, so the children's needs often cannot take precedence. The mother in our story can frantically attempt to enlist the help of a relative or friend, leave her son home alone and call him every hour, or tell her employer that she herself is sick. The parent will feel guilty whatever she does; the child left alone will be unhappy at best and, at worst, could be exposed to risk of harm.

Chronic illness poses other child care problems. Some of these are shared with children suffering from handicapping conditions, while others are unique to children with diseases that may be progressively debilitating or terminal. There were over a million such children in the United States in 1984.[17] The emotional and financial impact on a family whose child has a chronic illness can be devastating. Most parents in this situation need to work, to keep up medical insurance and to pay for costly services not covered by insurance. All need occasional time off from the physical and emotional drain of caring for their children, so child care may be needed even if one parent does not work outside the home.

Children with chronic illnesses need the same quality child care as well children do, but they have other needs in addition. For example, they may require medication throughout the day. A leukemic child may need more naps than peers; children with hormonal disorders such as diabetes may require special diets and must be watched closely so that they do not share another child's lunch or snack. Common injuries or falls might have to receive uncommon attention. There are intense emotional needs as well, both for the ill child and the well children in the program. The child must be made to feel like everyone else, although special treatment is required. The other children may be puzzled and frightened by their peer's disorder. Since he or she looks just about like them, but is not, they may worry about the integrity of their own bodies. The ill child's right to a secure and happy childhood, experienced both at home and in child care, is perhaps the most pressing need.

Depending on the specific illness, child care may be more or less difficult to obtain, but it is generally more difficult than obtaining child care under normal circumstances. Facilities are unlikely to have caregivers trained to work with the physical or emotional needs of children who are chronically ill or who can spare the extra time required. And caregivers and parents are not immune to persistent social attitudes surrounding illness and death. There are many people who fear contact with individuals suffering from diseases that are both nonacute and noncontagious.[19] Most people understand on one level that cancer is not contagious, for example, but there remains an underlying fear that it can somehow be "caught." When factual information is not so clear, such fears can border on hysteria. Autoimmune Deficiency Syndrome (AIDS) is a compelling case in point. An increasing number of children are being found to carry the HIV virus (which can result in AIDS), having contracted it before birth from infected mothers. The only risk a young child with the HIV virus poses to others is through blood contact. Caution in caring for a cut or scrape, and the use of inexpensive disposable gloves would eliminate this risk. Yet many caregivers would rather quit than have daily contact with a child who has, or may develop, AIDS. If they do admit the child, they may see enrollment decline as other client families withdraw their children. In sum, misinformation and illogical fears are potent obstacles to providing care for children with chronic or life-threatening illnesses. Their families are often unable to obtain the child care services that are available to other children, even though they may need them more.

PRACTICAL BARRIERS TO OBTAINING CHILD CARE

To be sure, public sentiments are not the only reasons why those with special needs are denied access to child care. There are a host of practical reasons why many child care facilities cannot accommodate a child with extraordinary needs, and why the child might not be able to attend.

Before discussing these more concrete hindrances, we should note that a big problem in the provision of child care for special populations is a lack of demographic data that can be used in planning services for them. For many of these special groups, no one is really sure about the actual number of children who are involved, especially before they reach school age. For example, the data regarding the number of children in migrant families are somewhat unreliable, largely because federal agencies have failed to establish a uniform definition of "migrant" and to set consistent eligibility requirements for migrant child care services. We do know that there are at least 500,000 American children under the age of six suffering from physical handicaps.[17] However, the lack of national data on either the child care needs of their families or the availability of services for this population makes it difficult to evaluate the extent to which their needs are being met. What data do exist suggest that need is far greater than supply, but how much more so than in the general population is unknown.

Without reliable data on how many children we are dealing with, it is difficult to form social policies responsive to their needs. In fact, some existing policies are more a deterrent than they are a help to making child care accessible. Laws prohibit child care facilities from admitting acutely ill children even if they could be kept in isolation. Relevant to those who are chronically ill are laws governing the administration of medications (although parents have no such restrictions in their own homes). For handicapped children, laws that specify physical layout and special amenities may be there to protect the child, but the expense of adding these features can defeat the most well-intentioned caregiver. An ironic barrier to providing child care services to migrant families is the law itself. The coordinator of the Child Development Program in Orange County, California told the Select Committee[17] that to be eligible for a Federal Migrant Child Care Program, a child must have moved with his or her family in the last five years. This effectively excludes very young children who were born within the local agricultural community, and undermines the intent of the act—which was to provide child care for small children so their older siblings could attend school instead of babysit.

Geographic Barriers

A minority of child care centers will accept children from one or more of the special populations. Family day care providers are typically more flexible than centers, and we can conjecture that at least some of them are willing to assume responsibility for an atypical child (most likely at extra cost). As will be noted later in this chapter, there are some special programs for these children operating in communities around the country. If the child is old enough, a Head Start program may be available. For families to have access to these rare centers or special programs, they must live within a reasonable commuting distance. Sometimes, however, even this is not enough.

Transportation for a physically handicapped child may always be a hassle, and the trip to the child care setting is no exception. Driving with a child who is in a wheelchair, or moving medical equipment needed at both home and child care, can be problematic. Couple these with the extra time that may be required to dress and feed even a more mobile handicapped child, and we can see that the parent has already done half a day's work even before arriving on the job. Many of these problems also afflict families with chronically ill children, who may have the added burden of driving long distances with medications or food that must be kept refrigerated. Although recent years have witnessed an increase in the number of child care programs for children with common illnesses, a parent may be forced to lengthen the commute to work considerably to get there, at the same time trying to keep the ill child comfortable. If a relative is found who is willing to care for the child, these same problems may appear if he or she has to be picked up and taken to the home, or the child taken there.

Bilingual and migrant families may have child care services available in their communities, but transportation can still be an obstacle. Many

non-English speaking families are poor and may not be able to afford
a car or public transportation to child care, then to work, then back
again. Since programs with bilingual caregivers are most likely to be
found in areas that have a large ethnic population, those who live in
suburban or rural districts would be unable to attend. Migrant families
in particular are likely to have transportation problems. Migrant housing
is generally placed close to the fields and far from towns where child
care may be available. This denies access for children whose parents
either have no means of transportation or whose work hours (beginning
very early in the morning) preclude their being able to bring their
children to the facility.

Physical and Material Barriers

The physical barriers to child care that immediately spring to mind
are those for handicapped children. Many child care centers are located
in churches and old school buildings, where indoor and outdoor stairways
are part of the structure. They do not have wide doorways or modern
bathrooms with support grips. A child who has limited mobility might
not be able to negotiate the facility, and a blind child would have to
be carefully taught to do so. There might not be sufficient room to
isolate an acutely ill child where he or she could be comfortable for
the day. Some states mandate an isolation area for a child who becomes
ill while at day care, but this is a temporary placement used only
until the parent (who has been called from work) arrives. Children
with chronic illnesses who need to rest more often than their peers,
perhaps with medical equipment, may not have a quiet space available.
Many child care facilities, whether family day care homes or centers,
operate on minimal profits. They could never afford the additions or
special amenities which would enable them to accommodate these special needs children.

The need for special materials is another reason why certain children
cannot be admitted to standard child care programs. Children who
are bilingual should be able to enjoy storybooks and records relevant
to their culture. These educational materials could provide a rich learning
experience for their English-speaking classmates as well. The problem
is that many facilities can barely afford the materials they would like
to have for their mainstream patrons; the cost of specialized products
is often out of the question. By the same token, centers that serve
mostly non-English speaking children may not be able to afford both
native materials and "American" ones to aid in the children's accultur-

ation. Even standard materials might pose a hazard to a retarded or developmentally disabled child. Some toys, for example, might have small parts or require skills that are appropriate for most children in the chronological age range the center serves, but are inappropriate for a retarded child who is not as developmentally advanced or a handicapped child who lacks the coordination required to use them.

Food poses another materials problem. Migrant and minority culture children may be unfamiliar with the food served in the facility, and this could make it difficult for them to adapt to their surroundings and feel comfortable there. Children with chronic illnesses may need specialized diets which the center might not be willing to prepare. Even if the parent brings meals and snacks from home, it is difficult for caregivers to serve them while trying to serve something different to the others. As anyone who has observed mealtime in a children's lunchroom knows, it can be next to impossible to keep children from exchanging food. The child who is highly allergic to milk is handed a milk carton by a good-natured three-year-old just learning to share. Or a disgruntled two-year-old grabs the diabetic child's fruit from his plate and substitutes a half-eaten cupcake. Feeding the chronically ill child in isolation is often not practical and can interfere with the child's socialization and strides to develop a sense of normalcy.

Lack of Qualified Staff

The lack of people trained in the skills necessary to provide good child care haunts day care facilities throughout the nation. Caregivers who have the technical training or specialized skills necessary to care for a child with special needs are an even rarer breed. The entire staff must have some preparation to deal with even one ill, handicapped, migrant, or bilingual child, but specific abilities may be required as well. To care for a chronically ill child, someone on the staff must know how to use special equipment or be certified to administer drugs or injections. Ideally, registered or practical nurses would be on hand to care for acutely ill children, but the nursing shortage and staffing cost usually preclude that possibility. For children with physical, emotional, or intellectual handicaps, the caregiver must be trained to identify what the child is capable of doing and how to proceed with developmental and learning tasks. She may have to be a physical therapist, or be capable of communicating or consulting with one. With a child who is in the process of learning English, someone on the staff must speak the child's home language fluently enough to understand attempts to communicate needs and pronounce native and English words. The same may be true for a migrant worker's child, whose caregiver also must be highly sensitive to the real need for continuity and familiar with the family's lifestyle.

Unfortunately, with the low wages most child care facilities can offer, their chances of hiring someone trained in therapies, special education methods, or other specialties are very slim. If they want to upgrade the skills of their current staff, their search for appropriate courses is likely to be as difficult as a parent's search for appropriate child care. Even where specialized training is available, workers might be unable to take advantage of it because of cost, timing, or transportation difficulties.

Finances: The Biggest Barrier

As can be gleaned from this discussion, the most severe restriction to the provision and procurement of child care services for those with special needs is money. If caregivers could be paid an appropriate wage, turnover would be reduced and children would benefit from more continuity in their care. If relevant training were more available and affordable, the skill level of the entire occupation would be raised. If those with specialized training could be paid salaries commensurate with their education and competitive with other businesses requiring the same skills, more specialists might be persuaded to enter the child care profession. If facilities could afford the remodeling and special materials these children might require, many would probably do so. They would also be able to reduce their staff-child ratios so the child could be afforded the extra time and services. Ironically, if all of these improvements were to happen, child care would be priced so high that most families could not afford it.

The cost of appropriate child care is already a heavy burden for parents whose children have special needs. For example, family day care (which is typically less expensive than center-based care) may cost two to three times more for a handicapped child than for those who pay the regular fee.[17] Since disabled and retarded children may require care far beyond the age when most children can safely care for themselves, these costs will be incurred over a much longer period of time.

Even a child whose special needs are limited to days when he or she is ill can strain the family budget. For example, a few day care centers provide home care by regular staff for children who are too ill to attend, but this is both rare and prohibitively expensive.[19] If an acute care program or provider is found, the cost represents an addition to the normal weekly child care expense.

The sorry conclusion is that neither caregivers nor parents can afford appropriate child care services for youngsters with special needs. This is the result of our narrow social focus on providing intervention and educational programs to the exclusion of meeting other needs. The general unwillingness of government and business to assume much responsibility for child care has hurt all American families. Children with special needs have surely suffered the most.

TO MAINSTREAM OR NOT TO MAINSTREAM

The question of what is the most appropriate type of care for a child with special needs may appear to be a matter of individual choice. Yet this question is the subject of an ongoing theoretical debate about the wisdom of full integration throughout American society. This debate is heard in the context of school desegregation and forced busing. For handicapped and retarded children, the wisdom of the law is that they be educated in the "least restrictive" environment, interpreted to mean alongside nonhandicapped peers, if at all possible. This spirit has also led to abandonment of most institutions for those with physical or mental disabilities. Just 20 years ago, retarded and handicapped children could attend residential or sheltered day programs, where special services were provided and child care was not a problem. Today, these special children are often remanded to home care and public education.

This is not to say that deinstitutionalization and mainstreaming are detrimental practices. The problem is that the "cart was put before the horse," as these policies were instituted before researchers could determine if they were uniformly beneficial and before adequate community supports for deinstitutionalization were in place. The evidence that has since accumulated suggests that "normalization" can be both good and harmful.[23] What remains to be determined is which children, with what particular disabilities and individual traits, will fare better in an integrated setting.

The issue is no more clear-cut in the case of bilingual children. There is no question that they should be afforded equal education and life opportunities. The puzzle is how to involve them in the mainstream without impairing their ability to function as members of their ethnic communities. In the context of both education and child care, how can we provide services without forcing them to lose a sense of connection with their linguistic and cultural origins? Even child-rearing practices can differ among ethnic groups, so the standard fare in an "American" day care setting can impose somewhat foreign treatment. If children are placed in the care of an English-speaking caregiver, they may eventually become linguistic and cultural exiles.[11] If they receive care inside their own culture, they will be "ghettoized" within their ethnic community. The dearth of bilingual caregivers who are already assimilated does not make for easy solutions to this predicament.

Integration of bilingual and handicapped children can certainly be achieved, albeit with some effort. Head Start, in which 22% of the enrollment is Hispanic, has designed bilingual-bicultural programs that focus on the needs of Spanish-speaking children. Curricula have been developed to provide instruction in two languages. There are models to train Head Start staff in bilingual-bicultural education, and resource centers that provide technical assistance to centers with programs for Spanish-speaking children and families.

Head Start is also the largest single provider of services to handicapped preschool children and their families.[18] In 1972, Congress mandated that at least 10% of Head Start's national enrollment consist of handicapped children. The project has successfully carried out the mandate; in the 1987–88 program year, handicapped children accounted for over 13% of the preschoolers enrolled.[1] These children are mainstreamed into the regular program. They receive the full range of Head Start services as well as services tailored to their special needs. Training materials are provided for staff, and technical assistance is given to Head Start centers to help them serve these children.

Another program that involves mainstreaming handicapped children is the innovative Utah Social Integration Program. This program, which merges special education services (assessment, individual lesson plans, and services by specialists) with child care, has demonstrated that handicapped children can receive education as well as care with their nonhandicapped peers. The effort is a cost-efficient model program that has resulted in important developmental gains for the children involved at less cost than would be engendered by a self-contained service.[14]

In spite of the success of these programs, those who design services for children with special needs must never lose sight of the single most important question in the mainstreaming controversy: What is best for the individual child? This question cannot be answered by reference to current social policies or treatment fads. It must be tackled the hard way—by painstaking examination of each child's and family's circumstances and needs.

COORDINATION OF CHILD CARE WITH OTHER SERVICES

Although our discussion thus far has focused on the needs of specific special populations, it should be understood that many children fit into more than one category. For example, many mentally retarded children are also physically handicapped. Bilingual children can also have handicaps or chronic illnesses. Certainly all of these children, like those without problem conditions, will be acutely ill on some days of their lives.

It is also apparent that child care is not the only service children with special needs require. There are medical treatments, physical and/or psychological therapies, and various types of social services and supports to help their families to function. Too often, families with children who have special needs are left to find their way through this maze of services with little or no guidance. A family with a handicapped child might be eligible for social security, food stamps, and subsidized child care and medical services. These supports would entail visits to at least four state and local agencies, and this does not count the facilities where the services are rendered. A doctor might refer a chronically ill child to psychological therapy and the parents to a family support group. These services might not be locally available; paying for them is another matter entirely.

In the educational establishment, the Education for All Handicapped Children Act requires that a team consisting of parents, administrators, and teachers be formed to plan and coordinate a program for each child with special needs. The usefulness of a similar team of other service providers is clearly indicated. Much could be accomplished by communication between those who deliver medical, social, child care, and other services to those with special needs. This would insure that families receive the services to which they are entitled, and all supportive efforts could be coordinated to avoid both overlap and vacancies. Families would also have a central place to turn as new problems arose and circumstances changed.

Child care providers can be an important part of this team. Because they are with the child for many hours each week, they must help to administer interventions. They are also in a good position to monitor progress and suggest modifications. They interact with the child's parent much more often than other service providers, and thus are better able to bridge the gap between the child's home and out-of-home treatments. Clearly, the child care provider can be a tremendous resource to the other professionals responsible to the child and family.

Here again, a model is provided by Head Start. Some 92% of Head

Start programs designate a specific person to coordinate services for each handicapped student.[5] For any parent who has tried to negotiate the labyrinth of health, education, and welfare services for those with handicaps, Head Start's coordinating role may be its most important function.

In recognition of the need for integrated services, Public Law 99–457 (amendments to the education of the handicapped act) requires that a multidisciplinary team and a case manager be assigned to each family with a disabled child. Although the main thrust of the new law is to expand intervention services for handicapped infants and preschoolers, these services do not appear to be limited to efforts directly involving the child. There is recognition that the family has the major influence over the course of the child's development, and the personal manager who works with each family will attempt to address their problems and needs so they are in a better position to help their child. Child care will certainly be one of these needs for some families. Peggy Pizzo of the National Center for Clinical Infant Programs suggests that qualified child care programs apply for funds provided by the new legislation and become sites where early intervention services are delivered.[12] Thus child care could be integrated with the child's specialized program, parents would have a familiar place to enter instead of receiving services in scattered locales, and service providers could interact closely with families and children on a daily basis instead of on a formal schedule.

PROMISING SOLUTIONS

We have already described a few programs created to meet the child care and other requirements of children with special needs. In particular, Head Start is the major provider of services to handicapped and bilingual preschoolers. Of course, Head Start is primarily an early education program, and individual centers may or may not offer full-day child care depending on resources and community need. And not all families are eligible for Head Start services. The project is open mainly to lower-income groups, with only 10% of the slots allocated to families with higher earnings. Nonetheless, Head Start has created a number of innovative models which could be adapted to programs serving younger children of all income levels. Legislators have recognized Head Start's success and unique position to design and test prototypic services. Many of the child care proposals considered by the 101st Congress included funds for expanding Head Start and developing a child care component.

A project with a somewhat different thrust is First Start, directed by Marilyn Krajicek at the University of Colorado School of Nursing.[8] This is a national training program to teach paraprofessionals to care for handicapped infants and toddlers. Regional, state, and local agencies sponsor instructors to take the First Start curriculum. They then return to their home areas and train caregivers to provide the special care a very young handicapped child requires. According to Ms. Krajicek, the program has been offered in more than a dozen states and nearly 500 caregivers have been trained. As states begin to implement PL 99–457, they will find the project a valuable resource in helping them train a corps of service providers for very young children with disabilities. First Start is a giant step in the direction of overcoming the fear that makes many providers reluctant to undertake the care of a handicapped baby, and it is an educational gold mine of ideas on the type of care that is appropriate and developmentally optimizing. The project takes yet another step by requiring sponsors to develop a plan to assure collaboration between other agencies serving handicapped children in their locales. First Start has the elements to make it a valuable model for caregiver training. It is hoped that it will spawn identical programs for providers of care to the other special needs populations.

The MATCH program, operating in several counties in North Carolina, is an effort to expand child care services for handicapped or at-risk infants and toddlers.[9] MATCH operates four child development centers with a combined capacity for 48 children. Faced with a waiting list of 500, staff began to contact certified family day care providers and to match them with waiting list families in their neighborhoods. Caregivers become part of a team with parents and medical personnel and assist with planning goals for the child and monitoring progress. The providers are paid a higher than average fee, and have the added benefit of reducing their number of vacancies.

Providers in child care centers are assisted when they enroll children with developmental disabilities through Project K.I.D.S. (Kids in Integrated Daycare Services). Developed by the Association for Retarded Citizens/Arkansas, this state-funded project places developmentally disabled children, from infancy to five years old, into child care and pre-school programs in the community. K.I.D.S. staff help parents in selecting a child care facility, and eligible families are given state assistance with tuition. A parent education component informs parents about their rights, special education laws, and developmental issues. Parents help to plan their child's program with a team of helpers that includes a services coordinator, case monitor, appropriate therapists, and other health professionals. Child care teachers join this team, and the team joins the teachers at the child care setting. K.I.D.S. staff deliver therapeutic services to the disabled child, sometimes involving all of the children in attendance in activities they too can enjoy. The professionals are also there to observe children suspected of having developmental problems. Although small, the K.I.D.S. project is reporting improvements in physical, social, and cognitive skills in the target children, increased peer acceptance of disabled children, and positive evaluations of the program by parents and caregivers.[20]

The models we have discussed so far are designed to serve very young children with disabilities. Once these children enter school, they too are affected by the shortage of before- and after-school care programs faced by their nonhandicapped peers (Chapter 6). Dale Fink describes in detail a number of programs operating throughout the country to provide care for disabled children during nonschool hours.[6] In Albuquerque, New Mexico, for example, both regular and special education students attend a program run by the parks and recreation department. The program is housed in a school, but disabled students from other schools may enroll (transportation is provided). Since many of the students have multiple handicaps, volunteers are enlisted to create a high staff-child ratio and the opportunity for individual attention. In Syracuse, New York, a private school (Jowonio: The Learning Place) that has historically integrated regular and special need students runs an after-school program in the Syracuse Public Schools. Here, too, some of the children require one-to-one supervision, so the extra staff needs are met by student interns. In Delmar, New York, a private nonprofit child care program received a grant from the state Office of Mental Retardation and Developmental Disabilities to expand their enrollment to include children with special needs. Other programs exist solely for disabled children. Whether separate or mainstreamed, Fink believes that after-school programs for disabled children greatly expand their experiences. They typically spend their school day with a small group of children and therapists. In a good child care setting, "they sit at tables and play with decks of cards or dominoes or marbles . . . they try on clothes and hats . . . eat at snack tables with everyone else."[6] Friendships with peers have time to develop in this more casual atmosphere.

For the children of migrant workers, the Texas Migrant Council Mobile Head Start Program does just what the name implies: The program operates 47 centers in Texas for most of the year, but during the summer moves to several states to the north where the families migrate to do seasonal harvesting. The entire staff, including teachers, aides, and nursing assistants, are moved to states as far away as Indiana and Ohio. According to Vicki Nino of the Texas Migrant Council, Inc., the families are told where the summer Head Start locations will be, and most attempt to secure work in those areas. Thus this program eliminates some of the disruptions generated by geographic mobility by offering continuous services to migrant families and children.

The Chapter I/Migrant Early Childhood Program provides child care for preschoolers of migrant workers in Palm Beach County, Florida.[10] Sponsored by the school board, each school that conducts the program has a resource coordinator who goes into the community to enroll children. Child care is operated for the full working day from dawn to dusk, and transportation is provided. The program is based on the assumption that parents have a vital role in their children's school success. The coordinator visits with parents in the fields or at home in the evenings. Workshops and parent meetings are often conducted as late as 9 P.M. when the long workday is over. These outreach efforts and flexibility show that it is possible to accommodate the needs of those families who do not have a normal workday schedule, who lack telephones at the work place and perhaps at home, or who may not have a permanent mailing address.

General family support, which also includes the provision and coordination of a variety of helping services, is the goal of the Children's Respite Care Center in Carmichael, California. The program provides trained staff to work with chronically and terminally ill children and their parents. It also offers stressed families a needed timeout from the care their children require, and assures a caregiving environment suited to their needs.[13]

There are many other fine programs throughout the country that strive to meet the needs of families and children with particular problems. A common theme of these innovative efforts, apparent in the examples described here, is a commitment to serving the entire family—an approach now recognized as more effective than exclusively child-centered approaches (Chapter 1). These programs also address a variety of needs, either through direct provision of supports or referral to outside resources. They thus attend to the family as the complex unit it is and attempt to strengthen it by facilitating all aspects of family functioning. By acting as the hub of services to the family, they offer a wide base of support and impose a semblance of order on what can be a stressed and complicated lifestyle. As the family is strengthened, their ability to cope with the problems of raising a special child is enhanced.

The child becomes the ultimate beneficiary. In essence, these programs follow the ideology and methods of the growing family support movement that is reshaping the social services delivery system in America.[21]

Absent so far from our discussion of exemplary programs are those designed for children with acute illnesses. Actually, such programs are designed for parents who must get to work, because the sick child's needs are for a familiar environment and a parent's loving care and pampering. Yet we must face the fact that this is not always possible in today's demanding economy. One solution is acute care programs, which are springing up in cities around the country. These services are often initiated by medical groups or hospitals as a means of keeping staff at work instead of home caring for their sick children, but many are open to the public as well. An example is Chicken Soup in St. Paul, Minnesota, which has trained nurses to provide care, high staff-child ratios, and flexible drop-off and retrieval times. Although subjecting an ill child to a commute to a strange place to spend the day with strangers may not exactly promote recuperation, it is much better than leaving the child alone at home. Other programs such as Care in Oregon provide registered nurses in the home, a practice that at least gives the child the benefit of staying in a familiar environment. Such programs may make more sense to employers than they do to a child who does not feel well, but they represent the next best alternative to the ideal caregiving environment—home with a nurturing parent—when the ideal is not attainable.

Another problem with acute care programs staffed by nurses is their potential expense. Trained pediatric nurses can command over $20 an hour in hospitals and doctors' offices, plus fringe benefits, and the child care job would have to offer competitive wages. A nurse would only be able to care for a very few sick children, so the cost of retaining him or her would have to be shared by a small number of parents. Fees must also cover salaries on the days when no child is in attendance, since it is unlikely that a nurse would take the position without a guaranteed weekly paycheck. On top of these costs, the regular caregiver must still be paid, since her expenses are the same regardless of whether or not one child is absent. Clearly, even where acute care programs are available, few families will be able to afford them without some help from their employer.

So what do parents do when children come down with a sore throat or fever? The sad truth is that many of them call in sick, consuming their own sick days for child care. We saw in Chapter 5 that in many nations parents are allowed time off from work each year not only to care for a sick child, but to deal with other parenting responsibilities. In America, a smattering of enlightened employers is beginning to offer paid child care days as part of their benefits packages. Some of these plans are described in Chapter 8, where we also discuss some company-financed arrangements such as home health aides and acute care facilities shared by a consortium of businesses.

Another part of the solution is for child care facilities to be more lenient when it comes to admitting a child who is mildly ill or recuperating.[2] Many common illnesses such as colds do not even daunt an energetic youngster and cease to be contagious soon after the symptoms appear. Barring the child from the setting serves no purpose other than to make life a bit easier for the staff. It would be a small matter to incorporate into their training ways to deal with a child who is a little cranky or not quite up to par. Of course, in some states caregivers are bound by strict regulations which require them to shut the door on any child who is not perfectly healthy. Today, when child care issues are among the hottest topics in state legislatures nationwide, the time is ripe for changing such unnecessary rules.

8

◆ ◆

Child Care as the New Business of Business

During the 1980s, support for what might best be described as "privatization" meant that responsibility for many services provided by the federal government since the 1960s was shifted to private organizations and concerned citizens. When politicians were asked how they would meet human needs of any kind—including educational improvements, child care, hunger, and the growing problem of homelessness—the response almost always included the buzz words "private sector" and "voluntarism." The private sector, popularly defined as including charitable foundations, volunteer groups, and businesses, was supposed to be able to take care of any needs of children and families that were not met by the families themselves, by the states, or by the federal government.

This reliance on the private sector increased appeals to foundations, who struggled to bridge the gap between social needs and their ability to fund means of assistance. In addition to financial pressures, groups that traditionally relied on volunteer labor found it difficult to enlist enough people to meet the growing need for their services. Although Americans have always prided themselves on their willingness to devote time and energy to charitable and civic causes, the decade that saw so many mothers and grandmothers join the labor force seemed an inopportune time to call for more volunteers. Not only did women—traditionally the mainstay of volunteer programs—have fewer hours free from work and family responsibilities, but many men with working wives also found it difficult to meet their job and family obligations and have time left over for community service.

Privatization has also propelled business into a new era in which family benefits such as child care are beginning to be demanded by employees and their unions. Yet pressure from unions and a conscien-

166

tious desire to pick up the slack where the federal government left off are by no means the only motivations for businesses to respond to the growing need for child care. Forward-thinking business leaders know that they have been presented with a tremendous challenge: the economic climate is rapidly changing, and they must change with it to survive.

In Chapter 1, we discussed the reasons that women work. In this chapter, we will explore the reasons that some employers have decided that providing working families with affordable child care is important. Attainable, quality child care is not only good for children and families, it is good for business now and into the 21st century.

CHANGES IN THE LABOR FORCE

One reason that employers are taking steps toward involvement in child care is to respond to a change in the labor market. There is increased competition for qualified workers in a shrinking labor pool. Despite the anticipated growth in population when the post-World War II "baby boomers" began having children of their own, the new baby boom is not that dramatic. Although there are more women of childbearing age than there were in past decades, they are having fewer children per family. This means fewer young adults in the years ahead. By the turn of the century, there will only be approximately 1.3 million new workers (age 16–24) per year, compared to annual averages of around 3 million during the 1970s.[23]

If there are not enough young workers to fill all the available jobs, employees will have to be found in other segments of the population, namely among new immigrants, retirees, and especially women. Of the 8 million new jobs created between 1979 and 1985, most were filled by women, and most of these women were mothers.[24] Projections for this decade are that two-thirds of all new entrants into the labor force will be women, most of whom will be in their childbearing years.[23]

One reason, then, that some employers provide child care and other related benefits is to attract mothers of young children as employees. They also do so to retain women workers. For example, the health care industry was the first to respond in numbers to their employees' child care needs. Faced with a growing shortage of nurses, many medical facilities began to offer on-site child care and shift choices to keep their largely female work force on the job. Of course, providing benefits and work policies that address family needs assists not only mothers but fathers as well. The employer also benefits by gaining a competitive edge in a tightening labor market.

MUTUAL BENEFITS OF CORPORATE CHILD CARE ASSISTANCE

Some employers have initiated child care assistance and other family benefits in the hope that such amenities would result in higher employee productivity and a lower turnover rate. Until recently, this intuition has lacked objective proof. Business leaders networking among themselves often shared anecdotes about the success of their new policies such as leaves for child rearing and child care assistance, but there were very few studies to support these claims of success. Of course, most industrial companies are more comfortable conducting marketing research than they are the empirical, longitudinal research necessary to evaluate child care policies. Further, companies that provide child care assistance often provide an array of other attractive personnel benefits, and it is difficult to separate the positive effects of one benefit from another.[11] Is a lowered turnover or absentee rate among parent employees related to the company's child care benefit or to some other practice such as flexible work hours, generous vacation time, or comprehensive medical insurance? In short, determining the effect of any one aspect of family-friendly policy on worker performance is as difficult as determining the effect of any one aspect of child care quality on children's development (see Chapter 3).

Some larger companies have conducted internal studies or contracted with outside consultants to attempt to quantify their experiences with family-oriented policy. Although such internal studies usually do not meet the rigorous design and analysis criteria social scientists would demand, they augment the work of professional researchers who have attempted more formal investigations. Both types of research combine with anecdotal evidence to demonstrate to the business community that corporate involvement in child care definitely pays off in the long run.

Employee Loyalty

Companies that offer some form of child care benefit report lower recruiting costs and higher employee retention rates. Many job seekers today say that child care assistance is one reason they choose to apply to one firm instead of another.[24] When Official Airline Guides in Oak Brook, Illinois, mentioned their on-site child care center in a recruitment ad, they had 10 times the number of responses as had been generated by previous ads.[5] Although many companies find they must advertise job openings for some time, those with child care benefits might attract a larger number of applicants for similar positions. This results in jobs being filled sooner and increases the likelihood of finding the right person for a particular position.

The effect of child care programs on recruitment options was confirmed by at least two national surveys, one by Sandra Burud, Pamela Aschbacher, and Jacquelyn McCroskey of over 400 businesses[3] and another by Kathryn Perry of 58 employers.[22] In both studies, over 85% of the companies responding (many of whom sponsored child care centers) believed that their child care policies helped to attract new employees. A survey of employees themselves by the Bureau of National Affairs, cited by John P. Fernandez, revealed that 38% chose their company because it sponsored child care, and half recommended their employer to others for the same reason.[7]

Attracting qualified employees is one benefit; keeping them after a company has invested time and money in their training is another. Employers who sponsor the Northside Children's Center in Minneapolis report that employees who use the center have one-third the turnover rate of other workers.[5] In Wilmington, Delaware, the Du Pont Company reported to *Working Mother* magazine that they increased many family-friendly benefits for their employees, including support of community child care centers, to keep turnover down. They had discovered that a quarter of their male employees and half of their female employees were considering seeking employment elsewhere for the express purpose of gaining better family benefits.[21] According to national studies, support for child care does increase employee loyalty. The survey by Burud and associates and another conducted in 1982 by the U.S. Department of Health and Human Services (see Reisman, Moore, and Fitzgerald[24]) both reported that 65% of the firms that offered child care assistance believed this benefit had decreased employee turnover.

When employee turnover is a heavy expense for certain businesses, the cost can sometimes be offset by the comparatively moderate price of child care benefits. John P. Fernandez, division manager of American Telephone and Telegraph (AT&T) Communications Headquarters Region in Short Hills, New Jersey, estimates that on the average a corporation spends $25,000 to train most employees and $50,000 to train skilled professionals.[7] Although these figures are on the high side, other corporations have estimated that new employees need about a year to become fully productive.[24] Even at this price, losing employees because of inadequate child care benefits would seem more costly than providing such benefits. The same principle may be applied to employee departures for lack of adequate family leave. As we discussed in Chapter 5, mothers of infants are more apt to return to the same employer if they receive a reasonable time for child care leave than if they do not. While reassigning tasks during an employee's leave for childbirth or a family emergency may seem inconvenient, employers must consider that finding and training a permanent replacement may be much more difficult, and in the end more costly, than providing benefits to employees in whom they have already invested training time and funds.

Companies can impose turnover problems on themselves through rigid relocation policies. Many employees refuse promotions that entail a move to distant company branches because they do not want to sever ties with family and community. Bill Needham (not his real name), a computer systems analyst working for a large East Coast firm, told a journalist writing about parenting and work that he had refused a promotion and move to another state because he was a divorced father with custody of two small children. The reason he gave his employer was that he did not want to disrupt the children's already shaky sense of permanence by moving them to another home and community.[25] When interviewed for our book, Needham said that part of the disruption he envisioned was moving his younger child from the child care center that he had attended for several years, and the father decided that consistency in school and child care arrangements was more important than a career move. Fortunately, his employer responded by helping him form alternate career plans that would keep him in his current location without jeopardizing future offers of advancement. If the firm had not had general policies sympathetic to employees' child care needs, Needham might have changed companies rather than change communities. This company was spared the expense of recruiting and training a new Bill Needham, and we can be sure that they gained from his strengthened loyalty.

Increased Productivity

Many employers find that conscientious workers tend to be conscientious parents as well. Those companies that have instituted policies to accommodate family needs have found that their workers respond by being better employees. Productivity is improved in a number of ways, including reduced absenteeism and tardiness, reduced stress, fewer errors, and increased employee flexibility in work assignments.

The most common effect that child care problems have on the work place is on attendance. A survey by Ellen Galinsky of three New Jersey companies revealed that 51% of employees questioned had come to work late or left early in the past three months because of child care problems, and 40% had been absent at least once for this reason.[12] The most frequent child care problem is likely to be child illness. In the J.P. Fernandez analysis mentioned above, 82% of the women and 58% of the men who had missed more than six workdays the previous year cited staying at home to care for ill children as the reason for their absences.[7] Without further data, it is impossible to guess whether these percentages were lower for men because mothers more often stay home with ill children or because men are more reluctant to report that their absences are child care related.

The problem of absenteeism for child care reasons is not always visible to supervisors and personnel departments, although most know it is there. In companies that do not accommodate child care needs, parents with ill children may simply call in sick themselves. Disruptions in their regular child care arrangement, such as school closings during severe weather or a caregiver's illness, sometimes force parents to invent excuses for coming to work late. They may take an entire "sick day" off because they know they will be penalized for being tardy or because they fear their deception will be discovered. On the other hand, parents who are allowed to take extra time in the morning to make alternative arrangements may be able to put in a full day's work when they arrive at the office.

Some employers may believe that having their employees deceive them occasionally is an acceptable trade-off for getting the message across that absence for child care reasons is not legitimate. Others are uncomfortable with forcing employees to lie, fearing that dishonesty undermines the employer-employee relationship in other areas. Whatever their broader reasons for adopting more open policies about occasional absences and tardiness, employers may discover that doing so actually results in fewer absences and greater efficiency on the job. Those companies that have gone a step further and instituted child care programs generally find the desired impact on attendance. In the survey by Burud and colleagues, 53% of the companies reported that child care benefits had reduced absenteeism,[3] as did 72% in Perry's survey.[22]

Employees with child care difficulties may not only call in sick when their children are ill; they may be more likely to become ill themselves. The American Academy of Physicians found that people reporting high levels of stress had two to four times more health problems than those who felt less stressed.[24] Problems related to stress are said to cause as much as one-third of employee absences.[28] Of course, family problems are only one of the many sources of stress, but they are a significant one for working parents. For example, businesses across the country complain of what has become known as the "three o'clock syndrome." At that hour, office and factory telephone lines are tied up while anxious parents call their children to see if they have arrived home safely, and lonely or nervous children call their parents at work to ask questions, tell about their day, or just hear a loving voice.

J.P. Fernandez noted that 76% of women—both married and single— reported experiencing some stress on the job because of their difficulties balancing work and family responsibilities.[7] Over half of married men reported that work/family stress affected their jobs. Galinsky cites numerous studies showing that worries over children and child care arrangements often lead to stress at work.[14] The percentages for fathers were typically lower than those for mothers, undoubtedly because for working women, "family responsibilities often take priority over work responsibilities, . . . for men, work responsibilities almost always take precedence over family," according to Fox, Biber, and Pleck.[7]

Employers are often aware of the high stress level among individual employees with children. This is why companies such as Aetna Life & Casualty in Hartford, Connecticut and Hallmark Cards in Kansas City, Missouri offer on-site counseling services for employees and their families.[21] Since family-related stress is not likely to respond to stress reduction plans such as corporate exercise programs offered during work time, some employers are beginning to realize that child care assistance might help ease some of the pressures on parents that affect their work. Although the effect of stress on productivity is difficult if not impossible to measure, many employers sense that there is a connection. In a survey conducted in Prince George's County, Maryland, a suburb of Washington, D.C., 79% of employers believed that child care services or support would have a positive effect on employee stress, and 54% felt it would improve productivity.[1]

Company Morale and Image

In setting up equations to determine the economic benefits of child care assistance (cost of the aid vs. return on investment), some elements are easier to translate into dollar amounts than others. Reduced turnover and increased productivity, for example, can at least be estimated in terms of monetary value through one statistical paradigm or another. Employee morale and corporate image ("good will," in accounting terminology), however, are intangible assets whose effect on profits is definite but difficult to calculate. Child care benefits undoubtedly have an impact on both, but to what extent is strictly a matter of conjecture and opinion.

Executives' opinions about the good will value of child care assistance do seem to lean toward the positive side of the balance sheet. In the Burud and colleagues survey, 85% of the employers interviewed felt that child care assistance positively affected the company's public image.[3] Only a small number of the people who responded to Official Airline Guide's employment ad were interested in using the on-site child care center; instead, they saw the center as an indication that the company was progressive and "a good place to work."[5] As the chairman of the board of Corning Glass (now Corning, Inc.) stated, "Child care is one of those small pockets of excellence by which corporations and their people are judged."[6]

The SAS Institute, Inc. in South Carolina is one company that has made a strong commitment to child care as part of its corporate image. SAS sells computer software with a wide variety of business and research applications and provides training programs for its customers. The training center's two free on-site child care centers attract not only potential employees but also potential clients, who may spend several days or weeks in residence at SAS training programs. In addition, the firm also has policies that enable parents and children to share reasonably priced meals together in designated company dining facilities.[21]

Employee morale is also thought to be boosted by child care assistance. Burud and colleagues reported that 90% of the companies they surveyed believed that child care benefits improved morale.[3] Research to date has not shown that higher morale results in higher productivity, but there is a connection between the two in business practice. A positive attitude toward one's work and employer might also have some bearing on turnover, absenteeism, stress, and other factors affecting job performance.

Corporate decision makers are slowly coming to appreciate the intangible benefits that derive from family-friendly policies. The more foresighted among them are also beginning to talk about perceived benefits to business that will be reaped in coming decades. Some of our nation's top business leaders are advocating more and better child care because they see it as an insurance policy to protect the future economic health of their firms. Hampered by the lack of trained and trainable workers today, which they attribute in part to a failure of the educational system, they fear that the mediocrity of much available child care will also contribute to educational failure. If today's generation of children is given a poor chance at optimal development, tomorrow's labor force will not be prepared to meet the demands of an increasingly complex economy. Then all of a company's past efforts to improve employee morale, corporate image, and market share will be nullified.

THE RANGE OF CORPORATE CHILD CARE BENEFITS

There are over 6 million employers in the United States. The majority are small businesses, some having as few as one or two employees. Seldom do these small concerns offer child care benefits of any kind. Some exceptions were noted in *Working Mother*'s list of the 60 best companies for working mothers, including one California firm that has only 29 employees, yet provides not only child care but also an on-site primary school licensed by the State of California.[21] Generally, however, the activities of the larger employers provide us with a sense of the growth of corporate interest in child care.

About 44,000 U.S. firms have been identified as having 100 or more employees. According to Dana Friedman of the Conference Board, in 1989 only about 4,150 of these larger firms—or 11%—offered their workers any help with child care. As low as the actual percentage is, today's employers are more amenable to the idea of providing child care assistance than ever before. In 1982, only 600 employers were involved in child care in some way; by 1984, that number more than doubled to 1,500. Two years later, 2,500 employers were offering child care assistance, and 3,300 were by 1988.[13] The significance of these statistics is that they show a trend, although they represent a tiny proportion of businesses in general. As we look at the types of assistance offered, keep in mind that these plans reflect the efforts of a relatively small number of corporate pioneers.

Direct Child Care Services

The acme of child care assistance is for a company to establish a child care center in or near the work place. Estimates provided us by Dana Friedman show there are only about 1,050 on-site or near-site centers in the United States; 750 of these are in hospitals and 100 in government installations.[13] Some companies construct and operate their own centers. Stride Rite, for example, has recently completed an intergenerational care center for children from the age of 15 months as well as for elderly relatives. More commonly, companies choose to provide space for a child care program and turn its operation over to a for-profit chain or a nonprofit organization. Another arrangement is to allow participating employees to form their own directors' board. This is the approach taken by Merck in Rahway, New Jersey, whose on-site child care center is being built with company funds but will be operated by a nonprofit parent group.[21] The benefits of an on-site center include the ease of finding and monitoring a child care setting and the convenience of reduced travel time for parents and young children. Since parents are always nearby, they can quickly respond to emergencies such as sudden illnesses or inconsolable crying. In some companies parents may share breaks and lunch hours with their children if they wish, as they do at the SAS Institute.

There are also some disadvantages, for both parents and employers, to an on-site child care center. First, such centers are practical mainly for children younger than school age. Employees' older children are likely to attend schools near their homes, so that transportation to and from the on-site center in the early morning and afternoon hours would not be possible. Second, if employees commute long distances to work, they may not wish to submit their infants and young children to the long daily trip. Those who use public transportation may find it unreasonable to take a young child on a crowded bus or train during rush hour. A third drawback to an on-site facility may be cost, both to the employer and to the families who use it. Although some employers operate centers at a loss, operational costs are more often shared by employer and employees or paid entirely by parents. Without company financial assistance, the lowest paid workers may be unable to afford the on-site center, despite its conveniences, and must seek a less expensive alternative. Prices at the on-site centers celebrated in the recent *Working Mother* article vary from below to above market rates, depending on the degree of employer subsidy. Reported fees ranged from $57 weekly for preschoolers to approximately $150 for infants.[21]

All of these potential problems point to the importance of a needs assessment survey among all employees to determine how many would actually use an on-site child care facility before a company invests in one. Careful corporate planning, usually with an outside consultant, can determine costs, quality, and compliance with state and local regulations. Employees, who will be the users of the center, are another valuable resource.

The location and nature of some work sites preclude the feasibility of on-site centers. Obviously, some manufacturing processes involve chemical or mechanical dangers, making the site unsuitable for children. Other sites do not lend themselves to physical expansion and the addition or reassignment of space sufficient for a child care center. Employers with a small work force may not have the funds or a sufficient number of workers who would use the center to cover operating costs. In these cases employers can work in consortium with other businesses and sponsor a shared facility. Ideal sites for consortium centers include centrally located downtown businesses and industrial parks. To encourage these arrangements, some communities, such as Hartford, Connecticut, require new or renovated business complexes to include space for a consortium child care center. Incorporating plans for a child care facility in the overall budget for new construction or major renovation earns tax breaks in some states, and can help attract tenants.

The Prospect Hill Parents' and Children's Center in Waltham, Massachusetts is an example of a consortium center. It is located in the Prospect Hill Office Park and is open to children whose parents work at the park as well as to community residents. Companies pay an annual membership fee, and employees pay for the cost of care, although some participating companies also provide financial assistance as an employee benefit.[4] Seven employers donated funds to the Burbank, California, school district to renovate an unused school for use as a child care center. The employers each receive 20 slots for their workers' children, with the remaining spaces reserved for area residents.[10]

Family Day Care Networks

Another way that companies can insure that there is sufficient child care to meet their employees' needs is to contract with family day care networks within the community. So few licensed family day care homes exist in some areas that employers may enlist a local agency to recruit, train, and assist potential providers to become licensed or registered. In exchange for agreeing to serve as caregivers for the sponsoring company's employees, providers may receive various benefits, such as support for continuing professional development, sick days, substitute caregivers, and insurance coverage.

One company that sponsors a family day care network for its employees is American Express, Inc., in New York City. American Express provides funds to family day care associations and to resource and referral agencies to enable them to attract and train new providers. Southland Corporation (7-Eleven Stores) employs Child Care Dallas not only to recruit and train but to monitor family day care providers located along commuting routes of employees.[10] The California Child Care Initiative is sponsored by Bank of America and 32 other employers to help expand family day care services in the state. Since 1984, over 1,700 licensed family day care homes have been created with slots for 6,800 children.[20] Similar support of family day care networks is a feature of the child care programs of America West Airlines in Phoenix and Las Vegas and those of Eastman Kodak in Rochester, New York.[21]

The advantages and disadvantages of family day care homes were discussed in Chapter 1. One advantage of employer-sponsored family day care is that the free training provided can increase the quantity and quality of licensed care in an entire community. Another advantage is that, as opposed to a centrally located facility, family day care homes in the company network can serve employees who live in a wider geographic area and children in a broader age range.

Emergency and Supplementary Child Care Services

As stated earlier, a common reason for employee absenteeism is to care for a child who is ill. A number of employers (particularly hospitals) have established infirmaries where parents can bring a child who is too ill to attend child care or school. Hewlett-Packard and Levi Strauss together contributed funds to a nearby child care center to establish an infirmary for their employees' children. Although such practices do assist parents when a child comes down with a sudden illness, they do more to meet the employer's needs than they do those of a child who does not feel well (Chapter 7). A better alternative to dragging a sick child out to a strange environment to spend the day with strange caregivers is for someone to come to the child's home. In the New York–New Jersey area, a pilot program of this type was recently initiated by a consortium of seven companies, including such giants as *Time* magazine and Home Box Office (both Time, Inc. subsidiaries) and Colgate-Palmolive. This group contracted with two home health care agencies to send certified home health aides into employees' homes to care for children not only when they are ill, but on days when their regular caregiver is ill or their school or child care facility is closed. The aides will earn about $10.50 per hour, with the cost paid mostly or entirely by the employer. This rate of pay should help to attract qualified caregivers. The companies anticipate savings by not having to pay fees to temporary agencies, which can be quite high in the metropolitan New York area. Nancy Platt of Home Box Office stated that a temporary word processor would cost $15–20 per hour, so the home caregiver's fee is a better bargain.[18]

School vacations and holidays are other times when working parents face a child care dilemma. When schools close, many after-school programs do too, and very few employees have as many days off as do the public schools. Concerned employers sometimes form cooperative enterprises with unions or community agencies to provide temporary child care programs when schools are not in session. Employees at 3M get a 20–25% discount at the company-sponsored summer day camp in the St. Paul, Minnesota YMCA, and transportation is provided near the 3M site.[4] Fel-Pro, Inc., based in Skokie, Illinois, runs its own day camp for employees' children. The camp operates the entire summer and costs only $15 weekly per family.[20] Single-day programs can also be arranged to provide child care on school breaks such as Columbus Day and teacher training days. By enlisting the services of local youth agencies and perhaps releasing a few parents to serve as volunteer chaperones, day trips to zoos, museums, and other resources in nearby communities can be planned.

Resource and Referral Programs

Resource and referral (R&R) services (see Chapter 1) appeal to companies who wish to assist their workers in finding child care with a minimum of expense. In fact, of the 4,150 companies reported to provide child care assistance, 1,000 of them offer R&R services as their only benefit.[13]

Either through their own personnel departments or by supporting outside R&R services, these companies can provide employees with information about the different forms of child care existing in the community and current availability. They can also provide counseling to help parents choose the best form of care for their children and can encourage new caregivers to become trained and licensed. For example, IBM, based in Purchase, New York, began a nationwide R&R network in 1984. The service is available to IBM employees at no charge and to other corporations and individuals for a fee. In order to form the network, IBM contracted with Work/Family Directions, Inc., a Boston-based consulting firm, to develop local referral agencies; IBM provides computers, software, and training.[14]

Parent Education Seminars

Because enforced national standards for child care seem unlikely to materialize in the near future, one of the ways companies can assist parents is by teaching them to evaluate and monitor their child care arrangements. In addition to the individual counseling some companies offer through their R&R services, parent education seminars can be held on a periodic basis. The company can use knowledgeable human resource staff or contract with an outside consultant to provide a forum where parents can share information about their experiences with various child care options and obtain checklists for evaluating child care centers, family day care homes, and in-home providers. Separate seminars may be offered on such topics as infant/toddler care and school-age child care. Release time can be granted to employees to permit them to attend these seminars during work hours, or they can be offered during lunch hours.

The extremely difficult burden of evaluating and monitoring child care has been placed almost entirely on working parents. Employers who offer parent education programs show their support for parents undertaking this complicated task and provide them with opportunities to learn from one another.

FINANCIAL ASSISTANCE FOR CHILD CARE

A number of employers provide some type of financial assistance to help their workers pay child care expenses. Sometimes this can be done at little or no cost to the employer. For example, some businesses contract with for-profit chains to provide slots for employees' children. In exchange for the employer advertising the chain to workers, the chain offers them a reduced rate for child care.

Another type of financial assistance is the flexible or cafeteria-style benefit plan. The approximately 2,000 employers who offer flexible benefits allow employees to choose among an array of benefits—including a child care reimbursement—and to make up their own individual benefit packages within certain limits. For example, an employee close to retirement age may choose the maximum retirement benefit, while a younger person might choose a minimum retirement benefit in exchange for a child care benefit.

There are several advantages of flexible benefit plans that include child care reimbursement. Companies may perceive these plans as the most fair because they can provide one valuable benefit to employees with children while providing equally valuable benefits to employees without children. Two-parent working families may be helped the most by this style of benefit because it allows them to draw on the best of plans from two employers, perhaps choosing the husband's health insurance and retirement packages and the wife's child care assistance and dental benefits. Should one spouse change employers, however, the new benefit plan may cover these elements to a greater or lesser extent, changing the balance of their chosen benefits. For families headed by a single parent, flexible benefits may also leave gaps in coverage, since choosing child care assistance often entails giving up needed medical or other benefits. The choice between reduced child care expenses or regular dental checkups is a grim but all too typical dilemma for these families.

Another type of direct child care payment to employees involves a voucher program, which can work in one of two ways. An employee might pay for child care and be reimbursed for part of the cost by submitting a voucher to the employer. Some employers pay the vouchered fees directly to the provider, and the parent pays only the balance. One advantage of some voucher systems is that parents can choose their own providers. Another is that voucher plans support child care services in the community. Company vouchers may represent a stable source of income for a family day care provider who otherwise may have trouble collecting from individual families. And vouchers may help raise caregiver salaries without increasing cost to parents. A disadvantage is that vouchers can represent a significant expense to employers, although the cost may be offset by employee responses mentioned earlier such as reduced turnover and increased productivity. Vouchers also do little to help parents in areas where there is insufficient child care available.

Voucher systems can be designed to serve a variety of employer purposes and employee needs. Friedman provides the following examples.[9] Cambridge Plan International offers vouchers covering half of the cost of child care, with different ceilings allowed for infant, preschool, and after-school care. Polaroid Corporation pays 80% of the cost of care to employees earning less than $25,000, and decreasing percentages to higher wage earners. Measurex Corporation pays a portion of child care costs for infants under one year of age, and *Parents* magazine offers a flat subsidy to be used for infants up to three months old—both efforts to encourage women to return to work after maternity leave. The most common type of voucher system, however, is a flat rate to cover a portion of costs. Baxter Travenol Laboratories, Inc. in Deerfield, Illinois pays $3.50 a day for child care fees for each child. Although the actual cost to the parents is considerably more than that, the company estimated that this benefit saves each employee $788 a year in child care expenses.[14] This is certainly more than a token effort and represents a greater child care benefit than the vast majority of U.S. businesses provide.

Another option employers may choose to assist employees in reducing child care expenses is the Dependent Care Assistance Plan (DCAP), authorized by Section 129 of the 1981 Economic Recovery Tax Act. Under this plan, an employee estimates at the beginning of the tax year how much the family's annual child care expense will be, and the employer deducts a percentage of that amount from each paycheck. The money is then reimbursed when the employee submits paid child care bills. Essentially the employee is still paying the full cost of child care expenses, but with pretax dollars. This can save a considerable amount in taxes for some families. Although there is a cap on the amount withheld (no more than $5,000), it is higher than the maximum permitted under the Child and Dependent Care Tax Credit (see Chapter 2). The only cost to the employer is for administering the funds, and this is more than offset by savings from social security and unemployment compensation taxes that do not have to be paid on the portion of salary withheld. Another advantage for the employer is that there are no equity problems—employees without children will not feel that the company is offering a benefit to workers with children that others do not receive.

The DCAP approach does have many disadvantages, however. It favors employees with higher earnings, since they have the most to gain by sheltering income from taxes. Families earning less than about $24,000 fare better by taking the Child and Dependent Care Tax Credit. Also, the salary reduction reduces social security and unemployment benefits, so participants who become disabled or lose their jobs will receive lower compensation. Parents who overestimate their child care expenses cannot have the excess withholding returned. Finally, Internal Revenue Service scrutiny of many DCAPs led to caps on allowable withholdings (to prevent $75,000 a year executives from deducting $12,000 for housekeepers who also help with child care), and past abuses of these plans have engendered complex eligibility and reporting requirements.[9] To some employers, DCAPs have become more trouble than they are worth.

WORK PLACE POLICIES TO SUPPORT WORKING PARENTS

As discussed in Chapter 5, employers have a challenge ahead of them that is more demanding than the already complex task of helping their employees find needed child care. They must change their thinking about personnel as workers first, family members second. What we have witnessed in the last quarter century is the increasing permeability of the boundaries between the world of work and the world of the family. Anything employers do to help employees maintain a healthy balance between work and family life is a step toward increased productivity and decreased stress on parents with children. This task is not insurmountable or exorbitantly expensive. Even small businesses can join in the effort. It is essential, however, for all supervisory personnel to be thoroughly briefed in the company's policies and held accountable for carrying them out. A study conducted by the National Council of Jewish Women reported that the success of an employer's family policy is largely determined by the immediate supervisor, who gives or withholds support to individual workers.[2] Without the cooperation of those who deal with employees on a personal and daily basis, even the most supportive and enlightened employer cannot counter the negative effects of attitudes that continue to cause stress to working parents.

Flexible Arrangements

The first and major step employers can take to demonstrate concern for employees' family needs is simply to be more flexible. Rigid policies that require workers to clock in at eight and clock out at four, take specific days off for holidays and vacations, and limit the reasons for excused absences can be replaced by more lenient practices. One such practice is flextime, in which all workers must be on the job during certain core hours (ten to three or nine to two, for example), but can begin their day much earlier or leave much later. In some areas flextime arrangements have benefited industry and community, resulting in decreased traffic congestion and parking problems. They also give businesses longer hours of operation and phone coverage without adding another shift. In industries where flextime schedules are not feasible (for example, on some assembly lines), employers can be more sensitive to working parents' dilemmas when they have sudden child care emergencies.

Demonstrating flexibility in dealing with employees with ill children is an important part of indirect employer support of child care. Some companies simply allow employees to use their own sick or personal days for the purpose of caring for a child who is ill. Reducing the need for employees to be dishonest about how they are using their sick days may promote openness and honesty between workers and their supervisors, but as a child care policy, its effect is limited. Parents who have used up all their sick days will be tempted to come to work when they themselves are ill, a practice not universally appreciated in offices and very risky in settings such as schools and hospitals. A partial solution to this dilemma would be to allow workers to earn extra time off in addition to contracted sick days. For example, an employee who performs exceptionally well on a project or who suggests time- or cost-cutting measures might be rewarded with earned time off. This time could be used for personal reasons in addition to emergency care of children and thus would provide an incentive to workers without children as well.

Flexibility in the use of accrued vacation time is also helpful to parents. If employees are permitted to take vacation days on an incremental basis rather than at one specific time, their employer is providing them the opportunity to use approved time off for family needs.

There are many other ways companies can demonstrate flexibility to benefit employees without harming business. Where more than one shift operates, employees can be allowed to exchange complete or partial hours with others. For example, one employee can cover for an absent worker for a few hours by working a little late on his or her shift; a second employee can pick up the remaining hours by coming in a little early. Instead of receiving overtime pay, these "pinch hitters" will have the extra hours of work repaid in kind by the absent worker. In places where not all employees have the same days off, workers can also trade days off with others so as to be free on a school holiday or when children are ill.

Employers who experiment with a more flexible approach to employees' requests for time off to meet personal or family needs do not find that their businesses suffer or work goes undone. In fact, in a flexible atmosphere, the employees themselves often cooperate in redistributing work during a co-worker's absence, and the co-worker is likely to try to pay back the favor through increased productivity. A more personal benefit comes from improved employee-employer relationships. Indeed, one law firm that rewrote its personnel policy to explicitly allow employees to use their sick days to care for an ill child did so to "reduce the need to lie."[7]

Alternative Work Arrangements

Parenting is a full-time job that does not always leave room for full-time paid employment. Allowing workers (particularly new parents) to change their schedules to part-time for specific periods can be an effective employer support for working families. In businesses that invest time and money to train workers with specific technical skills, retaining dependable, experienced employees on a part-time basis can be far less costly than training new people. In some companies, workers who reduce their hours to above a specified minimum retain full benefits, while in others benefits are prorated according to the percentage of full-time hours scheduled. Employers, at the least, should provide job security and retirement credit to those who wish to work part time for a specified period, such as the year after returning from an infant care leave. Otherwise they may lose good employees to more accommodating firms.

Job sharing is one form of part-time work in which two employees share a full-time position, along with the responsibilities and benefits of that position. Job sharers may split days or each work part of a week, sometimes overlapping their schedules briefly so they can divide tasks or communicate with one another about the projects they share. This allows for consistency of staffing while providing parents with a means of reducing the hours their children need supplementary care. It sometimes has additional benefits for the employer as well: having two people in a position often provides more complete coverage and broader perspectives to the tasks or problems at hand.

Some kinds of positions—especially those which rely heavily on the use of computers—readily lend themselves to work-at-home plans. Helen Axel reported that only about 15,000 employees now work at home, but the number is expected to rise to 10 million in the 1990s.[7] The benefits and drawbacks of working at home while caring for one's children were discussed in Chapter 1. Employers who offer this option benefit from reduced costs for space and retention of the skills of trusted employees.[7] Of course, they must establish clear guidelines about which employees are eligible, how the time schedules are to be drawn up, and how and when the arrangement is to be evaluated.

Evaluation of any flexible work arrangement is an important key to success. The evaluation should take into account the observations of each participating worker as well as those of supervisors. After a number of successes and perhaps a few failures, patterns may eventually emerge that show which kinds of employees work efficiently with flexible scheduling and which do not, what pitfalls there are to the experimental arrangement, and how to avoid them in future.

CONTROVERSIES OVER FAMILY-FRIENDLY POLICIES

One of the most often heard complaints about the family-friendly work place—albeit a whispered complaint at times—is that child care benefits and other amenities provided to help working families are only for the benefit of women, and only women with children. There is a vague uneasiness that somehow men and childless women are not receiving equal treatment, a feeling easily dispelled when employers such as those mentioned in this chapter include in their benefit packages other kinds of incentives for workers without children. As our discussion of infant care leaves in Chapter 5 makes clear, we do not believe that child care or other family policies—whether in the private or the public sector—serve only working mothers: they serve entire families, especially the children, and they serve the society's current and future labor needs.

A related question that has rarely been discussed openly is whether or not women in business, especially those women in high management positions, are likely to cost a company more in the long run if child care assistance and related family benefits are provided. Corporate leaders may have been hesitant to examine this issue because they realized they must woo women workers to fill jobs and meet affirmative action mandates.

The issue became impossible to ignore when Felice Schwartz published a controversial article in the January-February 1989 issue of *Harvard Business Review*, asserting that women in management do cost more than their male counterparts, and that this can make women less desirable management candidates.[26] Schwartz is president and founder of Catalyst, a nonprofit research and advisory organization dedicated to fostering career and leadership development in women. As a reputable businesswoman and women's advocate, she may have been unprepared for the storm of protest that arose in response to her article. What caused the furor was Schwartz's two startling and controversial assertions. The first was that training and benefits for upper management women with families are actually more expensive than those for men. The second—and highly debatable—assertion was that management women fit into two identifiable classes: the "career primary" woman and the "career-and-family" woman.

According to Schwartz, "career primary" women have work patterns almost identical to those of men on the way up the corporate ladder. They are willing either to forgo children or to leave their rearing to someone else while they dedicate themselves to the long hours, business travel, and other prerequisites to success. By contrast, "career-and-family" women are also willing to work hard, but they prefer to postpone advancement to the upper echelons of management so they can devote some of their time and energy to children and family.

Some women and corporate leaders hailed Schwartz's analysis and her accompanying suggestion that women be given more opportunities to choose between putting their careers on the slow track—or the "mommy track" as the press quickly dubbed this concept—or continuing to move along the fast track with their male peers. Her critics, however, were disturbed by her suggestions that the choice was clear-cut and that top management should use probing interrogation to discriminate between the two types of female employee. In this way they could identify "career primary" women early in their careers and clear their path to the top. "Career-and-family" women would be weeded out of the advancement track to save the company the effort and expense of cultivating their abilities. Many woman leaders, including U.S. Congresswoman Patricia Shroeder, work/family researcher Fran Rodgers, and Du Pont executive Fran Wohl feared the consequence of such a practice would be to shunt many gifted women into dead-end, meaningless, and low-paying jobs.[19]

We applaud Schwartz's suggestions for retaining and making the best use of employees who do wish to slow down their career paths while their children are small. Yet devising a "mommy track" or any other permanently two-tiered system of advancement for women managers or any other group strikes us as discriminatory and a step backwards for equal rights. Such a notion ignores the possibility that men, as fathers trying to raise families and plan their careers, also have periods of time when they would like to be able to slow down without getting off the path toward success. In fact, 80% of workers in a national survey conducted by the recruitment firm Robert Half International said they would trade rapid career advancement for more time with their families.[27] Certainly all workers, not just women who become mothers, experience periods of change in their lives and readjust their career goals occasionally. The wish to spend more time with children, the needs of elderly parents, and a desire for new and different kinds of challenges are only some of the reasons.

There are also some logical flaws in Schwartz's argument. First, the system of tracking she suggests rests on an either/or assumption that there are only two personality types among management women rather than a variety of styles of responding to the daily dilemmas of balancing work and private life. A second, more disturbing flaw is that the proposal begs the question of whether or not top management can identify a woman's ability to cope with work and family pressures before all the evidence is in, that is, before she gives birth. It would seem counterproductive and unfair to force women to commit to a specific career track before they have had sufficient infant care leave to adjust to life with a baby and to sort out the shifting priorities that come with increased family responsibilities.

Corporate management certainly faces a dilemma in trying to support all employees in efforts to be good parents as well as productive workers while at the same time protecting company investments in high-level managers. Although possible financial disparities in the cost of supplying men and women with appropriate training and benefits merit further study, executives must also look beyond the cost per worker and consider the impact of the company's policies on the total cost of doing business. If they also look to the future, they may realize that "mommy tracking"— or "daddy tracking" for that matter—can eliminate some of the best people from the promotion pool and severely limit a company's choice of leaders. It would seem to make more sense to offer all employees— regardless of whether or not they have children—the opportunity to slow or to change their career paths temporarily when expedient and to pick up the pace again when they need or can accept a new challenge. In order to offer that kind of opportunity to both men and women, it is necessary to give all workers as much support as possible in meeting their family as well as business responsibilities.

HELPING BUSINESS HELP FAMILIES

Given the host of child care assistance and general family support policies from which a corporation or small business may choose, how do individual businesses get help organizing needs assessments, choosing a child care assistance plan, and evaluating programs within the company? Some, as we have seen, turn to for-profit child care chains to analyze the market, set up a program, and run it. There are also companies that specialize in setting up voucher plans and supplying the necessary software and forms. Nonprofit groups such as Catalyst are excellent sources of information. Another possibility is to hire a consulting firm that specializes in researching child care and other family needs within businesses and suggesting practical and affordable solutions. For example, Work/Family Directions in Boston is an experienced consultant and provider of services to many national corporations.

Child care consulting has in recent years developed from a part-time business for a few hardy and poorly paid advocates to a full-time profession for people with backgrounds in both business and child development or early childhood education. Recognition of child care consulting as a professional endeavor has been boosted by the development of a professional organization, the Association of Child Care Consultants International, based in Atlanta, Georgia.[16] The association has an annual conference that features workshops for professional consultants. It also provides a list of local consultants to businesses that request it. Other groups, such as the Real Estate Division of the Institute for International Research, hold seminars for business leaders to explain various forms of child care assistance, tax and insurance issues, and practical steps toward implementation. No longer is it necessary for business executives to rely on word of mouth or to do without child care plans because they have no one on staff qualified to analyze the internal needs of the company or simply do not understand the details.

Many states are also trying to help businesses to help their employees with child care. According to the Child Care Action Campaign, 13 states offer tax credits to firms that establish child care programs, and similar bills were pending in 21 other states at the end of 1989.[29] Yet fewer than 1% of the companies eligible for the credits have taken advantage of them. In New Mexico, for example, only one company has claimed the tax credit since it was first offered six years ago, and Connecticut's credit has been used by only 45 of 80,000 eligible firms. There are several reasons for the lack of popularity of this type of incentive. According to a *Wall Street Journal* report, credits are typically offered for start-up expenses, not for long-term operating costs. The credits reduce state corporate tax liabilities, but many firms do not have high enough profits to incur these taxes in the first place.[29] The *Wall Street Journal* also blames "company disinterest and puny credits."[17] Although many state lawmakers are enthusiastic about these credits as a low-cost way to show their constituents they are working to solve child care problems, this approach has apparently done little to increase employer involvement in child care or to expand the supply.

With or without help, a growing number of business leaders are responding to the challenge offered them during the past decade by privatization and the demographics of the labor force. They are increasing the availability of child care for their employees, and they are helping employees find new ways to cope with the conflicting demands of work and family life. Still, no matter how hard individual companies try to help their own workers, such solitary efforts will not solve all of the child care problems of American workers and employers. Whatever demands are placed on the private sector to absorb the shock of change in the American work place and the American family, individual corporations cannot do it alone, any more than individual working families or the government can.

In recognition of the entire society's responsibility for supporting children who are the future generation of workers, many business leaders are pressing for major social reforms to improve services to children. In particular, executives have banded together to call for an overhaul of the educational system in the United States. Gathered at the Business Roundtable in June of 1989, the chief executive officers of 200 large corporations turned from their usual discussions of trade deficits and taxes to tackle the problem of public education.[8] The CEOs invited an additional 200 attendees from the American Business Conference, the U.S. Chamber of Commerce, and the National Association of Manufacturers to join them in a call for national educational reform with the involvement of both business and government.

Although not yet the subject of an annual conference of this magnitude, there is growing recognition in the business world that improved child care will have an impact on the nation, its people, and its economy. Through participation in organizations such as the Child Care Action Campaign and the Conference Board, both in New York City, the Family Resource Coalition in Chicago, and the National Center for Clinical Infant Programs in Washington, D.C., as well as a host of local, state, and national agencies, individual men and women in business are contributing time, money, and management expertise to the support of child care reform nationwide. If but a small proportion of the energy exhibited at that meeting of the Business Roundtable is directed toward the problems of child care, we will owe the segment of business that consists of influential corporations and their leaders a tremendous debt of gratitude.

Yet insuring that there are sufficient able workers to meet the demands of the nation's economy in the 21st century cannot be the province of business leaders alone. Remember that the vast majority of employers are small businesses without the resources to help employees and their families as much as they might like. Even companies that are large and successful today may be replaced in earnings and power by other corporations tomorrow. But the needs of a nation's children remain constant and have the same urgency, no matter where their parents work and no matter which corporations are currently leading in profits. What the children need—and what business leaders seem to want also—is a supply of adequate and affordable child care that is not dependent upon a small fraction of companies, but is a responsibility distributed throughout society. Although their continued willingness to offer child care assistance supports the child care system as a whole, there must be a better organized system for them to support. We offer our vision of a workable system in the next two chapters.

9

The School of the 21st Century: A Step Toward a Unified System of Child Care and Family Support

America began the 20th century with an unmet need for child care; as the century ends, the need is ever more pressing. After all this time, the problem is finally being recognized throughout the society, and recognition is the first step toward remedy. Parents, beset with problems in finding and paying for child care environments where their children will be safe and happy, have received a small but growing response from some employers. Several state governments have enacted legislation designed to increase the supply of child care for their residents or to improve its quality. At the federal level, our nation's lawmakers have spent countless hours in recent sessions attempting to forge an agreement about how best to help working parents with their child care problems. As we discussed in Chapter 2, however, several barriers to federal legislation remain as of this writing. Yet with support coming from so many points along the ideological spectrum—and from such prominent advocates as President Bush and Senators Ted Kennedy, Christopher Dodd, and Orrin Hatch—we are close to the formation of a national policy on child care. The question of whether or not there should be federal assistance with families' child care needs seems to have been settled. Policymakers are now asking what form such assistance should take.

Although the sheer volume of activity on the part of state and federal governments is encouraging, the problem of supplying good quality child care for all the families who need it can be only partly addressed by legislation. Policy proposals to date have been responses to a crisis, just as efforts to create child care systems in the past were responses to crises (see Chapter 2). As such, they can generate only limited, short-term solutions. Imagine how difficult it would be for American public schools to design and deliver educational programs if their continued existence depended on the passage of a new bill in Congress every other year or so. If, as we maintain, the need for child care while parents work is not a passing trend, successful solutions must be comprehensive in scope and must include long-range plans. And if, as we believe, the current state of crisis is perpetuated by the mixed system of child care, what is obviously needed is a more stable and organized system, one that is capable of responding to future needs as well as to present ones.

The child care system of the future must support the child, the family, and the society as they enter the 21st century. In this chapter, we propose one part of such an organized child care system: what has been described by Zigler as the School of the 21st Century.[16] It is designed to meet the child care needs of children of all ages and to provide greater support for their families. Because of the specialized needs of very young children and the cost of supplying them with quality care, we will discuss financial aspects of infant/toddler care and its alternatives in Chapter 10. First, however, we will review some of the issues discussed earlier in this book that must be addressed in any effective effort to meet the child care needs of our nation.

WHAT A COMPREHENSIVE SOLUTION MUST INCLUDE

The formation of a meaningful child care policy—and the child care system it generates—can be guided by several principles derived both from research on the developmental needs of children and from practical experience with programs that have been successful in meeting these needs. A unified commitment to action is the main prerequisite for making quality child care a reality for all families who entrust their children to supplementary care for some portion of their young lives.

The first principle is that *all* children must have access to stable, good quality child care when and if they need it. Good care is the right of every child and should not depend upon family income, ethnicity, or the neighborhood where they happen to live. We should not adopt any solution that perpetuates the two-tiered system we have now or one that allows children to be segregated along socioeconomic or ethnic lines. Here we can learn from one mistake of Project Head Start. The program has been highly successful in integrating bilingual and disabled children, but not those across the socioeconomic spectrum. By regulation, the overwhelming majority of families served by Head Start must be poor. The result is that poor children are sent to one set of centers and middle-class and affluent children are sent to another. Let us not make the same mistake with child care. We as a nation must resolve that good quality child care, like public education, is an entitlement for all children who use its services, not a privilege.

The second principle is that the caregiver is the single most important determinant of child care quality. Any system that would best meet the needs of children, therefore, would also meet the needs of the adults whose behavior determines in large part the kind of care children receive. Caregivers must receive appropriate training, including both classroom work and on-site supervision, so they can learn to recognize and respond to the individual needs of children, interact with them in a positive manner, and insure that the children's activities and environment are conducive to their growth and development. To alleviate the shortage of good caregivers, we must enhance the incentives for entering and remaining in the child care field. Salary, benefits, and professional status must be raised to a level commensurate with the service caregivers perform—a service no less crucial than that performed by educators in the formal school system.

The third principle is that child care must provide for the needs of children in all areas of development. Throughout this book, we have differentiated child care from other education and intervention programs for children and families. This distinction is actually between *systems* of child care, of education, and of other services, although the purposes of these systems are not mutually exclusive. All of these systems are part of the total environment in which the child's learning and development take place. For the individual child as he or she grows, there is no distinction between child care and education. This notion was recognized in a report by the Council of Chief State School Officers, which emphasized "the growing consensus among researchers and practitioners that child care and early education are inseparable issues and must be considered as one . . . ."[5] The Council cited a paper presented to them by Anne Mitchell, who said, "Children cannot be cared for well without educating them and children cannot be educated well without caring for them."[5] Bettye Caldwell, Donaghey Distinguished Professor of Education at the University of Arkansas at Little Rock, has coined a term to describe this interaction: she suggests that we abandon the term "child care" altogether, substituting the term "educare."[3]

To provide for the wide range of children's developmental needs, any child care program must promote sound physical, social, emotional, and intellectual growth. Thus all child care environments must be above the critical level at which they would otherwise cease to support healthy development in these areas—the environmental threshold discussed earlier. In practical terms, quality control must be basic to all caregiving arrangements. We outlined in Chapter 3 the quality components that need to be addressed: health and safety practices; sufficient numbers of trained adults to care for the children served; appropriate patterns of grouping and staffing, including consistency of caregivers; developmentally appropriate activities; and parent involvement. We know what quality child care entails and how to provide it. What we need are the will and financial resources to do so.

The fourth guiding principle is that child care, as one of the significant elements of the child's total environment, should be well integrated with the other systems that support the child in the society. These include the family, the school, the health care system, and the myriad social institutions that influence children's experiences as they grow. We will discuss linkages between child care and the school later in this chapter, but the need for connections with other human services should not be overlooked. Because children and their families are a heterogeneous group with different strengths and different needs, universal benefits can only come from a broad base of social support. We cannot expect supplementary care of children while parents work, no matter how good that care may be, to solve the multiple problems that confront many individual families today, any more than we can expect formal schooling to solve them. Poverty and unemployment, poor health, parenting by teenagers, drug and alcohol abuse, physical handicaps, and the like present the need for specialized services for affected families. As we discussed in Chapter 7, child care for these families can become part of other interventions coordinated to assist them. A comprehensive child care system, when integrated with other social service delivery systems, will be able to link families with other community resources and supports should the need arise.

An important corollary to the integrated systems principle is that child care must be predicated on an ongoing partnership between parents and caregivers. We have learned that such proven programs as Project Head Start derive much of their success from having parents take an active role in the services provided to children.[2,12,14] Parents should be able to participate as much as they wish in planning goals and activities for their children. Child care programs must be flexible enough to incorporate parents' desires and needs and to make room for their continuous involvement. Child care is an adjunct to parental care—both systems must support one another to make the constant transition between environments as nondisruptive for the child as possible.

Any proposed child care system must embrace a fifth principle—the importance of accommodating the heterogeneity of children and families. It must present true options to parents, offering them choices between a variety of caregiving settings and philosophies. Families should not be forced to give up the type of child care they believe is best for their children in exchange for financial subsidy, and they should not be forced to trade a style of caregiving that supplements their own parenting efforts for any vacant child care slot that is on the bus line and is within their budget. Parents need guidance in choosing among child care options. They need to retain some degree of control over their choice. They should be allowed roles in monitoring and evaluating child care environments, and they should be trained to assume these roles.

Finally, the child care system must adhere to a sixth principle of continuity: it must represent a permanent commitment to children, families, and society. For children, continuity means that the same caregiver and caregiving setting will be there until they are ready to move on, thus avoiding disruptions in their experiences and sense of security. As children grow and change, caregiving must be available that meets their new developmental needs. Thus the child care system must offer the types of care appropriate for children as they progress from infancy through the preschool and school-age years. Continuity among the various types of programs that both care for and educate children—such as between preschool and primary grade programs—is also essential,[4] so that children are not suddenly exposed to contradictory goals, teaching styles, and strategies. Caldwell points out that such continuity is "downward as well as upward," with adaptations necessary in both primary grade and preschool programs.[4]

For parents, continuity means a coherent child care system that is readily available to them whenever they decide they need it. The current hodgepodge of child care offerings is barely understandable even to the parents who are forced to use it. An established organization would engender familiarity and become easy for parents to enter. Families should also be able to depend on the system to supply whatever type of care they require, whether for an infant or preadolescent, work-day or work night, during a temporary work assignment, part-time position, or daily nine-to-five (or seven-to-three) routine.

Finally, the child care system must furnish a permanent service to the society as it too develops and its needs change. The interdependence of child care and society has been noted throughout this book. Although we have emphasized the needs of the children in child care and the needs of families who raise them, we are also aware that those children and those families are affected by the economic strength and health of the society itself. Society needs child care of sufficient quality to support children's development in order to promote its prosperity now and in the future.

Although the child care system must be a permanent fixture, it must be flexible enough to respond quickly to social changes such as sudden shifts in population and employment patterns. As we have seen, the current patchwork system has grown rapidly in the past two decades in response to the demand for services; yet without a national policy for planned growth, the development, sponsorship, funding, and administration remain fragmented and unresponsive to emerging social needs. Further, society invests a fair amount of its resources into improving knowledge about how children develop and learn, but the benefits of these efforts cannot be fully realized without a child care system that is organized and flexible enough to incorporate new findings and innovative approaches to meeting children's needs.[4] Thus society owes child care recognition as a vital human service and must provide it with an institutional framework so it can accomplish its—and society's—mission.

WHO IS IN CHARGE OF THE SOLUTION?

It is one thing to assert, as we have done throughout this book, that child care must be a shared responsibility of all segments of society, not parents and providers alone, not business alone, not communities alone, and not government alone. It is another thing to determine what roles each of these parties should play in initiating a new child care system.

Beginning with the system itself, fundamental, systemic changes are required. Simply spending more money on the patchwork system we now have would exacerbate the problems and postpone reform; more drastic renovations would then be necessary in the future. The diversity in the forms of child care, as discussed in Chapter 1, can be an asset rather than a drawback, but only when all child care environments are brought up to the critical level of quality that children, families, and the society deserve. Diversity need not mean fragmented and substandard services. The hundreds of thousands of child care providers who work in countless settings across the nation need a unified professional discipline and an "auspice," as Caldwell calls it, to give them professional linkages to others working in the early childhood field.[4]

Unity has a proven impact. Many local efforts to form family day care networks and associations for center directors have successfully raised the quality of care delivered locally and improved working conditions. On a larger national scale, cohesiveness can extend these benefits to all children and caregivers. National professional networks can share successes and begin to influence the form and direction the child care system should take. Today, unfortunately, the lack of a coherent structure for child care delivery makes it difficult for the child care profession to disseminate its ideas and continues to work against the possibility of a comprehensive national policy.

In national attempts to work toward a more coherent structure as well as to address the problems of access and quality, there have been calls for both lesser and greater government involvement in child care. Some groups have advocated limiting the role of government to tax credits; other groups have argued for increased government spending and control in matters such as the regulation of child care facilities. These and other views are represented in the more than 200 different child care bills that were introduced in Congress in the past two years. The fact that members of Congress are discussing the matter indicates that the child care issue is finally being recognized as a national priority. However, the existence of so many different proposals is also a sign that there is not yet consensus on the legislative approach we should take to solving our nation's child care problems.

The disagreements on the part of policymakers stem, in part, from differences in ideology. Such disagreements not only prolong the debate, they also mean that acceptance of a national child care plan, whether comprehensive or minimal, will not be universal. Whatever policy is eventually enacted will not put an end to the intense controversy over the proper role of the federal government in the affairs of families and private concerns. Because of this philosophical stalemate, and because child care is a local service delivered at the local level, many are coming to regard child care, like public education, as a state and local rather than federal responsibility. If this is the direction the child care system will take, leadership is especially needed at these levels. As we will discuss below, several states and communities have already implemented portions of a child care system independent of federal initiatives.

This of course does not mean that our national government has no role to play in insuring equity and universal access to good quality child care. A national policy, based on the expertise of those in the many professions devoted to children, would serve as an exemplar for states working to shape their own efforts. The government should also continue to subsidize the cost of care for low-income and handicapped children, similar to what it currently does in education with Chapter I of the Elementary and Secondary Education Act and the Education for All Handicapped Children Act. The government should also assist with funding for research in child care quality and for the design and implementation of model child care programs that can be adapted by states and municipalities.

In considering a possible solution to the child care problem, it is important to be realistic about unavoidable limitations that can restrain efforts by federal or state governments or by the child care field itself. One major limitation is financing. Since the federal government is struggling to contain the massive budget deficit, its ability to fund child care initiatives is severely restricted. Many states are having difficulty maintaining already existing services after suffering reductions in federal assistance, and their residents are facing continuous tax increases. As it stands, those who work in the child care profession are basically subsidizing, through low wages, the labor of families who have higher incomes than the caregivers do. Parents also bear the brunt of the lack of child care funds by straining their budgets, sometimes to the breaking point.

The problem of cost is highly significant because the cost and quality of care are related. Care that is above the environmental threshold of quality generally costs more than care that is not. And, when higher income parents are paying more for child care than do other parents, the two-tiered child care system is perpetuated. Some families are able to purchase good quality care for their children. Others are lucky to secure slots in subsidized facilities, some of which provide excellent care. For many families, however, the choice of child care is limited to low-cost and, often, low-quality services.

The federal government has partially addressed the high cost of child care through the Child and Dependent Care Tax Credit and subsidies to low-income families made available through Title XX of the Social Services Block Grant. However, as we saw in Chapter 2, neither provision is adequate to provide all families with access to good quality child care.

At the state level, there is variation in ability and commitment to address the child care needs of families. Some states have been able to piece together funding from various sources to fill the gap left by Title XX cutbacks, but these states are few in number. California, for example, has established an information and referral network that provides subsidies for child care, referral services, and provider training. However, even in California, where the response to the child care problem has been highly progressive, government funds alone were not sufficient and had to be used primarily as leverage to obtain private sector funds. Thus a consortium of corporations and local and state governments was created in order to raise $700,000 to fund six demonstration projects across the state which aim to expand the supply of child care and improve the quality of the services.

The results of the California program support our claim that a coherent child care system makes improvements possible. All early childhood and child care programs in California are housed in the Child Development Division of the Department of Education. Having a single administrative agency has been an effective means of coordinating services, trying innovative ideas, and establishing uniform quality. This central hub has also enabled funds for many programs to be combined, making California the distant leader in expenditures for early childhood services.[10]

Some states are attempting to replicate the California initiative. Five states, including New York, Connecticut, and Massachusetts, are making financial commitments to improve the working conditions and salaries of child care workers in an attempt to meet market demands and insure continuity of care for children. Many other public and private efforts have been mounted in various localities. All of these initiatives represent circumscribed attempts to address child care problems. Most of the individual as well as state efforts operate without assurance of long-term funding. A national child care policy would serve as a framework for otherwise isolated state and local commitments and enable the total to become greater than the sum of its parts.

THE SCHOOL OF THE 21ST CENTURY

The need for a child care system that is accessible to all children is not unlike the need for universal education that our nation addressed in the last century. In fact, there are so many parallels between child care and education that Zigler has drawn plans to connect the two in the form of the School of the 21st Century. The program calls for implementing a child care system within the already existing educational system and making use, where possible, of available school buildings, which taxpayers are already subsidizing. Responsibility for the program would be shared by federal, state, and local governments, as well as by parents who use the system.

Designed to address multiple family needs, the School of the 21st Century program provides a variety of child care and family support services. In and of themselves, these services are not unusual; they are already provided in many communities, but they are delivered in a piecemeal fashion. Bringing them under one umbrella will enhance the availability of services and establish a comprehensive child care and family support system that is operated under the auspices of the school but functions separately from the regular academic programs.

Major Components

Included in the program are two on-site child care components. The first is all-day, year-round child care for preschoolers from age three to kindergarten entry. The programs and activities offered to this age group will be developmentally appropriate and will not resemble formal schooling. The second component is before- and after-school and vacation care for children from kindergarten through at least grade six, with activities that reflect the individual interests and growing autonomy of grade school students (see Chapter 6). In schools that have half-day kindergarten sessions, children would attend school in either the morning or afternoon, and could return to the child care program for the remaining hours of the day. Planned activities in the school-age component would be informal, relaxed, and an enjoyable way for children to spend their out-of-school hours.

Three other components of the School of the 21st Century program comprise outreach services to benefit all families in the school district, even those who do not use the preschool or school-age child care programs. The first is the creation of a network of licensed or registered family day care providers in the district, with the school's child care system as the hub. Program personnel would offer training and general support to the at-home providers, which could improve the quality of local child care arrangements. The network would also be an integral extension of the school's child care components. Because school-based child care would not be available to children under the age of three, family day care homes could provide the caregiving environments for younger children. Caregivers in the network would also reap some benefits. Among the greatest difficulties family day care workers identify are isolation, lack of convenient education opportunities, and the need for substitute caregivers during the provider's illness or vacation time. A professional network can alleviate many of these problems and can encourage more providers to enter or remain in the business.

The second outreach service is a resource and referral system (see Chapter 1). Either physically based in or linked with the school, the R&R service would provide area families with information about child care facilities and places that provide care during irregular hours or for children with special needs. Homes in the family day care network would be among those listed, which would help parents of children under age three locate and evaluate potential providers in the community. Families could also obtain referrals to community agencies offering specialized services such as financial assistance for child care or living expenses, health care, mental health services, and other supports.

The third outreach component creates a home-based family support and parent education program, based on the Parents as Teachers model in Missouri. This program provides guidance to parents from the third trimester of pregnancy to the child's third birthday. Outreach workers based in the school offer information about child development, answer questions, and address problems parents may have while they raise small children, either exclusively at home or with supplementary child care services. These workers are trained to conduct screening programs to identify possible problems that may arise in the child's development, including hearing and vision difficulties. Through home visits and regular parent meetings, parents can share child-rearing information among themselves and learn from the child care workers about access to any special help their children may require.

Although we envision all five components of the School of the 21st Century program as interdependent, implementation of the entire program at once is not mandatory. One or more of the components can be initiated after an assessment of the community indicates what the greatest needs are and what resources are available. Components can also be started on a small scale and later expanded. Implementation issues will be discussed later in this chapter.

Requirements

Because every community is different, numerous variations among 21st Century School programs are expected. However, several requirements have been built into the design of the program in order to insure its integrity.

First, the program would be noncompulsory. It would be utilized only by parents who need child care and would represent one choice among already existing options.

Second, School of the 21st Century programs would share a common goal of making available good quality child care to all children who need it. Universal access can be guaranteed by having the program operate on parental fees for service, with fees adjusted to family income on a sliding scale, but there are other methods as well. In terms of quality, although schools are generally exempt from state licensing requirements for the operation of child care facilities, it is suggested that School of the 21st Century programs apply for a state license and that they further insure quality by adhering to professional standards. For example, the National Academy of Early Childhood Programs (NAECP) offers accreditation to child care facilities that provide care that meets the guidelines of the National Association for the Education of Young Children, the parent organization of NAECP.[1]

The third safeguard insures adequate staff training and developmentally appropriate environments. The program, although delivered in or administered by the school, would be coordinated by an early childhood education professional and staffed by providers with training in child development, such as that offered by the Child Development Associate program. The preschool child care program would focus not on academic subjects, but on play and social interactions, which are of prime importance during the early years. The school-age program would be based on the premise that after the school day, children need to take time off from school work. It would provide them with opportunities to engage in physical and recreational activities and would allow for a diversity of individual interests and needs. Providers in the family day care network would receive training in child development and learn to provide appropriate interactions and activities.

Benefits of the Program

Sheila Kamerman, a Columbia University professor of social work and a national expert on child care issues, told a *Chicago Tribune* reporter that the School of the 21st Century program's main asset is its connection with "an institution that's well established, well accepted, known to parents and lends itself to universal access."[13] Certainly a major benefit of the program is that it assures families of local access to quality care for children of all ages. Transportation to distant child care settings is reduced, and coordination of locally available services

eases families' transitions from one form of child care to another as
children grow. Benefits for children include not only higher quality
care throughout the stages they need it, but also the potential for early
identification of developmental problems, such as hearing and visual
handicaps or learning disabilities.

There are benefits for child care professionals as well. The component
creating a central hub for encouraging, training, and supporting family
day care providers will increase their visibility within the community.
Connections with potential clients will be easier, as will the parents'
task of finding, evaluating, and monitoring the care their children receive
in such settings. Ongoing training programs for all child care workers
in the area will give them techniques and resources to enhance their
work with children. Within the context of the program, employment
issues such as pay upgrades and the provision of worker benefits may
also be addressed. In addition to such practical supports, treating child
care workers as respected members of the early childhood profession
should raise their status and sense of self-worth.

The School of the 21st Century program is also expected to have a
positive impact on school districts. They will be able to identify special
needs children before school entry and begin to provide remedial services that will eventually help the students in school. Educators will
be in a better position to coordinate existing educational programs with
those serving younger children. The school may also bolster its image
as a community institution dedicated to the service of families and
children.

Because the continued funding—and hence the existence—of family
support programs hinges on confirmed evidence that they are indeed
effective,[17] all School of the 21st Century programs must be submitted
to continued evaluation. A design for measuring specific program objectives has been offered.[18] The plan includes assessments of most of the
benefits discussed here as well as items such as reducing the number
of hours children are in self-care and the amount of time parents miss
from work because of failures in child care arrangements. The number
of changes in caregivers and settings individual children experience is
another essential measure of how successful the program is in promoting
continuity of care.

Implementation Issues

"Every once in a while, an idea comes along that makes such eminent
good sense, it's hard to see why no one thought of it earlier . . . .

[T]he 21st Century School's program . . . is a project that fits into that category."[7]

Although the School of the 21st Century is an idea that has numerous benefits and a growing number of supporters, controversy surrounds the implementation of the program. Those in favor of the theory of the program contend that child care and family support programs fit logically within the mission of the schools and have the added benefit of reducing child care fees, because many administrative costs can be absorbed in existing school budgets. Proponents further note that incorporating child care and ancillary services in the school could raise the quality and legitimacy of programs because of education's professional standing and its adherence to various standards.[8] A school's involvement in services for young children will not only benefit children and families, but supporters believe it may also have a positive influence on learning and instruction modes in the primary grades, resulting in less academically rigid programs in the elementary school. The emphasis on developmentally appropriate activities in the preschool child care program may lead to a rethinking of the ways to shape kindergarten and the early primary grades to allow for a smoother transition from preschool to grammar school.

New programs in public schools tend to meet with a certain amount of resistance. Opposition to the School of the 21st Century concept has not been the general reaction of educators, however. In fact, in 1988 the National Association of Elementary School Principals surveyed 1,175 principals and reported that two-thirds of them were willing to provide child care services if they were given the necessary resources.[15] As early as 1974, the American Federation of Teachers supported public school involvement with early childhood programs to eliminate the need for an additional bureaucracy for preschoolers.[10] Because the need for child care is widely acknowledged, the questions raised about the program deal less with its *raison d'être* than with more material concerns such as where the space and operating funds will come from and how staff will be trained and paid. Other questions concern the appropriateness of the school environment for young children, whether there will be a reduction in the number of child care choices for parents, and how flexible school administrators will be to change the regular school schedule or respond to the needs of families whose children do not attend school.

Space. Readily accessible, suitable space is mandatory for any child care program. The School of the 21st Century proposes to use schools, where space is often at a premium. Opponents of the program ask where space will be found, whether it will decrease the amount of space available for the regular school program, and whether the physical environment will be appropriate and safe for preschool children.

School administrators agree that space is always a problem: yearly fluctuations in enrollment require innovative approaches to space allocation and frequent adjustments and room changes. In a survey of North Carolina school principals and superintendents by Lubeck and Garrett, a variety of attitudes emerged toward incorporating prekindergarten programs into the public schools. Because space is already tight in most North Carolina schools, some administrators resisted the idea. However, several other administrators contended that facilities rarely precede programs. As one superintendent noted, "If we wait until facilities are available, these early childhood programs will never come."[8] The message here is that unless a strong commitment to a program exists, the program cannot exist; the will to bring the program to fruition is instrumental to the process. If there is commitment to child care, school board members will take child care into consideration when they make space allocations. For example, in Ontario, Canada, any new school being built must include space for child care.

In the meantime, a number of short-term solutions have been implemented by educators who are committed to the idea of school-based child care but who do not yet have sufficient space available. In North Carolina, for example, solutions to the space problem included renting or purchasing a nearby building, constructing a separate facility on the school grounds, using modular buildings, or joining forces with child care programs in the community. This latter solution has been used in Wyoming, as will be described later in the chapter, as well as in other parts of the country. In Milwaukee, one school not only uses space in a nearby child care center, but also sends teachers there to conduct kindergarten classes. In this case, a child care program did not reduce academic space but contributed to a solution to the district's overall space shortage.

The space issue is also relevant with respect to child care for school-age children. Having space available for before- and after-school and vacation programs is not usually a major problem, because school is not in session when these programs operate. We mentioned in Chapter 6, however, the need to accommodate teachers' desires to have jurisdiction over and use of their classroom space and materials after school hours. Additionally, when children are in school-age child care, they need to feel that they are out of school and on their own time. Although existing space such as a cafeteria, gym, or large classroom may be used for school-age child care, it may be unsuitable unless provisions are made to modify it for child care purposes. Some programs temporarily alter such space by using easily movable furniture, rugs, room dividers, and cabinets where supplies used in the program can be stored.

Developmental Appropriateness. Another concern voiced about the School of the 21st Century program comes from those who believe schools may be inappropriate locations for young children, both physically and developmentally. Opponents fear that standardized curricula and homogeneous teaching methods, common in many public schools, would be used in the child care setting. These practices would not be suitable for preschoolers, since their developmental levels and abilities vary even more widely than those of school-agers. A related concern is that child care in the schools might lead to an academically oriented curriculum that would impose cognitive learning experiences on young children before they are ready. The potential for such an orientation exists not only in school-based child care programs, but also in other child care and early intervention programs. One reason is that some providers and parents mistakenly believe that early formal and structured schooling, rather than developmentally appropriate learning environments, will enhance children's later academic performance.

The fear that child care delivered in, or in conjunction with, the school will be academic or developmentally inappropriate appears to be unfounded. A national survey of existing prekindergarten programs found that the physical location of a program (whether in a school or a community organization) is not an indication of the quality and age-appropriateness of the care delivered.[10] School of the 21st Century programs are expected to guard against an academic orientation by adhering to program requirements, noted earlier, that include a curriculum geared toward the needs of children in the age levels served and staff who are knowledgeable in child development and early childhood education.

Staffing. With the current shortage of trained caregivers, it is natural that a school district considering implementing a school-based child care program will have staffing concerns. It is important first to allay teachers' fears that they will be unwillingly drafted from their classrooms into the child care program. The program's staff must be separate from personnel in the academic program but will maintain professional relationships with them. The School of the 21st Century is not formal schooling, so supervisory staff and caregivers should be trained specifically in child development or early childhood education rather than in primary school teaching.

Because states vary in the requirements child care workers must meet, 21st Century Schools should impose their own uniform standards in addition to state regulations. Suggested credentials for district-wide and site supervisors are a master's degree in early childhood education, child development, or a related field. Teachers for ages three to five should have a bachelor's degree in the same disciplines. Those working with school-agers should have degrees in recreation or specialized experience that suits them to work with children of that age in a nonacademic setting. Teaching assistants and family day care providers need a high school diploma or equivalent as well as training and supervised experience in the child care field. All staff should be given opportunities for continuing education.

To be most successful, the staffing plan should incorporate a career ladder to encourage professional advancement. In order to attract the best caregivers and to keep them in the program, administrators will want to send a clear message that those who work in the child care program are not second-class teachers, but are providing a specialized service in a field where training and experience count toward salary increases and promotion. We cannot emphasize enough how important it is to supply caregivers with benefits and salaries that reward them for their work and allow them to improve their financial and personal status without leaving the profession.

In programs that will rely primarily on parent fees, especially in districts where few parents can afford the full amount, there will be some hard fiscal decisions to make. The most imposing will be how much to pay caregivers, since personnel costs account for the major share of the budget in any child care program. Those who make salary decisions must see that the already low pay scale for those in the child care profession is not perpetuated. Although relying on parent fees might be a good way to initiate a school-based child care program, local planners should begin to explore alternative funding sources early in the development of the system. Innovative ways to approach funding will be discussed later in this chapter.

Parental Choices. A fundamental goal of the School of the 21st Century program is to increase the availability of good quality child care so that all children have access to it. Critics of the program fear that parents would face a loss rather than expansion of choice if a school-based child care system is nationally implemented. It is pointed out, for example, that since many School of the 21st Century programs would have the advantage of rent-free space, they may have lower operating costs than other child care services and thus charge lower

fees. Their potentially below-market rates, coupled with accessible location and link with the school's reputation as a good environment for
children, may be so attractive to parents as to drive neighborhood
child care providers out of business. Undue competition from school-
based child care programs would, if this reasoning were correct, restrict
parental choice, and hurt the local economy.

The demand for child care in this country is so great, however,
that we believe the School of the 21st Century will never replace existing
good quality services. There will always be parents who are not comfortable with their local schools or who would prefer to have their children
in a facility based in a church, synagogue, or particular private setting.
If we look at the success of private schools in our country, even in
areas where public education is excellent and school transportation is
free of charge, we can predict the successful coexistence of school-
based centers with a variety of other child care programs in the same
community. In addition, the program suggested includes options other
than school-based centers, such as family day care networks. Further,
we believe that unlicensed and poor quality care continues to be offered
because it meets an unmet need for services. Once all parents have
access to help in locating, evaluating, and monitoring care delivery in
the community, there is a real possibility that poor quality settings
will be driven out of business. We welcome that possibility.

There are several ways that legislators, school administrators, and
others who are implementing School of the 21st Century programs
can share concerns about issues such as those mentioned above. At
the Yale Bush Center in Child Development and Social Policy, Matia
Finn-Stevenson has developed a flexible strategy appropriate for successful implementation of the program at the local, state, and eventually
federal levels. She leads an annual three-day training institute, funded
in part by the Ford Foundation. Plans are underway to publish a newsletter that will link communities in the School of the 21st Century network.
There will be information about ongoing projects, solutions to problems,
and opportunities for further training.

FROM THEORY TO PRACTICE

The desire of many educators to be responsive to the needs of families
is now evident in thousands of schools across the United States. Many
school districts have some involvement in child care services that are
components of coordinated services for preschoolers. Examples of these

programs are described in a report of a national survey by the Public School Early Childhood Study.[10] In addition, several communities have already implemented the School of the 21st Century program. To illustrate how the concept has been translated into practice, we will describe three models of the program in the states of Missouri, Wyoming, and Connecticut.

The Missouri Model

Robert Henley, superintendent of schools in Independence County, Missouri, was instrumental in pioneering a School of the 21st Century in September 1988. A community-wide needs assessment indicated that parents in Independence not only needed child care, but would welcome a school-based program. Financial support from the Greater Kansas City Community Foundation and Affiliated Trusts made possible the renovation of school space to make it suitable for preschool children. The program is supported primarily by parental fees for service, which range from under $20 weekly for the school-age program to approximately $50 weekly for the full-day program for three- and four-year-olds. The school board contributes the space and pays for custodial and administrative services and for utilities incurred in the use of the buildings from six in the morning to six at night, year round. After its first year of operation, the Independence program reported a balance between income and costs, so there was no additional expense for the school system.

All 11 elementary schools in the Independence district offer before- and after-school and vacation child care, and two of the schools offer all-day child care for children ages three, four, and five years and a "flip/flop" program for kindergarten children featuring half-day kindergarten and half-day child care. Although it is located in only two schools, the preschool child care component is available to all families in the district. Two other components of the program have been in operation in the school district for several years. These are R&R services and the Parents As Teachers program, described earlier in this chapter, which is provided in all public school districts in Missouri.

Another component of the School of the 21st Century, outreach to family day care providers, has also been implemented in Independence. School principals and program coordinators invited the family day care providers in their school neighborhoods to discuss their specific needs and goals and to help organize the program. Many of the providers accepted the invitation and have formed a network centered in the

school. There they meet with colleagues, receive training, share resources, and get help with finding substitute providers in the event of
illness or other emergency. Thus, in Independence family day care
providers have found ways to alleviate some of the major difficulties
inherent in being independent caregivers.

The Wyoming Model

Unlike the Missouri program, which is in a suburban, high-growth
area, the School of the 21st Century in Wyoming is in a small rural
community. The area suffers from an extreme shortage of child care
providers. To address this problem, district superintendent Ron White
initiated an adaptation of the School of the 21st Century child care
component as a first stage in implementing the program. Rather than
opening a child care center in the school buildings, the district schools
forged a partnership with existing child care facilities within the community. In the initial stage, only programs that serve preschoolers will
be involved. The staff in these programs will receive regular training
administered by the school and paid for by the state Department of
Education, which will also provide technical assistance. This training
will not only give experienced providers the opportunity to expand
their skills, but it is hoped it will encourage new providers to enter
the field.

The cooperation and support of Lynn Simmons, state superintendent
of schools, has been instrumental in getting funding and technical assistance from the state. The cost of the child care services is supported
primarily by parent fees, with some additional assistance coming from
local corporations.

This variation of the School of the 21st Century, namely contracting
for services with community-based organizations, is common in communities that develop programs for school-age children, as we discussed
in Chapter 6. The Wyoming model further demonstrates the flexibility
of the program; school officials can address the area of greatest need
first, adopting a plan that they can realistically administer and can
afford.

The Connecticut Model

The Connecticut version of the School of the 21st Century was initiated
at the state level in 1988 by legislation appropriating $500,000 a year
to the Department of Human Resources (DHR). John Larson, president

pro tempore of the state senate, helped gather political support to initiate the model programs. DHR commissioner Eliot Ginsberg, in conjunction with the Department of Education, implemented three demonstration programs, one each in a suburban, rural, and urban public school, in 1989. As proof that schools are not apprehensive about taking on responsibility for preschoolers and for child care, the state was inundated with requests from school districts that wanted to be chosen as sites for the models.

The Connecticut programs are supported by public rather than private funds and are administered by a state agency rather than the local school board, as is the case in Missouri and Wyoming. There are other differences among the three models. In the other states the programs are implemented on a district-wide basis, thus having an impact on the entire community. In Connecticut, each program is available in one public school and serves families from only one neighborhood. The purpose is to gain experience with the program in different types of community so that variations of the model will be available to suit differing local needs. Also, whereas the Missouri and Wyoming programs focus on components of the original School of the 21st Century plan, the Connecticut programs are implementing the five components within a framework of school-based Family Resource Centers. In addition to the School of the 21st Century services, these centers provide programs for teenage pregnancy prevention and adult literacy.

Because the Connecticut programs are administered by the Department of Human Resources, which has jurisdiction over child care subsidies in the state, they have been able to implement a sliding scale fee schedule and to subsidize the cost of care for low-income children. The Missouri and Wyoming programs have not yet tapped into funds that may be available in their respective states for child care assistance, so all parents must pay the same fees. However, both states have established scholarship funds, which are supported by corporate contributions, to partially offset the cost of care for families with financial need.

In Connecticut, the program is already expanding. There will be three more School of the 21st Century model projects by the 1990–91 academic year. In addition, a large Connecticut defense contractor is considering funding the program in the school districts from which it draws workers. The Connecticut Education Association, a professional organization to which many of the state's teachers belong, has made a commitment to the general concepts embodied in the School of the 21st Century and is developing its own model program. Evaluation of all current models will be taking place while the expansion continues.

Other Models

The Lake County school district in Colorado has recently joined the School of the 21st Century network. The district has a high percentage of low-income residents. Members of the community initiated The Center, a child care and early childhood enrichment program for children ages two and one-half to five. In addition, child care is provided for school-age children both during the school year and throughout the summer. Renovations were made to a previously closed school building where the program is now housed. A broad base of financial support was arranged to establish and run The Center. Operating funds are provided by the state Department of Education, Department of Social Services, handicapped education programs, and grants from businesses. In addition, support services are delivered by several state and local agencies. This cooperative venture illustrates that quality child care programs can be realized even in poor communities if everyone shoulders part of the responsibility.

As of this writing, communities in Texas, Iowa, Wisconsin, Ohio, and other states are planning to adopt one or more components of the School of the 21st Century plan. Similar programs are also being developed across the country. For example, the Pomona (California) Unified School District, under the directorship of Bill Ewing, has school-based child care that serves children from infancy to 14 years. Pomona's school system also offers a host of family support services linked to the schools through a resource and referral program, including comprehensive services to teenage parents and their infants.[10] In Florida, state representative Michael Friedman recently proposed a bill to the state legislature to establish "First Start Schools," which include elements of the School of the 21st Century. In North Carolina, former superintendent of schools Craig Phillips inspired one local district to develop a program similar to the School of the 21st Century, to serve the children of teenage mothers. He is also working on a separate proposal to set up preschool programs throughout the state, to be funded by an extra one-cent tax on cigarettes.

LOOKING TOWARD THE FUTURE

For the School of the 21st Century movement to foster a more organized system of child care nationally, the model would have to be adopted by every school district in the country. The history of the kindergarten movement and educational reform in the United States illustrates that such national acceptance happens slowly, on a state-by-state and district-by-district basis. Financial incentives offered by Congress can hasten the process. It is conceivable that by the year 2000 we could have an organized system of child care and family support in place in most communities, one that serves children from birth to the early teen years with programs that do not fall below the environmental threshold for each age group.

Our optimism arises from the favorable reactions of so many individuals, groups, and public and private entities that have a stake in our children's future. It is evident from the models and programs discussed above that when educators are committed to addressing the needs of children and families, they propose creative solutions and sidestep the numerous obstacles to good quality child care for all. Parents also are supportive of the idea of school-based child care; at least one survey showed an overwhelming majority of parents would like to see schools offer such programs.[11] Numerous national organizations—such as the National Education Association and the Parent-Teachers Association—support the idea, as do hundreds of state and national policymakers. Many of the various legislative proposals entertained by the U.S. Congress included the provision of funds for states to start school-based child care programs and expanded subsidies for children whose parents cannot afford the cost of child care.

Although members of Congress appear to recognize the need for a national child care policy, disagreements about the details have prevented one from being enacted. As a result, federal financial supports of whatever magnitude have been withheld from those eager to begin. Currently, child care programs for children under school age, operated by school districts and supported by tuition payments made by parents, make up only 3% of a host of early childhood programs across the country.[10] This estimate was derived from the Public School Early Childhood Study, which described the typical school-based, all-day child care program as located in the Midwest in a predominantly middle-class community where parent fees can support the program. While not surprising, this profile underscores two important points. First, there is a need for more communities to consider child care for children of all ages when planning school-based programs. Second, there is a need to be creative in securing funding sources so quality child care programs can be established in school districts in poor neighborhoods where families cannot afford fees that would cover the full operating costs.

School districts are accustomed to acquiring funds from local government sources, such as property tax revenues, and from the states or
federal government through state boards of education. These coffers
are not unlimited, however, and there is no reason why schools cannot
seek assistance from nontraditional sources. Some possibilities are suggested by the programs described above. Funds have been obtained
from national and community foundations, state and private agencies
responsible for various children's services, and major local employers
who stand to benefit from supporting an organized child care system
in their communities. Some federal assistance is necessary; however,
it should be kept in mind that only 6% of the total budget for education
in the United States comes from federal funds. Child care is unlikely
to receive a higher proportion.

As it stands, middle-class and affluent communities are in the best
position to duplicate current models of success in School of the 21st
Century programs. In poor urban and rural neighborhoods where relatively few parents can afford to subsidize the child care component by
paying full fees, schools must undertake the arduous process of fund
raising in addition to standard planning and implementation tasks. The
federal government could expedite the development of child care programs in such school districts by making a clear financial commitment
to meeting the child care needs of poor families.

A major impediment to this commitment is that in all the policy
proposals discussed by Congress in recent sessions, no agreement has
been reached about the overall national cost of supplying child care
to all those who need it. Minnesota Senator Dave Durenberger has
estimated the cost of providing child care to all the preschoolers alone
at $75 billion annually,[6] although neither Durenberger nor anyone else
has ever proposed asking the federal government to contribute such a
sum. Such estimates, some much higher and some much lower, are
generally off-the-cuff guesses used to express the enormity of the cost
of child care to the nation as a whole. Because the School of the 21st
Century would be developed in each local district, it is at the local
level that goals must be set and needs assessments done. The next
logical step is for communities to decide what the total cost of meeting
these goals would be and what combination of funding would be most
effective. Charging full fees for service to those who can afford them
may be necessary in the short term while states and school districts
organize their child care systems. For the long term, we should be
moving toward the eventual goal of entitlement, as America has achieved
with universal public schooling.

There is no doubt that the form of child care that will always carry the highest pricetag in any community will be care for infants and toddlers. We now turn to a discussion of possible means of easing the considerable burden of that expense on families and communities.

10

◆ ◆

A Child Allowance Trust Fund: Expanding Child Care Options for Families of Infants and Toddlers

As noted in the previous chapter, the School of the 21st Century plan is designed to increase the quality and availability of child care for children of all ages. For infants and toddlers, however, quality child care is an expensive proposition. A specially trained adult who cares for a very small number of children must have her salary needs met by a small number of parents, and each family's share may be more than many of them can realistically afford. Any effective national child care policy must include provisions to insure that quality for infant and toddler care is not compromised because of parents' inability to pay and that their choice about what is best for their children is not restricted by economics.

In this chapter, we propose that the United States establish a child allowance trust fund as a means of assisting parents to care for their very young children with whatever combination of parental and supplementary care best suits their circumstances. The trust fund would expand the social security system to provide an annual stipend to all families for each of their children from birth to age three. The stipend could be used to help defray the cost of child care, but it could also be used as partial replacement income for parents who choose to care for their infants and toddlers at home.

The concept of a national child care policy that assists families regardless of their employment status has been promoted by President George Bush, whose plan for a refundable tax credit would give parents extra income to pay for child care or to provide care themselves. The child allowance trust fund proposed here also enables parents to make such a choice; however, it differs from the Bush plan in several significant respects. First, President Bush's refundable tax credit would be available only to those who have little or no tax liability—in other words, to the very poorest families. This group does not even include all those whose incomes are below the official poverty standard,[1] not to mention the many middle-class families whose earnings are depleted by the high cost of infant/toddler care. The child allowance trust fund, by contrast, would be a cash benefit available to all families who have contributed to the social security system. Second, Bush's proposed tax credit was capped at $1,000 annually per child, hardly enough to cover the annual child care bill for one child, conservatively estimated at about $3,000 for center care.[3] The cost for infant/toddler care can be at least twice that much. Nor would $1,000 be sufficient compensation for a parent to stop working for very long in order to raise a young child. The child allowance trust fund, however, would provide an annual stipend generous enough to assist in the purchase of good quality care or to supplement the income of parents who wish to remain at home while their children are small.

FREEDOM OF CHOICE

Throughout this book, we have emphasized parental choice in the total rearing of children, including child care arrangements. Today many parents actually have little choice in how they can raise their young children. Many would prefer for one parent to stay at home, but the need for income precludes that option. When infant/toddler care is the most viable alternative for a family, it must be in an environment that fosters the baby's healthy growth and development. But many parents do not have this choice either, because such an environment is not available in their community or because they cannot afford it. A national child care policy must provide all parents with genuine options on both fronts: they must have freedom to choose the type of caregiving they want for their child, and they must have freedom to enter a child care system of universal quality.

Many child care proposals entertained by Congress in recent sessions address only the choice of supplementary care, detailing methods to expand the supply, raise the quality, and/or help parents with the expense. Such approaches may pit parents who strongly believe that young children should be cared for exclusively at home against those who need or want supplementary child care. The children's allowance trust fund would extend support to families in both positions, and it would make either option available to all.

Most parents as well as most professionals seem to agree that newborn and newly adopted children should be cared for by their families. In Chapters 4 and 5 we detailed the needs of infants and parents to have time together to form secure attachments, establish mutual relationships, and adjust to their new lives together. Leaves that would allow parents time to care for infants have been debated in Congress for some time (see Chapter 5). While progress at the federal level has been slow, 14 states, or 28%, have enacted some form of parental or family leave policy on their own.[6] With some exceptions, most limit the period of leave to six to ten weeks. We would not call this parental leave, but maternity leave, as it covers only enough time for the mother's recovery. It also severely limits a family's choice about when to place their baby in child care. The Yale Bush Center's Advisory Panel on Infant Care Leave[20] recognized that families need more time than many have now— several months at least—to adjust to and provide a firm foundation for an infant. The panel recommended that a national policy be established to allow one parent to stay home for three months with compensation and for an additional three months unpaid without loss of job security, health coverage, and other benefits. While this would certainly give more families and babies the opportunity to develop secure relationships, some families will need more than three to six months to adjust to the stressful changes in family life that accompany the birth of a child.

Although placing an infant in supplementary care at a few weeks of age is, we believe, an unwise practice that cannot be sanctioned by research to date, individual variations in infant development and personality make it impossible to say for certain at what age entry into a high-quality child care setting is advisable. One infant may adjust to supplementary care quite well at six months, another may do so at nine months, and some special needs infants may not do well in a supplementary child care environment at all. To have choices that accommodate each family's and each baby's circumstances, parents need a buffer considerably greater than that provided by current parental leave legislation in some states and greater than that which would be provided by a national family leave policy, even if one is eventually enacted.

The proposed child allowance trust fund would complement leave policies by paying parents a fixed amount that would give them some support during whatever unpaid leave is provided by employers, by states, or by future national laws. Further, by making this supplement available to parents for the first three years of their children's lives, the fund would extend the period of choice between home and paid child care for many families. Equally important, the allowance might alleviate some of the guilt and loss of self-esteem experienced by mothers who stay at home to care for their children, many of whom feel discriminated against by policies that address only supplementary child care options. The message inherent in the concept of a children's allowance is that caring for children is recognized by the society as an important task worthy of social support, whether it is performed by parents or with the help of supplementary caregivers.

Of course, a child allowance will not enable all parents to choose to stay at home with their children for up to three years. Some mothers will want to work for personal reasons, while others will have to do so for financial ones. For many families in the lower and middle classes, the allowance would be helpful but would certainly not meet their income requirements. Young families with children have experienced sharp decreases in income over the last few years—a 26% decrease for under-30 heads of household from 1973 to 1986, as compared to a 15% decrease for families with heads of household over 30 years old.[3] Bane and Ellwood[1] note that of the 20% of the nation's children living below the poverty line, half live in two-parent families; in the majority of those families, one or both parents work, yet they remain poor. Low wages, rather than unemployment (which would obviate the need for child care, but not for other forms of assistance), is the usual cause of poverty in these families. In 1987, 13% of the men who worked year round and full time had wages that could not support a family of four above the poverty line, which was $12,000 that year. Bane and Ellwood also point out that even in female-headed poor families, 69% of the mothers work to support their children, about the same percentage as women who work in two-parent families. These figures seem to indicate that families who are not on welfare, but are working as hard as they can, may still face the specter of poverty.

Of course, many more families would be officially poor if both spouses did not work. And many working families live in areas—in major cities, for example—where wages somewhat above the official poverty line can still result in hunger and homelessness because the cost of living is higher than the national average. Even middle-class parents often feel that the quality of life they can achieve is much lower than that which their own parents enjoyed, and this is particularly true for those at the lower end of the middle-income spectrum. A national child allowance would thus not eliminate the need for infant/toddler child care.

Whether parents have more or fewer choices about using infant care, they must all be able to obtain care of sufficient quality. As outlined in Chapter 4, good quality care for infants and toddlers is dependent on the availability of trained staff, suitable adult-child ratios (1:3 for infants and 1:4 for toddlers), and small group size. Care that meets these criteria is expensive, costing from \$80 to \$200 per week in East Coast metropolitan areas. Further, the supply of infant care arrangements has not kept pace with the burgeoning demand. For these reasons, many parents must choose child care for their young children that is of questionable quality—even though the price is still high.

Recent proposals to address the problems that stem from the high cost of infant and toddler care are characterized as supply or demand subsidies. Proposals considered "supply subsidies" aim to expand the availability of good quality services and to reduce the cost to parents by offering providers training opportunities and direct financial support. Proposals classified as "demand subsidies" are designed to increase the resources parents have to spend on child care. Demand subsidies, such as payments to low-income families and tax credits, are popular among policymakers, but as currently conceived they have serious limitations. Some of the proposals set the amount of the subsidy so low as to render it almost useless in the face of actual child care costs. Others are targeted solely to the poorest families. Proposed subsidies to poor families may be attempts to correct problems with current mechanisms, namely the Child and Dependent Care Tax Credit and the Dependent Care Assistance Plan, both of which benefit families with relatively higher earnings. Although assistance to low-income families should be a priority in any child care policy, it must be recognized that working-class and middle-income families also need support if they are to be able to afford quality care. Recent reports by Peter Moss[11] and the National Child Care Staffing Study[19] make it clear that a substantial number of children from middle-income families are receiving the poorest quality care.

The child allowance we propose is a form of a demand subsidy, but it would be a universal cash benefit not necessarily restricted by income. Because one of its purposes is to help parents pay for quality child care, it would be calculated on the basis of estimates of the cost of such care. Having a child allowance would not guarantee, of course, that parents could purchase quality care for infants and toddlers. The shortage of child care slots for this age group would have to be remedied. However, if a child allowance is instituted together with national acceptance of the School of the 21st Century (Chapter 9), there will be more support for potential providers to enter this market. Further,

parents will get more help in making child care choices, increasing
the likelihood that more of the nation's infants and toddlers will be
placed in care that is above the environmental threshold for healthy
growth and development.

CHILD ALLOWANCES IN OTHER NATIONS

The concept of a child allowance is neither new nor radical. Precedents
for such a mechanism to assist parents in raising young children have
long existed throughout the world. In Canada, for example, a universal
family allowance based on number of children under age 18 is available to
all families. According to Elaine Valin of the Department of Health
and Welfare Income Security Division, families apply for the allotment
at the hospital when they give birth; adoptive parents or recent immigrants can apply at their local Income Security Program office. The
family allowance is given regardless of income, but it is taxed like
other income. Although the amount of the allowance is small, it can
be supplemented with other provincial welfare programs if necessary.

In France, a family allowance is part of a comprehensive family policy
designed to benefit all citizens with small children. As described by
Kamerman and Kahn,[7] Moss,[11] and others, the objectives of French
family policy are to equalize the economic burdens of families who
have children and those who do not, to insure a minimum standard of
living, to make child rearing and parent employment compatible national
goals, to encourage families to have more than two children, and to
assist parents with the care and rearing of small children.

To some extent, French family policy is pronatalist; that is, it is
designed to encourage an increase in the population by making it easier
for parents to manage larger families. For example, there is a family
allowance supplement for single parents with low incomes and a universal
young child allowance for nine months, beginning with the fifth month
of pregnancy. Long-term allowances (up to three years) are available
to parents who meet income guidelines; 80% of French parents are
eligible to receive a long-term allowance. An additional tax-free family
allowance is given to any family when they have a second or later
born child, the only conditions being that the mother receive prenatal
care and the child receive immunizations and regular physical exams.
(One result of this policy is that the infant mortality rate in France is
the fourth lowest in the world.[10])

The French government not only supports parents when they have
children, but also is committed to assuring all children of high-quality

child care. This goal is achieved by a number of means. First, the government provides center care at low cost to parents. About 79,000 infants and toddlers in France are cared for in "creches," or infant/toddler centers, the majority of which are operated by the state. The creches are open up to 11 hours per day to accommodate a variety of work schedules, and they cost parents the U.S. equivalent of from $3 to $17.50 daily.[2] The creches are very popular and are often filled to capacity. The government is not only scrambling to build more, opening new centers at the rate of two a month in Paris alone,[8] but is supporting private child care providers to insure that all infants and toddlers can obtain good supplementary care. To increase the supply of child care, direct grants are provided to municipalities and to centers run by non-profit groups, and subsidies are available for the services of in-home caregivers and family day care homes.

Quality in both government-sponsored and private child care arrangements is promoted largely by recruiting trained caregivers and treating their profession with respect. Child care workers in France are integrated into the total economy and enjoy the same benefits that all French workers do. For example, French child care providers are protected by the national social security system, regardless of whether they work for the state or are self-employed. They receive sick and vacation pay and retirement benefits. Parents who employ an in-home caregiver receive a direct grant to cover the cost of their contributions to social insurance for the provider. Parents who prefer the French equivalent of family day care providers receive similar monthly grants if the caregiver is approved by the local Department of Health and Social Affairs, the government agency responsible for the care and education of children under three.[11] As a result, over 75% of family day care providers in France are licensed,[10] compared to fewer than 10% in the United States.

Child care workers in France are part of a profession spanning both health and education. In the infant/toddler centers, directors are pediatric nurses; staff who care for toddlers have the equivalent of an associate's degree and two years of added training in early childhood education and child development; and infant caregivers have at least one year of special training after high school.[10] All of these workers receive salaries competitive with those in the professions of teaching and nursing.[8] Licensed family day care providers receive training and assistance from a public health nurse and are guaranteed a minimum wage.

The cost of all of these child care benefits in France is supported by employer contributions and, to a lesser extent, by general revenues.[7] As reported by Carol Lawson,[8] up to 80% of the cost of child care services is paid for in some way by public funds. The parents' share is never more than a fraction of their incomes, averaging about 14%. The poorest families pay only $195 per year, less than the weekly cost of infant care in some areas of the United States.

Other countries in Western Europe also have a variety of policies to support child care services, provide family or child allowances, promote child health, and help parents balance work and family responsibilities. In Austria, for example, all families receive an allowance for each child worth approximately 15% of the average female wage.[7] This is a substantial benefit considering the limited resources of that nation. In West Germany, a child-rearing grant was introduced in 1986. Its goal is to encourage parenting and it is universal for the first six months. Thereafter, the grant is available to families according to financial need. West German parental leave policies, combined with the child-rearing grant, give all parents the ability to choose between staying at home with a baby or purchasing child care.[7]

In Finland, a tax-free child allowance equaling about 5% of the minimum wage is universally available. In addition, families who meet income guidelines can receive a taxable cash benefit averaging about one-third of the minimum wage in that country. This allowance was implemented gradually, initially targeting families with children under two and then, by 1990, made available to families with children up to three years old. Future plans are for the allowance to cover children up to age seven. As in West Germany, the objective of the Finnish policy is to give parents the choice between staying home and receiving a small income supplement, or working and purchasing government subsidized child care.[7]

The goals of Sweden's comprehensive family policy are to promote equality between men and women and to assist families in achieving a balance between work and family life throughout the society.[7] Within this framework, an elaborate infrastructure in Sweden supports working parents with benefits such as subsidized health and child care services, a paid parental leave for parents of infants, and the option of reduced work hours for any worker with children under eight years old. Parents also receive up to 60 days of paid child care leave each year, which may be used to care for children when they are ill, to meet with teachers, to attend school functions, or to perform other parental responsibilities. Sweden also provides a tax-free child allowance for each child up to 18 years old.

This brief description of family benefits in other countries suggests some trends in the social regard of children and parents. The majority of industrialized countries recognize the importance of giving support to families with young children. After birth, paid leaves give infants and parents time to develop secure relationships and obviate the need for supplementary child care for babies in the first months of life. Parents are then supported in their choice between staying home to look after infants and toddlers and going to work outside the home. A child or family allowance is typically one of several benefits granted to help families with the expenses of child care and child rearing. In the majority of countries, a basic amount for a child allowance is universal, although in many cases poorer families are given more financial assistance in some form than those with higher incomes. When supplementary care is required, the allowance and government support of child care workers and facilities help to make quality care available and affordable to all families.

The examples described here represent just a few of the more than 100 countries that have some type of national family policy. Yet most of these countries have resources that in no way compare to the wealth of the United States. While we are well aware than a child allowance will add a burden to this nation's finances, we see that most of the world's governments are willing to shoulder that burden and give families high priority in their national budget decisions. Benefits such as parental leaves and child allowances reflect national philosophies that the society is responsible for addressing the developmental needs of children and the economic needs of employees and employers.

It is these philosophies, rather than specific modes of implementation, which can provide models for child care policy in this country. When we discussed infant care leaves in Chapter 5, we explained that the United States cannot simply imitate the family programs in other nations, because these programs are delivered through each country's unique social service structure. For the United States to institute any family policy that is both acceptable to its citizens and effective in achieving desired goals, the policy must be implemented within the framework of democratic principles and our traditional bureaucratic structures. We suggest the social security system as the supporting structure for a child allowance because it is an established mechanism for providing for the special needs of adults and, to a lesser extent, dependent children. Methods of revenue collection and distribution are already in place. Expanding the system to deliver a child allowance thus appears easier and less costly than devising a new service system would be.

SOCIAL SECURITY FOR CHILDREN

Our motivation in proposing a child allowance trust fund stems from our concern that in the United States the current lack of a national family leave policy and the high cost of infant/toddler care stand as barriers to the healthy development of many of our youngest citizens. By supplying families with some financial support during a child's first three years of life, more parents would be able to provide environments—whether at home or in a quality child care setting—that support their children's development in all areas. Although this goal is part of the rationale for child allowances in other countries, here the similarity to a proposed U.S. child allowance program ends. In some nations, the motivation behind the allowances may be to encourage people to have more children or to encourage mothers to remain at home (or, in some cases, to enter the labor force). In the United States, the policy would exist solely to insure choice in child-rearing matters. Another major difference between our proposal and the family allowance policies of other nations lies in the method of funding. Unlike the governments of several countries that support such benefits in part or in whole from general revenues, the U.S. government has neither the history of supporting universal benefits in this way nor the current fiscal capability to do so. By financing the child allowance through a special trust fund linked to the social security system, the program can be designed to be self-supporting.

Background

The notion of expanding the social security system to address the needs of families with children is based on a proposal by Jule Sugarman, [16] who played a central role in the nationwide Head Start program during its first five years. Sugarman suggested increasing funding for essential programs serving children, youth, and families—including child care, family services, primary and secondary education, maternal and child health, and youth employment training—by creating what he has called a children's investment trust. The trust would draw revenues from general funds as well as from a new payroll tax added to social security deductions. Money in the trust would be separate from other social security accounts and no exchanges of funds between the two systems would be possible.

Sugarman's goal is to increase federal funding levels for child and family programs by approximately 50%. He suggests phasing in the new tax so that this increase can be possible within five years. According to his calculations, in the first year of the trust each employee (within certain income guidelines) would be taxed at the approximate rate of 0.1% of income, with a matching employer contribution. This rate would increase to 0.3% in the fourth year. At these levels, the trust would produce revenues of $6.5 billion in the first year and about $24.8 billion in the fifth year of the program. This pool of money would be appropriated by Congress each year to help support new and existing programs through tax credits and through grants to states, local governments, and private organizations that provide family services.

The program we are proposing bears many similarities to the Sugarman model. However, funds from the child allowance trust fund would be distributed directly to families with children up to three years of age rather than to service agencies. Parents would thus be able to use the money at their discretion.

Compatibility with Social Security Philosophy

The idea of integrating a children's benefit into the social security system may appear to represent a departure from the original goals of this established program. Yet the social security system has always existed in order to maintain a fund to assist citizens of many types. The system provides a pension not only for retired workers, but also for those who are disabled and can no longer work. In addition, social security provides a monthly allotment for minor children and other qualified dependents of disabled or deceased workers. Workers who contribute to this system—or their dependents—may draw from it when their contribution ends. One rationale for the passage of the Social Security Act of 1935, and for its subsequent revisions, was to relieve families from the extraordinary economic burden of supporting elderly and handicapped family members who could no longer support themselves. Financial support of children was not considered such an extraordinary burden unless a wage earner in the family died or became unable to work.

Although the range of social security beneficiaries is not limited to the elderly, retired workers do receive the bulk of social security entitlement. Further, more than half of the outlays of the federal government (excluding defense spending and interest payments) go to benefit the elderly.[12] While older Americans have suffered some loss in disposable income and standard of living as a result of the economic climate in recent years, as a group their financial condition is far superior to that of children. One out of every five children under the age of 18 is poor; among infants and children under the age of three, one out of four lives in poverty.[3] If their parents are working, 7.65% of the family's income is placed into the social security fund to ward off poverty at some future date.

Not only poor parents but those of all income levels might welcome the idea that some of the contributions they make to the social security system could provide benefits to them while their families are young, not when their children are grown and on their own. And not only do younger workers have to wait many years before they can draw on their social security investment, but many worry that they will never reap any benefits from the system. By the time the current population of workers reaches retirement age, some reason, the nation may be unable to sustain the fund.[12] If, as we have suggested in previous chapters, we consider the healthy development of today's young children an investment in human capital, even those workers closer to retirement might consider the positive impact of social security for children on the capability of the next century's smaller labor force to support a much larger number of retired people.

In a discussion of the history of the social security system, Phillip Longman[9] notes that the original architects of the program considered children in exactly those terms. They believed that it behooved a nation to insure that its children would eventually be able to achieve a productivity level that would support the aging population and other dependent members. The long-term security of the society depended upon children growing up to be competent wage earners and thus contributing members to the system and to the nation.

Recent controversies about the current status of the social security system are making many Americans acutely aware of the need to insure the healthy development of a future generation of workers. In a report analyzing the social security system, the Committee for Economic Development (CED) states that given the dramatic demographic changes our nation has experienced, those working after the first decade of the 21st century will face a growing burden as they attempt to fulfill the promises made to retired workers in earlier years.[12] The CED argues that unless certain adjustments are made, current social security surpluses will not be sufficient to avoid undue hardship and unfair burdens, not only for future retirees but also for the young workers who must support them. The recommendations in the report are primarily financial ones, such as changes in the way the assets of the social security trust funds are invested and the way the surpluses are used. Yet in past statements the CED, a national organization representing corporate America, has recognized the value to the nation in general and business in particular of investing in children during their early childhood years.

Political Hurdles

Although the benefits to children, families, and the society are numerous, the notion of a universal child allowance is likely to generate controversy. Opposition may be directed toward the principle of offering such an allowance in a nation firmly committed to the doctrine of domestic privacy. A more pragmatic concern stems from linking the allowance to what is perceived as a troubled social security system.

A bonus paid to families with young children may be regarded by some as governmental interference in the private lives of citizens. One reason is that support of this type can be seen as a fertility incentive, as it sometimes is in other countries. Kamerman and Kahn note such possible opposition, writing that critics would "worry that people (or the 'wrong' people) might be encouraged to have more children."[7] Yet research on the French family allowance indicates that providing financial help to parents does not result in larger families. The French policy, as discussed earlier in this chapter, was formed in part because of concern over low fertility rates in that country during the past two decades. Although the child allowance in France is a significant source of income supplement to families, it has not increased family size as was hoped. The fertility rate in France is at 1.7 per woman of childbearing age, which is well below the conservative goal of 2.1 children, considered necessary for population replacement.[7] Similarly, Sweden has reported no dramatic rise in birth rates after granting considerable increases in child allowances for each child after the first two.[14]

The fear that the "wrong" people (that is poor and/or unmarried women) will be tempted to have more children in order to collect a larger child allowance is probably groundless. In the United States, the closest thing we have to a child allowance is Aid for Families with Dependent Children (AFDC), which is available through the welfare system to single-parent families who meet income and other eligibility guidelines. Concern has been expressed in the past that the availability of AFDC might have been one of the primary influences on changing family structures in the last two decades, encouraging married women to divorce or unmarried women to bear more children. The reasoning was that women no longer needed to marry or remain married in order to support their children, as they could always obtain AFDC payments if their incomes dropped below a certain level. Yet an analysis of the statistics on AFDC use and single-parent families, offered by Bane and Ellwood,[1] does not bear out this possibility. In the 1970s and

1980s, inflation and cuts in benefits reduced the actual value of AFDC payments for those who received them by 25%, and the tightening of eligibility rules held the percentage of children in the United States receiving them at a stable level. Yet during that same period, the number of children living in single-parent homes rose sharply, from 12% of the general population to 20%. Such evidence indicates that cutting benefits and making them more difficult to collect does not reduce the number of divorces or the number of births to unmarried mothers. If reducing the current levels of assistance to poor single-parent households has not checked the rate of their growth, it is clear that increasing assistance to families is unlikely to increase the birth rate among these groups.

Another reason why the proposed allowance should have little influence on the birth rate is that it will supplement family income for a relatively short period of time. The expense of child rearing certainly extends beyond three years and will be much higher than the allowance provides even during that period. Further, no matter how much the allowance is for the first three years of a child's life, it will never approach the average cost of raising a child to age 18, estimated to be $90,000.[5] It is likely that this long-term economic reality would outweigh the short-term benefit of a child allowance in a family's private decisions concerning whether or not to have children, how many to have, and when to have them.

There may also be opposition to having the allowance available to all families with young children, regardless of need. Universalism, or not limiting government-sponsored programs to the poor, has been proposed for a number of other programs and services for children.[7,15] Kamerman and Kahn point out that it is "very difficult to do special things for [the poor] without creating or seeming to create perverse incentives or inequalities."[7] Because families across the socioeconomic spectrum face the same problems of cost, availability, and appropriateness of supplementary child care programs for infants and toddlers, they would all welcome the assistance the allowance would provide. Universality would thus give the proposal a broad base of popular support. Practically, however, granting the allowance to everyone would mean that money must be given to those who are not in need. Several possible distribution options will be discussed later in this chapter to adjust a universal child allowance according to financial need.

Other arguments against a child allowance trust fund stem from disagreements about the means of raising the revenue to finance it. The Reagan years began an era of staunch opposition to any form of tax increase, and President Bush has vowed to continue this political course. Yet increases in social security taxes have been imposed as scheduled, suggesting perhaps that this is the one area where taxes can be raised without presidential resistance. However, opposition may be expected from an aging population. The growing number of adults whose children are no longer young might object to increasing their social security contributions to provide benefits to young families. Questions may also be raised because of the current controversy over the status of the social security system. Today, many workers fear that the future retirement savings of millions of people in the next century may be jeopardized by current administrative practices. They may insist that instead of expanding the social security system, our nation should be making efforts to strengthen it. These are all legitimate concerns, and they must be addressed if the idea of a universal child allowance linked to the social security system is to be generally accepted by the public.

Actually, affiliation with the social security system can be an advantage for the child allowance trust fund. The allowance would not necessitate government spending from the general revenue. Income for the program would be generated through employer and employee contributions. Administrative costs would be paid either through these contributions or from other government funds, but the price would be lower than if an entirely new system had to be built. Businesses and individuals would not have to fill out yet another tax form and send payment to yet another government agency.

IMPLEMENTING A CHILD ALLOWANCE IN THE UNITED STATES

A universal child allowance that would meet the objective of insuring that parents can afford either to stay home or to purchase quality care for their infants and toddlers will be expensive. The most obvious questions are: "How expensive?" and "How would the money be raised?" The overall cost, of course, depends on how much each family will be granted. We approached this question by determining the cost of one year of supplementary care for an infant and two years for a toddler. This type of care is so expensive that an allowance equal to this amount would allow many parents the choice of caring for their children for part or all of the time before their third birthday. Concerning how the money will be raised, we considered two possible means of obtaining the needed funds: a flat tax rate and a progressive taxation scheme.

Calculating the Cost of the Program

The annual revenue necessary to support the child allowance trust fund was estimated for the years 1990 through 2000 to provide figures based on at least some known statistics and to avoid the uncertainty associated with longer term population projections. First we determined the number of children who would receive the allowance. For each year, the population of children zero, one, and two years old was calculated. (These statistics, based on Census Bureau data, may be obtained from the Yale Bush Center in Child Development and Social Policy.) The population projections used were based on fertility and mortality rates experienced in the mid-1980s, on the assumption that these rates will hold over the near future.

After determining the number of infants and toddlers in each year, we estimated the annual cost of providing each of them with supplementary child care. As noted in previous chapters, estimates about the average cost of child care vary widely depending on the source of the information. Therefore, we present calculations for a base case and two other scenarios using slightly higher estimates of the cost of infant/ toddler care. The base case scenario uses estimates from the Bureau of the Census that we consider extremely conservative: $39.40 to $41.10 weekly, or $1,970 to $2,055 per year.[18] In our two other scenarios, the annual cost of care per child is assumed to be $3,500 to $4,750 ($70 to $95 weekly) and $5,000 to $7,500 ($100 to $150 weekly). These figures are based on our own estimates on the cost of quality child care and on findings from two recent studies, the Philip Morris Companies' 1988 survey[13] and the National Child Care Staffing Study.[19] The estimates of the average weekly cost of care for each age bracket (zero to one year, one to two years, and two to three years) were multiplied by 50 weeks (representing the typical work year) to produce estimates of annual cost per child.

Total annual revenue necessary to support the child allowance trust fund was calculated for each of the scenarios by multiplying the assumed cost of care for a child in each age group by the number of children in that age group. These calculations, presented in Table 1, are in constant 1989 dollars. No increase in the average cost of child care is assumed, and no administrative costs are included. Depending on the method used to administer the funds, the administrative costs could vary widely, but we assume they would be relatively small if the fund is linked to an already existing federal administrative structure. Thus our projections for total revenue needed are a very rough estimate, to

TABLE-1.   **Revenue Needed to Fund the Child Allowance for One Decade (in Billions of Dollars)**

	SCENARIOS		
YEAR	BASE CASE	MODERATE EXPENSE	HIGH EXPENSE
1990	$22.85	$45.15	$67.23
1991	22.76	44.96	66.95
1992	22.60	44.63	66.44
1993	22.38	44.18	65.78
1994	22.12	43.66	64.99
1995	21.84	43.10	64.16
1996	21.55	42.55	63.34
1997	21.30	42.04	62.59
1998	21.07	41.61	61.96
1999	20.90	41.27	61.45
2000	20.77	41.02	61.09

be used only as a guideline in planning for a universal children's allowance.

Estimated rates for the added social security contributions necessary to fund the three scenarios are based on total household income of American workers.[17] Over 90% of workers contribute to the social security system, but we were unable to obtain data about the income levels of noncontributors. Calculating the tax on the income of all workers was the only feasible alternative but results in slightly lower contributions than will be required.

For a flat tax rate, the total tax necessary to generate the desired revenue is calculated and divided equally between employee and employer. For a graduated tax rate, this tax revenue is divided equally between total employer and employee contributions. The employee tax rate is adjusted so that households with annual incomes of less than $9,999 will pay no additional taxes and households with annual incomes of $30,000 will pay 100% or more of the flat tax rate (see Table 2). At present, social security taxes are paid only on the first $51,300 of income; however, in our calculations we have shown the effect of using no income ceiling for only that portion of the social security contribution designated to the child allowance trust fund.

The flat tax rates that would be necessary to fund the three scenarios for the proposed child allowance trust fund are presented in Table 3. Examples of the estimated annual increase in individuals' social security

TABLE–2.   **Graduated Tax Rates to Fund the
Child Allowance**

INCOME LEVEL	PERCENT OF FLAT TAX RATE
Under 9,999	0.00
10,000–19,999	33.33
20,000–29,999	66.67
30,000–49,999	100.00
50,000–74,999	125.00
75,000 and over	150.00

taxes in both the flat and graduated tax rates to meet approximate base case costs appear in Table 4.

The base case scenario rests on the assumption that actual child care costs are consistent with current Census Bureau figures. Thus the amount of allowance per year per child would be $2,055 for children from birth to one year and $1,970 for children ages one to three. The total revenue generated from the fund would be $22.85 billion for 1990, decreasing to $20.77 billion in the year 2000. Total revenue needs, in constant 1989 dollars, decline over time because the total number of children in the birth-to-three age bracket is projected by the Census Bureau to decline over the next decade. To obtain this level of revenue, an additional social security contribution of 0.42% of wages (at a flat tax rate) would be needed from employer and employee alike.

In the moderate expense scenario, the annual cost of child care used to calculate the funds needed for a universal child allowance is increased to $4,750 for infants and $3,500 for children ages one to three. This assumed cost of care is considered by child development experts to be closer to the amount of money needed to purchase quality care.

TABLE–3.   **Flat Tax Rate to Fund the Child Allowance: Percent of Income per Household, Matched by Employers**

	SCENARIOS		
CONTRIBUTORS	BASE CASE	MODERATE EXPENSE	HIGH EXPENSE
Employee	0.42	0.82	1.22
Employer	0.42	0.82	1.22
Total	0.83 (rounded)	1.64	2.44

TABLE–4. **Average Annual Cost of the Child Allowance per Household: Base Case Scenario, 1990**

ANNUAL INCOME	FLAT TAX COST	TOTAL REVENUE (BILLIONS)	GRADUATED TAX COST	TOTAL REVENUE (BILLIONS)
Under 2,500	$ 2	$0.01	$ 0	$ 0.00
2,500– 4,999	16	0.07	0	0.00
5,000– 7,499	26	0.15	0	0.00
7,500– 9,999	36	0.17	0	0.00
10,000–12,499	46	0.24	15	0.08
12,500–14,999	57	0.27	19	0.09
15,000–17,499	67	0.33	22	0.11
17,500–19,999	77	0.34	26	0.11
20,000–22,499	88	0.41	58	0.27
22,500–24,999	98	0.39	66	0.26
25,000–27,499	109	0.46	72	0.31
27,500–29,999	119	0.42	79	0.28
30,000–32,499	129	0.52	129	0.52
32,500–34,999	140	0.42	140	0.42
35,000–37,499	150	0.50	150	0.50
37,500–39,999	161	0.44	161	0.44
40,000–44,999	175	0.87	175	0.87
45,000–49,999	196	0.73	196	0.73
50,000–59,999	225	1.31	282	1.64
60,000–74,999	276	1.18	344	1.47
75,000 and over	448	2.20	671	3.30
Total taxpayer revenue		11.42		11.41
Total employer revenue		11.42		11.41
Total revenue		22.85		22.82

The total revenues needed, given this scenario, are $45.15 billion in 1990, decreasing to $41.02 billion in 2000. An additional social security contribution of 0.82% per employer and employee would be needed to raise the necessary funds.

In the highest expense scenario, the annual allowance is increased to $7,500 per child under age one and to $5,000 per child aged one to three, based on estimated annual child care costs in those amounts. This higher cost estimate raises the total revenue needed to $67.23 billion in 1990, decreasing to $61.09 billion by the year 2000. To achieve this level of revenue, an additional social security contribution of 1.22% would be needed from each employer and employee.

Other Cost/Distribution Options

The three scenarios described above are presented to provide a sense of the scope of the proposed child allowance trust fund and the potential costs involved, as well as to illuminate how, during these times of growing national budget deficits, the needs of families can be addressed. We do not intend them to be used as exact formulas and models.

All three scenarios are based on the assumption that a child allowance must be universal if it is to win widespread political support.[7] However, although a universal cash benefit is an important income supplement to poor families, it also enhances the income of wealthy families who already have the option of not working and the means of purchasing quality infant/toddler care. If a graduated tax rate is adopted, these families will pay more into the trust fund than those with lower earnings, thus reducing the net value of their allowances and the perception that they are gaining an undeserved benefit. Another way to target more of the funds to families most in need without undercutting political viability of a child allowance is to consider the benefit income and tax it accordingly.

A different option is to grant part of the allowance universally and distribute the rest on an income-tested basis. In this plan, a basic amount (one-third of the suggested grant, for example) would be guaranteed to all families with children under age three. Progressively higher amounts would then be available to families in descending income brackets. Another approach would be to have a universal child allowance for all families with children under six months, or under one year of age, and then an income-tested allowance for families with children up to age three. This option would at least insure that all infants could be cared for at home if their families desire.

These and other proposals to limit the allowance according to need could reduce the total amount of revenue needed for the fund. Such plans might be more feasible ways to introduce the idea of a child allowance to the United States. They must not undermine the purpose of the allowance, however, which is to give all parents the means to care for their own children in early life or to purchase care of good quality. The allowance must not be so small or so brief that it does not provide the necessary support, nor must eligibility be so restricted that it is perceived as a benefit for a limited population and creates dissent among the majority who will be asked to pay for it.

OTHER PROBLEMS, OTHER PROMISES

Although the child allowance would bring a smaller paycheck each week over a worker's entire career, the amounts suggested in our scenarios would be relatively small. Social security already requires substantial contributions from workers: 7.65% of their earnings up to $51,300, and double that for those who are self-employed. Depending on the amount of the allowance, the increases may amount to as little as 0.42%, 0.82%, or 1.22% of an individual's annual income, based on flat tax rates described earlier. To a family earning $30,000 per year, this would mean having approximately $126, $246, or $366 witheld in additional social security taxes each year (at a monthly rate of $10.50, $20.50, or $30.50). These costs could be even less if other cost/distribution options are developed.

Although we have argued the benefits of administering the child allowance trust fund through the social security system, some problems can be foreseen. There will of course be objections to applying social security taxes to incomes above the current ceiling of $51,300. On the other hand, subjecting higher incomes to just the child allowance tax rate might appease those who believe the current ceiling gives a tax preference to the wealthy who end up paying a lower proportion of income. Another problem is that distributing the allowance through social security would mean abiding by that system's eligibility rules. This would disfranchise those who pay into other retirement funds such as teachers and some government workers. Teenage parents and others who have never worked the required number of calendar quarters would also be ineligible—and these are families who are likely to need child care support the most. Current means of assisting them would have to remain in place.

The increase in employers' social security contributions is likely to generate opposition from business people who think they are already paying excessive taxes. Further, if many people choose to use the allowance as an income supplement while they stay home with small children, labor shortages will only intensify. Employers will understandably resist having to pay higher taxes only to exacerbate their labor problems. Yet a growing number of businesses are already spending more to provide family-friendly policies, and these policies are resulting in mothers entering and remaining in the work force (see Chapter 8). The availability of the child allowance might not affect these results that dramatically, and these employers would be able to reduce the sums they spend for partial wage replacement for those workers who choose to remain at home. Mothers who do return to work may well be more productive if they know their young children are in good caregiving environments that the allowance enabled them to purchase. Given this secure foundation, these young children will have an increased chance of growing up into adults who have acquired the educational and personal skills to contribute to business in the future.

Helping parents with the high cost of child care is an endeavor some employers have already undertaken. They must be joined by all employers, and all employees, if this help is to be extended to the broader population as a universal child allowance. Although high cost is only one of several contributors to the current national child care crisis, many of the problems discussed throughout this book stem from cost issues. The high staff turnover and lack of adequate training in the child care profession, for example, are not only inconvenient for parents, but also potentially harmful to children who do not get consistent and appropriate care. A child allowance, unlike direct subsidies for training and caregiver salaries, would not address these issues directly. Its indirect effects, however, would be to allow parents to afford to pay caregivers a living wage and to reject care by inexperienced or uncommitted caregivers. Higher wages will permit more providers to stay with their jobs and lure others to the profession. While this will affect supply and to some extent quality, improved caregiving depends on the availability of training programs.

If employees and employers are to pay for the allowance, perhaps the government's share of responsibility should come in the area of training. This can be done by expanding the existing Child Development Associate program. The curriculum and administration of the program are already in place and would not have to be created at additional cost. Federal funds would be needed to help more schools to offer CDA training and to subsidize students who could not afford tuition. This would be a minor contribution compared to that of taxpayers but might be realistic in light of the government's current financial predicament. Local governments could promote training by supporting provider networks as well as resource and referral systems to enhance parents' abilities to choose among providers. These services can be relatively inexpensive when linked to the School of the 21st Century program, described in Chapter 9.

If every child is a national resource, then every child's welfare is a national responsibility. Unless we make every effort to insure that all children have an opportunity to grow and develop as they should, we will be shortchanging not only the children but our nation's future. Our proposal for a child allowance entails relatively small financial contributions from employers, citizens, and various levels of government. If each element of society assumes a share of the responsibility for young children, the child allowance trust fund could be fiscally feasible in the short term and beneficial to the health of the nation and its economy in the long term. This investment in our children will be repaid many times over.

Epilogue: Caring for the Society of the 21st Century

Politicians and educators are fond of saying, "Our children are our future." But we must consider the kind of future we expect them to live in and how best to provide them with the tools for meeting it. Those tools include the technical skills we imagine they will need. However, our predictions of the technology of the future have, as often as not, been proven to be wrong. For example, in the 1950s we imagined that by the end of this century people would be able to live or work on the moon or in space stations. Although these advances have not yet occurred, our children are learning technical skills we never imagined—operating videocassette recorders and personal computers, for instance. Since we cannot guess the future, we can do no better than to give them more enduring personal and social resources: self-confidence, the capacities for leadership and cooperation, self-discipline, inventiveness, concern for others, loyalty, and dedication to the principles of democracy. These are the skills they will need in the 21st century, no matter what specific technological or social challenges arise, just as we needed these skills in the 20th century. And they will develop them or not develop them in an environment that adults determine and control.

The total environment that adults are providing our children is composed of the family, the educational system, the child care system, the health care system, and all the other systems that make up our social infrastructure. Of all these components, child care receives the least social support but has far from the least responsibility in shaping our children's lives. During this century we have seen the child care system develop haphazardly from one serving a small proportion of families to one that affects the rearing environments of the majority of American children. We are convinced that a child care system that works with rather than without the other social systems that influence children will assist in producing a society of adults who are capable of meeting whatever challenges the next century brings.

Since economic and human resources are not unlimited, social systems must sometimes compete for their share. Yet children are not simply another special-interest group, whose needs must be weighed against the needs of other populations and systems, such as the elderly, the work force, the economy, the natural environment, and the national defense system. Children will be those populations and the navigators of those systems in time. If society is willing to compromise children's development, they may soon become adults who lack the ability and the motivation to take over that which we fought so hard to preserve at their expense.

Just as it is difficult for an individual family using the current fragmented child care system to balance its own needs with those of the work place, it will always be difficult for a nation to balance the needs of families with all the other needs of society. Balancing the needs of children, families, and society in the present is also an exercise in balancing the future needs of society with its immediate demands. It is not a balance we are likely to strike perfectly, so we must give top priority to producing a generation that has not lost the heart to continue the effort.

The proposals that we have offered in this book, although focused on improving the quality and quantity of child care services, attempt to address the current problems of our other social systems so their future vitality will be enhanced. Improved child care will benefit them all, so we have asked them all to contribute to its improvement. Families and caregivers must continue to do the best they can, but with the support of the other systems that their efforts already support. We have suggested that business dedicate some of its energy and its profits to future workers and business leaders and those who care for them. We have suggested that the educational system devote a portion of its resources to children below the age of five, who will become the future students and teachers in the system. We have suggested that workers give a percentage of their income now to those who will provide them with a living in the future, through social security contributions and a healthy economy. And we have suggested that the federal government support research and help to create models for enhancing the development of those who will inherit the democracy. Only by recognizing that children are quite literally the families and the society of the future will we be willing to give them their rightful place in the society of the present.

References

Preface

1. Klein, E. (1989, June). *Public opinion polls on family policies: 1984 through 1989*. New York: Ms. Foundation for Education and Communication.

Chapter 1.
The Mixed System of Child Care

1. Bronfenbrenner, U. (1979). *The ecology of human development*. Cambridge, MA: Harvard University Press.
2. Bureau of Labor Statistics. (1987, August 12). *United States Department of Labor News*, USDL No. 87–345.
3. Children's Defense Fund. (1987). *A children's defense budget FY 1988*. Washington, DC: Author.
4. Children's Defense Fund. (1988). *Vanishing dreams: The growing economic plight of America's young families*. Washington, DC: Author. Quotation on p. 176.
5. Children's Defense Fund. (1989). *A vision for America's future*. Washington, DC: Author.
6. Corsini, D.A., Wisensale, S., & Caruso, G. (1988, September). Family day care: System issues and regulatory models. *Young Children*, pp. 17–23.
7. Cox, D., & Richarz, S. (1989). Traditional and modernized characteristics of registered and unregistered family day care providers. ERIC Document Reproduction Service No. ED 290 577.
8. Day care's cosmic crapshoot. (1987, June 26). *New York Times* (editorial), p. B1.
9. Feldman, D. (1989, January). Pricey daycare insurance. Ripoff or safeguard? *Management Review*.
10. Fields, R.G. (1989, May 14). For many mothers, child care means economic

survival. *Waterbury* (CT) *Sunday Republican*, pp. Al, 10. Quotation on p. 1.

11. Goelman, H., & Pence, A. (1987). Effects of child care, family and individual characteristics on children's language development: The Victoria Day Care Research Project. In D. A. Phillips (Ed.), *Quality in child care: What does research tell us?* (pp. 89–104). Washington, DC: National Association for the Education of Young Children.

12. Hofferth, S. (1989). Testimony before the Subcommittee on Children, Families, Drugs and Alcoholism, U.S. Senate, Washington, DC.

13. Hofferth, S.L., & Phillips, D. A. (1987). Child care in the United States, 1970 to 1995. *Journal of Marriage and the Family, 49*, 559–571.

14. Institute for American Values. (1989, March). *How the child care market works: An economic analysis*. Family Policy Brief. New York: Author.

15. Kagan, S.L., & Newton, J.W. (1989). For-profit and nonprofit child care: Similarities and differences. *Young Children, 45*(1), 4–10.

16. Keyserling, M.D. (1972). *Windows on day care*. New York: National Council of Jewish Women.

17. Knight-Ridder News Service. (1988, August 5). Problems in child care raise national debate. *Amarillo Globe-Times*.

18. Lewin, T. (1988, July 12). Day care centers, school doors close. *New York Times*, pp. B1–2.

19. McMillan, P. (1989, July 24). More talk than action; child care comes of age as issue, yet need grows. *Los Angeles Times*, p. 1.

20. Meisels, S.J., & Sternberg, L.S. (1989, June 7). Quality sacrificed in proprietary child care. *Education Week*, p. 36.

21. Mendels, P. (1989, July 11). Paying for day care. *Newsday*, pp. 1, 6.

22. Morgan, G. (1987). *The national state of child care regulation 1986*. Watertown, MA: Work/Family Directions.

23. Morgan, G. (1986). Summary of the Ad Hoc Committee Meeting Discussing Policy Issues in Child Care for Infants and Toddlers (February 12 and 13, 1986).

24. National Association for the Education of Young Children. (1985). *The child care boom: Growth in licensed childcare from 1977 to 1985* (Pamphlet No. 761). Washington, DC: Author.

25. Phillips, D.A., Howes, C., & Whitebook, M. (1989, April 28). *Child care quality: The real options facing parents*. Paper presented at the Society for Research in Child Development symposium, "The National Child Care Staffing Study." Kansas City, KS.

26. Reardon, P. (1989, October 8). Poverty wages take toll in child care. *Chicago Tribune*, Section 2, pp. 1, 8.

27. Reisman, B., Moore, A.J., & Fitzgerald, K. (1988). *Child care: The bottom line.* New York: Child Care Action Campaign.

28. Select Committee on Children, Youth and Families. (1988a, February 25). *Children and families in poverty: The struggle to survive.* (Opening statement of a Committee hearing.) Washington, DC: U.S. Government Printing Office.

29. Select Committee on Children, Youth and Families. (1988b, December). *Children and families: Key trends in the 1980s.* Washington, DC: U.S. Government Printing Office.

30. Select Committee on Children, Youth and Families. (1989, September). *U.S. children and their families: Current conditions and recent trends.* Washington, DC: U.S. Government Printing Office.

31. Seligson, M., et al. (1989). *School-age child care.* Paper prepared for the Bush Center in Child Development and Social Policy, Yale University, New Haven, CT. Unpublished manuscript.

32. Shank, S.E. (1988). Women and the labor market: The link grows stronger. *Monthly Labor Review, 111*(3), 3–8.

33. Stephan, S. (1988, June 3). *Child day care: Federal policy issues and legislation.* Congressional Research Services Issue Brief No. IB 87193. Washington, DC: Library of Congress.

34. U.S. Bureau of the Census. (1982). *Trends in child care arrangements of working mothers.* Current Population Reports, Series P-23, No. 117. Washington, DC: U.S. Government Printing Office.

35. U.S. Bureau of the Census. (1987). *Who's minding the kids? Child care arrangements: Winter 1984–85.* Current Population Reports, Series P-70, No. 9. Washington, DC: U.S. Government Printing Office.

36. U.S. Department of Health, Education and Welfare (1976). *Statistical highlights from the national child care consumer study.* Washington, DC: DHEW Publication number OHD 73–31096, Office of Human Development.

37. U.S. Department of Labor. (1988, April). *Child care: A workforce issue.* (Report of the Secretary's Task Force.) Washington, DC: Author.

38. Whitebook, M., Phillips, D., & Howes, C. (1989, April 28). *Adult caregivers in typical child care centers: Characteristics, compensation, and working conditions.* Paper presented at the Society for Research in Child Development symposium, "The National Child Care Staffing Study." Kansas City, KS.

Chapter 2.
Where Is the Child in Child Care?

1. Ariés, P. (1962). *Centuries of childhood.* New York: Knopf.

2. Biber, B. (1984). *Early education and psychological development*. New Haven: Yale University Press.

3. Brigham, A. Quoted in Pence (1987), p. 154.

4. Bureau of Labor Statistics. (1987, August 12). *United States Department of Labor News*, USDL No. 87–345.

5. Butts, R.F., & Cremin, L.A. (1953). *A history of education in American culture*. New York: Holt, Rinehart & Winston. Quotation on p. 241.

6. Cahan, E. (1989). *Poverty and the care and education of the preschool child in the United States, 1820–1965*. New York: Columbia University, National Resource Center for Children in Poverty.

7. Children's Defense Fund. (1987). *A children's defense budget*. Washington, DC: Author.

8. Dratch, H. (1974). The politics of child care in the 1940s. *Science and Society, 38*, 167–204.

9. Federal Interagency Day Care Requirements. (1980, March 19). *Federal Register, Part V*, Vol. 45, No. 55, pp. 17870–17885.

10. Friedman, D. (1985). *Corporate financial assistance for child care*. Conference Board Research Bulletin No. 117. New York: The Conference Board.

11. Johnson, L.B. (1979). Remarks on Project Head Start, May 18, 1965. In E. Zigler & J. Valentine (Eds.), *Head Start: A legacy of the war on poverty* (pp. 67–69). New York: Free Press.

12. Kahn, A.J., & Kamerman, S.B. (1987). *Child care: Facing the hard choices*. Dover, MA: Auburn House. Quotation on p. 76.

13. Latimer, L.Y. (1989, September 3). Suffer the children: The church-state day care controversy. *Washington Post*, p. C5.

14. Letchworth, W.P. (1876). *Homes of homeless children: A report on orphan asylums and other institutions for the care of children*. Reprinted 1974. New York: Arno Press.

15. Mitchell, A., Seligson, M., & Marx, F. (1989). *Early childhood programs and the public schools*. Dover, MA: Auburn House.

16. National Commission on Excellence in Education. (1983). *A nation at risk: The imperative for educational reform*. Washington, DC: U.S. Government Printing Office.

17. *New York Times* editorial. (1880, July 22). Quoted in Zelizer (1985), p. 177.

18. *New York Times* editorial (1904, December 9). Quoted in Zelizer (1985), p. 37.

19. Nixon, R.M. (1971, December 10). *Congressional Record*, S21129.

20. Pence, A.R. (1987). Child care's family tree: Toward a history of the child and youth care profession in North America. *Child & Youth Care Quarterly, 16*, 151–161.

21. Pestalozzi, J.H. Quoted in Thompson (1951), p. 46.

22. Skolnick, A. (1980, Summer). The paradox of perfection. *Woodrow Wilson Quarterly, 4,* 112–121.

23. Steiner, G.Y. (1975). *The children's cause.* Washington, DC: The Brookings Institution.

24. Thompson, M.M. (1951). *The history of education.* New York: Barnes & Noble.

25. Winget, W.G. (1982). The dilemma of affordable child care. In E. Zigler & E.W. Gordon (Eds.), *Day care: Scientific and social policy issues* (pp. 351–377). Boston: Auburn House, 1982.

26. Zelizer, V.A. (1985). *Pricing the priceless child: The changing social value of children.* New York: Basic Books.

Chapter 3.
The Search for Quality in Child Care

1. Bloom, D.E., & Steen, T.P. (1988). *The labor force implications of expanding the child care industry.* New York: Child Care Action Campaign.

2. Bredekamp, S. (Ed.). (1987). *Accreditation criteria and procedures.* Washington, DC: National Association for the Education of Young Children.

3. Carew, J.V. (1980). Experience and development of intelligence in young children at home and in day care. *Monographs of the Society for Research in Child Development, 45* (Nos. 6–7, Serial No. 187).

4. Child Welfare League of America. (1984). *Standards for day care service,* revised ed. Washington, DC: Author.

5. Children's Bureau. (1942). *Standards for the day care of children of working mothers.* Washington, DC: Children's Bureau Publication No. 284.

6. Children's Defense Fund. (1987). *A children's defense budget.* Washington, DC: Author.

7. Clarke-Stewart, A. (1984). Day care: A new context for research and development. In A. Collins (Ed.), *Minnesota Symposium on Child Psychology* (Vol. 17, pp. 61–100). Hillsdale, NJ: Erlbaum.

8. Clarke-Stewart, K.A. (1987a). Predicting child development from child care forms and features: The Chicago study. In D.A. Phillips (Ed.), *Quality in child care: What does research tell us?* (pp. 21–41). Washington, DC: National Association for the Education of Young Children.

9. Clarke-Stewart, K.A. (1987b). In search of consistencies in child care research. In D.A. Phillips (Ed.), *Quality in child care: What does research tell us?* (pp. 105–119). Washington, DC: National Association for the Education of Young Children. Quotation on p. 114.

10. Federal Interagency Day Care Requirements. (1980, March 19). *Federal Register, Part V,* Vol. 45, No. 55, pp. 17870–17885.

11. Finkelhor, D., Williams, L.M., & Burns, N. (1988). *Nursery crimes: Sexual abuse in day care.* Beverly Hills, CA: Sage.

12. Gamble, T.J., & Zigler, E. (1986). Effects of infant day care: Another look at the evidence. *American Journal of Orthopsychiatry, 56,* 26–42.

13. Goelman, H., & Pence, A. (1987). Effects of child care, family, and individual characteristics on children's language development: The Victoria Day Care Research Project. In D. A. Phillips (Ed.), *Quality in child care: What does research tell us?* (pp. 89–104). Washington, DC: National Association for the Education of Young Children.

14. Harms, T., & Clifford, R.M. (1980). *Early Childhood Environment Rating Scale.* New York: Teacher's College Press, Columbia University.

15. Hartmann, H.I., & Pearce, D.M. (1988). *Wages and salaries of child care workers: The economic and social realities.* New York: Child Care Action Campaign.

16. Howes, C. (1987). Quality indicators in infant and toddler child care: The Los Angeles study. In D.A. Phillips (Ed.), *Quality in child care: What does research tell us?* (pp. 81–88). Washington, DC: National Association for the Education of Young Children.

17. Kontos, S., & Fiene, R. (1987). Child care quality, compliance with regulations, and children's development: The Pennsylvania study. In D.A. Phillips (Ed.), *Quality in child care: What does research tell us?* (pp. 57–79). Washington, DC: National Association for the Education of Young Children.

18. Lewin, T. (1989, January 29). Small tots, big biz. *New York Times Magazine,* pp. 30–31, 89–92. Quotations on pp. 89, 91.

19. Morgan, G. (1985). The government perspective. In G. Morgan, N. Curry, R. Endsley, M. Bradbard, H. Rashid, & A. Epstein (Eds.), *Quality in early childhood programs: Four perspectives.* (High/Scope Early Childhood Policy Papers, No. 3.) Ypsilanti, MI: High/Scope.

20. Morgan, G. (1987). *The national state of child care regulation 1986.* Watertown, MA: Work/Family Directions.

21. Nelson, J.R., Jr. (1982). The politics of federal day care regulation. In E. Zigler & E.W. Gordon (Eds.), *Day care: Scientific and social policy issues* (pp. 267–306). Boston: Auburn House. Quotation on p. 270.

22. Petrie, P. (1984). Day care for under 2's at child minders and in day nurseries. *Early Child Development and Care, 16,* 205–216.

23. Phillips, D. (1984). Promoting collaboration between research and policy-making. *Journal of Applied Developmental Psychology, 5,* 91–113.

24. Phillips, D.A. (1987a). Preface. Epilogue. In D.A. Phillips (Ed.), *Quality in child care: What does research tell us?* (pp. ix–xi; 121–126). Washington, DC: National Association for the Education of Young Children.

25. Phillips, D.A. (Ed.). (1987b). *Quality in child care: What does research*

tell us? Washington, DC: National Association for the Education of Young Children.

26. Phillips, D.A., & Howes, C. (1987). Indicators of quality in child care: Review of research. In D.A. Phillips (Ed.), *Quality in child care: What does research tell us?* (pp. 1–19). Washington, DC: National Association for the Education of Young Children. Quotation on p. 15.

27. Phillips, D.A., Howes, C., & Whitebook, M. (1989, April 28). *Child care quality: The real options facing parents.* Paper presented at the Society for Research in Child Development symposium, "National Child Care Staffing Study," Kansas City, KS.

28. Phillips, D.A., Scarr, S., & McCartney, K. (1987). Dimensions and effects of child care quality: The Bermuda study. In D.A. Phillips (Ed.), *Quality in child care: What does research tell us?* (pp. 43–56). Washington, DC: National Association for the Education of Young Children. Quotation on p. 54.

29. Phillips, D., & Zigler, E. (1987). The checkered history of federal child care regulation. In E.Z. Rothkopf (Ed.), *Review of research in education* (Vol. 14, pp. 3–41). Washington, DC: American Educational Research Association. Quotations on pp. 14, 18.

30. Reardon, P. (1989, October 22). Child-care centers a hit-miss deal. *Chicago Tribune*, sec. 2, pp. 1, 3.

31. Reisman, B., Moore, A.J., & Fitzgerald, K. (1988). *Child care: The bottom line*. New York: Child Care Action Campaign.

32. Ruopp, R.R., & Travers, J. (1982). Janus faces day care: Perspectives on quality and cost. In E. Zigler & E.W. Gordon (Eds.), *Day care: Scientific and social policy issues* (pp. 72–101). Boston: Auburn House.

33. Ruopp, R., Travers, J., Glantz, F., & Coelen, C. (1979). *Children at the center*. Cambridge, MA: Abt Books.

34. Spitz, H.H. (1986). *The raising of intelligence: A selected history of attempts to raise retarded intelligence*. Hillsdale, NJ: Erlbaum.

35. Strickland, J. (1988). Human services meet tort reform. In National Council of Churches, Ecumenical Child Care Network (Ed.), *In the eye of the storm: Liability insurance and child care* (pp. 31–37). New York: National Council of Churches.

36. U.S. Department of Health and Human Services (1985, January). *Model Child Care Standards Act: Guidance to states to prevent child abuse in day care facilities*. Washington, DC: Author.

37. Whitebook, M., Howes, C., & Phillips, D.A. (1989). *Who cares? Child care teachers and the quality of care in America* (Executive Summary, National Child Care Staffing Study). Oakland, CA: Child Care Employee Project.

38. Whitebook, M., Phillips, D., & Howes, C. (1989, April 28). *Adult caregivers in typical child care centers: Characteristics, preparation, compensation, and working conditions.* Paper presented at the Society for Research in Child Development symposium, "National Child Care Staffing Study," Kansas City, KS.

Chapter 4.
The Caregiving Needs of Infants and Toddlers

1. Ainslie, R., & Anderson, C. (1984). Daycare children's relationships to their mothers and caregivers. In R.C. Ainslie (Ed.), *Quality variations in daycare.* New York: Praeger.

2. Ainsworth, M.D., & Wittig, B.A. (1969). Attachment and exploratory behavior of one-year-olds in a strange situation. In B.M. Foss (Ed.), *Determinants of infant behavior,* Vol. 4. London: Methuen.

3. Belsky, J. (1986). Infant day care: A cause for concern? *Zero to Three,* 6(5), 1–9.

4. Belsky, J. (1988). The "effects" of infant day care reconsidered. *Early Childhood Research Quarterly, 3,* 235–272. Quotation on p. 266.

5. Bronfenbrenner, U. (1988). Strengthening family systems. In E. Zigler & M. Frank (Eds.), *The parental leave crisis: Toward a national policy* (pp. 143–160). New Haven: Yale University Press.

6. Clarke-Stewart, A.K. (1988). "The 'effects' of infant day care reconsidered" reconsidered. *Early Childhood Research Quarterly, 3,* 293–318.

7. Dittman, L.L. (1985). *Finding the best care for your infant or toddler* (pamphlet). Washington, DC: National Center for Clinical Infant Programs; National Association for the Education of Young Children.

8. *Early Childhood Research Quarterly* (1988). Infant day care. Vol. 3, No. 3

9. Fein, G.G., & Fox, N. (1988). Infant day care: A special issue. *Early Childhood Research Quarterly, 3,* 227–234. Quotation on p. 233.

10. Federal Interagency Day Care Requirements (1980, March 19). *Federal Register,* Part V, Vol. 45, No. 55, pp. 17870–17885.

11. Gamble, T., & Zigler, E. (1986). Effects of infant day care: Another look at the evidence. *American Journal of Orthopsychiatry, 56,* 26–42.

12. Greenspan, S., & Greenspan, N.T., (1985). *First feelings: Milestones in the emotional development of your baby and child.* New York: Viking Penguin.

13. Harlow, H. (1971). *Learning to love.* New York: Ballantine Books.

14. Lamb, M.E. (1981). The development of father-infant relationships. In M.E. Lamb (Ed.), *The role of the father in child development* (2nd ed.). New York: Wiley.

15. National Center for Clinical Infant Programs (1987, November 10). *Consensus on infant/toddler day care reached by researchers at NCCIP meeting* (press release). Washington, DC: Author. Quotation on pp. 1, 3.

16. Phillips, D.A., Howes, C., & Whitebook, M. (1989, April 28). *Child care quality: The real options facing parents.* Paper presented at the Society for Research in Child Development symposium, "National Child Care Staffing Study," Kansas City, KS.

17. Phillips, D., McCartney, K., Scarr, S., & Howes, C. (1987). Selective review of infant day care research: A cause for concern. *Zero to Three,* 7(3), 18–21. Quotation on p. 20.

18. Ruopp, R., Travers, J., Glantz, F., & Coelen, C. (1979). *Children at the center: Final report of the National Day Care Study: Summary findings and their implications.* Cambridge, MA: Abt Books.

19. Sroufe, L.A. (1988). A developmental perspective on day care. *Early Childhood Research Quarterly, 3,* 283–291. Quotation on p. 290.

20. Stern, D.N. (1977). *The first relationship: Infant and mother.* Cambridge, MA: Harvard University Press.

21. Thomas, A., Chess, S., Birch, H.G., Hertzig, M.E., & Korn, S. (1963). *Behavioral individuality in early childhood.* New York: New York University Press.

22. Thompson, R.A. (1988). The effects of infant day care through the prism of attachment theory: A critical appraisal. *Early Childhood Research Quarterly, 3,* 273–282.

23. Young, K.T., & Lang, M.E. (1984). Examining state day care licensing requirements. *The Networker, 5*(4), 5–6.

24. Young, K.T., & Zigler, E. (1986). Infant and toddler day care: Regulations and policy implications. *American Journal of Orthopsychiatry, 56,* 43–54. Quotation on p. 50.

25. Zigler, E., & Finn-Stevenson, M. (1987). *Children: Development and social issues,* pp. 289–291. Lexington, MA: D. C. Heath.

26. Zigler, E., & Frank, M. (Eds.) (1988). *The parental leave crisis: Toward a national policy.* New Haven: Yale University Press.

Chapter 5.
The Crisis of Infant Care

1. Allen, J.P. (1988). European infant care leaves: Foreign perspectives on the integration of work and family roles. In E. Zigler & M. Frank (Eds.), *The parental leave crisis: Toward a national policy* (pp. 245–275). New Haven: Yale University Press.

2. Bond, J.T., & Lovejoy, M. (1988). *Mothers in the workplace working*

paper: The role of managers/supervisors in easing work-family strain.
New York: Center for the Child, National Council of Jewish Women.

3. Brazelton, T.B. (1988). Issues for working parents. In E. Zigler & M. Frank (Eds.), *The parental leave crisis: Toward a national policy* (pp. 36–51). New Haven: Yale University Press.

4. Farber, E.A., Alejandro-Wright, M., & Muenchow, S. (1988). Managing work and family: Hopes and reality. In E.F. Zigler & M. Frank (Eds.), *The parental leave crisis: Toward a national policy* (pp. 161–176). New Haven: Yale University Press.

5. Friedan, B. (1986). *The second stage* (revised ed.). New York: Summit Books.

6. Hopper, P., & Zigler, E. (1988). The medical and social science basis for a national infant care leave policy. *American Journal of Orthopsychiatry, 58*, 324–338.

7. Kagan, S.L., Powell, D.R., Weissbourd, B., & Zigler, E. (Eds.). (1987). *America's family support programs: Perspectives and prospects.* New Haven: Yale University Press.

8. Kamerman, S.B. (1988). Maternity and parenting benefits: An international overview. In E. Zigler & M. Frank (Eds.), *The parental leave crisis: Toward a national policy* (pp. 235–244). New Haven: Yale University Press.

9. Kamerman, S., Kahn, A.J., & Kingston, P. (1983). *Maternity policies and working women.* New York: Columbia University Press.

10. Moroney, R.M. (1987). Social support systems: Families and social policy. In S.L. Kagan, D.R. Powell, B. Weissbourd, & E. Zigler (Eds.), *America's family support programs: Perspectives and prospects* (pp. 21–37). New Haven: Yale University Press.

11. "Open Air New England" (1989, January 17). Broadcast on Connecticut Public Radio. Hosts: Faith Middleton and Bill Henry.

12. Piccirillo, M. (1988). The legal background of a parental leave policy and its implications. In E. Zigler & M. Frank (Eds.), *The Parental leave crisis: Toward a national policy* (pp. 293–314). New Haven: Yale University Press.

13. Powell, D.R. (1987). Day care as a family support system. In S.L. Kagan, D.R. Powell, B. Weissbourd, & E. Zigler (Eds.), *America's family support programs: Perspectives and prospects* (pp. 115–132). New Haven: Yale University Press.

14. *Programs to strengthen families.* (1983). New Haven and Chicago: Yale Bush Center in Child Development and Social Policy and Family Resource Coalition. [Available from Family Resource Coalition, 230 N. Michigan Avenue, Suite 1625, Chicago, IL 60601.]

15. Schroeder, P. (1989). *Champion of the great American family.* New York: Random House.

16. U.S. Chamber of Commerce. (1989, February 7). *Testimony before the Subcommittee on Labor-Management Relations of the House Committee on Education and Labor,* by Dr. Earl H. Hess.

17. Wandersman, L.P. (1987). New directions for parent education. In S.L. Kagan, D.R. Powell, B. Weissbourd, & E. Zigler (Eds.), *America's family support programs: Perspectives and prospects* (pp. 207–227). New Haven: Yale University Press.

18. Williams, J.H. *Psychology of women: Behavior in a biosocial context.* New York: Norton.

19. Women returning to work. (1989, August 21). *Newsweek,* p. 4.

20. Zigler, E., & Frank, M. (Eds.). (1988). *The parental leave crisis: Toward a national policy.* New Haven: Yale University Press.

Chapter 6.
School-Age Child Care

1. Baden, R.K., Genser, A., Levine, J.A., & Seligson, M. (1982). *School-age child care: An action manual.* Boston: Auburn House.

2. Bredekamp, S. (Ed.). (1987). *Accreditation criteria and procedures of the National Academy of Early Childhood Programs.* Washington, DC: National Association for the Education of Young Children.

3. Cohen, A.J. (1984). *School-age child care: A legal manual for public school administrators.* Wellesley, MA: School-Age Child Care Project, and San Francisco: Child Care Law Center.

4. Coolsen, P., Seligson, M., & Garbarino, J. (1985). *When school's out and nobody's home.* Chicago: National Committee for the Prevention of Child Abuse.

5. Elkind, D. (1981). *The hurried child: Growing up too fast too soon.* Reading, MA: Addison-Wesley.

6. Evans, S. (1989, September 3). Many working parents rely on neighbors and relatives. *Washington Post,* p. A16.

7. Fink, D.B. (1986a). *Latchkey children and school-age child care: A background briefing.* Wellesley, MA: School-Age Child Care Project.

8. Fink, D.B. (1986b). School-age child care: Where the spirit of neighborhood lives. *Children's Environments Quarterly,* 3(2), 9–12. Quotation on p. 9.

9. Finkelhor, D. (1986). *A sourcebook on child sexual abuse.* Beverly Hills, CA: Sage.

10. Galambos, N.L., & Garbarino, J. (1985). Adjustment of unsupervised children in a rural setting. *Journal of Genetic Psychology,* 146, 227–231.

11. Kagan, S.L., & Zigler, E. (Eds.). (1987). *Early schooling: The national debate.* New Haven: Yale University Press.

12. Kyte, K. (1983). *In charge: A complete handbook for kids with working parents.* New York: Knopf.

13. Long, L. (1984). *On my own: The kids' self-care book*. Washington, DC: Acropolis Books.

14. Long, L., & Long, T. (1982). *Latchkey children: The child's view of self-care*. Baltimore: Loyola College (ERIC Document Reproduction Service No. ED 211 299).

15. Long, T.J., & Long, L. (1983). *The handbook for latchkey children and their families*. New York: Arbor House.

16. National Safety Council. (1987). *Accident facts*. Chicago: Author.

17. Noble, K.B. (1988, February 15). Library as day care: New curbs and concerns. *New York Times*, pp. A1, A17. Quotation on p. A17.

18. Olsen, D., & Zigler, E. (1989). An assessment of the all-day kindergarten movement. *Early Childhood Research Quarterly, 4*, 167–186.

19. Phillips, J.D. (1987). *Breakaway human resource planning and the* Bottom Line *through family issues management* (working paper). Copyright author (Senior Director for Corporate Planning for Merck & Co.). Quotation by Thomas Long on p. 5.

20. Public housing becoming home to SACC programs. (1987). *SACC Newsletter, 4*(2), 1–6.

21. Richardson, J.L., Dwyer, K., McGuigan, K., Hansen, W.B., Dent, C., Johnson, C.A., Sussman, S.Y., Brannon, B., & Flay, B. (1989). Substance use among eighth-grade students who take care of themselves after school. *Pediatrics, 84*, 556–566.

22. Rodman, H., Pratto, D., & Nelson, R. (1985). Child care arrangements and children's functioning: A comparison of self-care and adult-care children. *Developmental Psychology, 21*, 413–418.

23. San Francisco voters give school-agers a boost with Prop D. (1987). *SACC Newsletter, 4*(2), 3.

24. Select Committee on Children, Youth and Families. (1984). *Families and child care: Improving the options*. Washington, DC: U.S. Government Printing Office. Quotation on p. 26.

25. Seligson, M. (1987). Keeping in touch (editorial). *SACC Newsletter, 4*(2), 2.

26. Seligson, M., & Fink, D.B. (1989a). *No time to waste: An action agenda for school-age child care*. Wellesley, MA: School-Age Child Care Project.

27. Seligson, M., & Fink, D.B. (1989b, April). School-age child care in America: Providers survey. In *School-age child care in America: A twelve-month research action study*. Unpublished report submitted to Smith Richardson Foundation.

28. Smock, S.M. (1977). *The children: The shape of child care in Detroit*. Detroit: Wayne State University Press.

29. Steinberg, L. (1986). Latchkey children and susceptibility to peer pressure: An ecological analysis. *Developmental Psychology, 22,* 433–439.

30. Swan, H., & Houston, V. (1985). *Alone after school: A self-care guide for latchkey children and their parents.* Englewood Cliffs, NJ: Prentice-Hall.

31. Systems recruit, support home caregivers for school-agers. (1986). *SACC Newsletter, 4*(1), 7–10.

32. U.S. Bureau of the Census. (1987). *After-school care of school-age children.* Current Population Reports, Series P-23, No. 149. Washington, DC: U.S. Government Printing Office. Quotation on p. 5.

33. Vandell, D.L., & Corasaniti, M.A. (1988). The relationship between third graders' after-school care and social, academic, and emotional functioning. *Child Development, 59,* 868–875.

34. Winn, M. (1983). *Children without childhood.* New York: Plenum.

35. Woods, M.B. (1972). The unsupervised child of the working mother. *Developmental Psychology, 6,* 14–25.

Chapter 7.
The Challenge of Providing Child Care for Children with Special Needs

1. Administration for Children, Youth and Families. (1989, January). *Project Head Start statistical fact sheet.* Washington, DC: Department of Health and Human Services.

2. Aronson, S.S., & Osterholm, M.T. (1986). Infectious diseases in child day care: Management and prevention. Summary of the symposium and recommendations. *Reviews of Infectious Diseases, 8,* 672–679.

3. Berk, H., & Berk, M. (1982). A survey of day care centers and their services for handicapped children. *Child Care Quarterly, 11,* 211–214.

4. Children's Defense Fund. (1989). *A vision for America's future.* Washington, DC: Author.

5. Fifteenth Anniversary Head Start Committee. (1980, September). *Head Start in the 1980's.* Washington, DC: U.S. Department of Health and Human Services.

6. Fink, D.B. (1988). *School-age children with special needs.* Boston: Exceptional Parent Press. Quotations on pp. 28, 71.

7. Johnson, C.M., Sum, A.M., & Weill, J.D. (1988). *Vanishing dreams: The growing economic plight of America's young families.* Washington, DC: Children's Defense Fund.

8. Krajicek, M.J., Robinson, J., & Moore, C.A. (1989, May/June). First Start: Training paraprofessionals to care for children with special needs. *Pediatric Nursing.*

9. MATCH facilitates day care for children with handicaps. (1988, Spring/ Summer). *Family Support Bulletin, 11.* (Publication of the United Cerebral Palsy Associations.)

10. Mitchell, A., Seligson, M., & Marx, F. (1989). *Early childhood programs and the public schools: Between promise and practice.* Dover, MA: Auburn House.

11. Moret, M. (1987, October 23). *Surviving in the inner city: A profile of Hartford's Puerto Rican children.* Paper presented at the Yale University Bush Center in Child Development and Social Policy, Social Policy Luncheon Series, New Haven, CT.

12. Pizzo, P. (1988). New law can help child care programs with children who have special needs. *Child Care Information Exchange, 64,* 27–28.

13. Rhodes, M. (1984, June 18). Testimony presented at hearings before the Select Committee on Children, Youth and Families.

14. Rule, S., Stowitschek, J., & Innocenti, M. (1986). Day care for handicapped children: Can we stimulate mainstream service through a day care–special education merger? *Child Care Quarterly, 15,* 223–232.

15. Salisbury, C. (1986). Adaptation of the questionnaire on resources and stress—short form. *American Journal of Mental Deficiency, 90,* 456–459.

16. Select Committee on Children, Youth and Families. (1984, January). *Federal programs affecting children.* Washington, DC: U.S. Government Printing Office.

17. Select Committee on Children, Youth and Families. (1984, September). *Families and child care: Improving the options.* Washington, DC: U.S. Government Printing Office. Quotation on p. 38.

18. *Status of handicapped children in Head Start programs: Seventh annual report of the U.S. Department of Health, Education and Welfare to the Congress of the United States on services provided to handicapped children in Project Head Start.* (1980, February). Washington, DC: Department of Health, Education and Welfare.

19. Sterne, G. (1987). Day care for sick children. *Pediatrics, 79,* 445–446.

20. Stone, C. (1989, Fall). Kids are kids: Integrated day care works. *Family Support Bulletin,* 8–9. (Publication of the United Cerebral Palsy Associations.)

21. Weissbourd, B., & Kagan, S.L. (1989). Family support programs: Catalyst for change. *American Journal of Orthopsychiatry, 59,* 20–31.

22. West, P., Illsley, R., & Kelman, H. (1984). Public preferences for the care of dependency groups. *Social Science and Medicine, 18,* 287–295.

23. Zigler, E., & Hodapp, R.M. (1986). *Understanding mental retardation.* New York: Cambridge University Press.

Chapter 8.
Child Care as the New Business of Business

1. Bailey C.A. (1988). *A report on child care: The business perspective in Prince George's County.* Prince George's County, MD: Prince George's County Economic Development Corporation, Prince George's County Department of Social Services.

2. Bond, J.T., & Lovejoy, M. (1988). *The role of managers/supervisors in easing work-family strain.* Mothers in the Workplace working paper. New York: Center for the Child, National Council of Jewish Women.

3. Burud, S., Aschbacher, P.R., & McCroskey, J. (1984). *Employer supported child care: Investing in human resources.* Boston: Auburn House.

4. Child Care Action Campaign (no date). *Examples of employer involvement in child care assistance.* Information Guide #24 (flier). New York: Author.

5. Coolsen, P. (1983). *Strengthening families through the workplace.* Chicago: National Committee for Prevention of Child Abuse. Quotation on p. 24.

6. Fernandez, H.C. (1988). *Child care and family sensitive policies: A survey of Philadelphia area businesses.* Philadelphia: Temple University School of Social Administration. Quotation on p. 7.

7. Fernandez, J.P. (1986). *Child care and corporate productivity.* Boston: D.C. Heath. Quotations on pp. 32 and 73.

8. Fiske, E.B. (1989, June 6). Concerns raised on school quality: Business leaders join in calls for reforming educational practices in the U.S. *New York Times,* p. A19.

9. Friedman, D.E. (1985). *Corporate financial assistance for child care.* (Conference Board Research Bulletin No. 177). New York: Conference Board.

10. Friedman, D.E. (1986). *A national overview of employer-supported child care.* New York: Conference Board Work and Family Information Center.

11. Friedman, D.E. (1987). *Family supportive policies: The corporate decision-making process.* New York: Conference Board.

12. Friedman, D.E., & Gray, W.B. (1989a, March 9–10). *The corporate response to health and family needs.* Paper presented at the Conference on Health and the Family, Henry J. Kaiser Family Foundation, Menlo Park, CA.

13. Friedman, D.E., & Gray, W.B. (1989b). *The corporate response to family needs: A life-cycle perspective.* New York: Conference Board.

14. Galinsky, E. (1986). *Investing in quality care: A report for AT&T.* New York: Bank Street College.

15. Galinsky, E. (1988). *The impact of child care problems on parents on the job and at home.* Unpublished paper prepared for the Child Care Action Campaign Wingspread Conference.

16. Kleiman, C. (1989, August 14). Child care consultants gain stature. *Hartford (CT) Courant*, p. B4.

17. Labor Letter. (1989, November 28). *Wall Street Journal*, p. A1.

18. Lawson, C. (1989, September 7). 7 Employers join to provide child care at home in a crisis. *New York Times*, pp. A1, C12.

19. Lewin, T. (1989, March 8). "Mommy career track" sets off a furor. *New York Times*, p. A18.

20. Mernit, S. (1989, June). The newest in family-friendly benefits. *Working Mother*, pp. 64–69.

21. Moskowitz, M., & Townsend, C. (1989, October). The 60 best companies for working mothers. *Working Mother*, pp. 74–98.

22. Perry, K.S. (1982). *Employers and child care: Establishing services through the workplace*. Washington, DC: Women's Bureau, U.S. Department of Labor.

23. Phillips, J.D. (1987). *Breakaway human resource planning and the* Bottom Line *through family-issues management* (working paper). Copyright author (Senior Director for Corporate Planning for Merck & Co.).

24. Reisman, B., Moore, A.J., & Fitzgerald, K. (1988). *Child care: The bottom line*. New York: Child Care Action Campaign.

25. Rubin, N. (1984). *The mother mirror: How a generation of women is changing motherhood in America*. New York: Putnam.

26. Schwartz, F.N. (1989). Management women and the new facts of life. *Harvard Business Review*, 89(1), 65–76.

27. Skrzycki, C. (1989, September 3). Family concerns spark changes at work. *Washington Post*, pp. A1, A17.

28. Strohmer, A. (1988). *Returns on investment for corporations investing in child care*. Unpublished report for Merck & Co.

29. Trost, C. (1989, November 14). Few use credits for child-care plans, study finds. *Wall Street Journal*, p. A8.

Chapter 9.
The School of the 21st Century

1. Bredekamp, S. (Ed.). (1987). *Accreditation criteria and procedures of the National Academy of Early Childhood Programs*. Washington, DC: National Association for the Education of Young Children.

2. Bronfenbrenner, U. (1974). *A report on longitudinal evaluations of pre-school programs. Vol. 2. Is early intervention effective?* Washington, DC: Office of Human Development. DHEW Publication No. OHD74–25.

3. Caldwell, B. (1989, Spring). A comprehensive model for integrating child

care and early childhood education. *The Teachers College Record*, pp. 404–415.

4. Caldwell, B.M. (1989, August 12). *Early intervention at home and abroad.* An invited address to Division 37 of the American Psychological Association, New Orleans, LA.

5. Council of Chief State School Officers. (1988, November). *A guide for state action: Early childhood and family education.* Washington, DC: Author. Quotation on p. 29.

6. Durenberger, D. (1989, June). Senator Durenberger's office confirms that this figure appears in several of his oral remarks about the Act for Better Child Care, although it does not appear in the written form of his speech before the Senate published in the *Congressional Record*.

7. Independence, Mo., greets 21st century. (1990, January 27). *St. Louis (MO) Post Dispatch*.

8. Lubeck, S., & Garrett, P. (1989). *Pre-K programs in North Carolina: Preferences of superintendents and principals*. Chapel Hill, NC: Frank Porter Graham Child Development Center. Quotation on p. 17.

9. Mitchell, A.W. (1988, August 15). Paper presented to the Council of Chief State School Officers and cited in CCSSO, 1988, p. 29.

10. Mitchell, A., Seligson, M., & Marx, F. (1989). *Early childhood programs and the public schools*. Dover, MA: Auburn House.

11. Philip Morris Companies, Inc. (1989). *Family survey II: Child care.* Conducted by Louis Harris and Associates. New York: Author.

12. Powell, D.R. (Ed.)(1988). *Parent education as early childhood intervention: Emerging directions in theory, research, and practice*. Vol. 3 of I.E. Sigel (Ed.), *Advances in applied developmental psychology*. Norwood, NJ: Ablex.

13. Reardon, P. (1989, December 17). No recess for child care needs. *Chicago Tribune*, section 2, pp. 1, 12.

14. Ryan, S. (1974). *A report on longitudinal evaluations of preschool programs.* Vol. 1. *Longitudinal evaluations*. Washington, DC: Office of Human Development. DHEW Publication No. 74–24.

15. Wright, R. (1990, January). Who's watching the children? *McCall's*, pp. 22–30.

16. Zigler, E.F. (1989). Addressing the nation's child care crisis: The school of the twenty-first century. *American Journal of Orthopsychiatry, 59*, 484–491.

17. Zigler, E., & Black, K.B. (1989). America's family support movement: Strengths and limitations. *American Journal of Orthopsychiatry, 59*, 6–19.

18. Zigler, E., & Finn-Stevenson, M. (1989, November). *Evaluation of the School of the 21st Century*. Proposal to the Ford Foundation, unpublished manuscript.

Chapter 10.
A Child Allowance Trust Fund

1. Bane, M.J., & Ellwood, D.T. (1989). One fifth of the nation's children: Why are they poor? *Science, 245,* 1047–1053. Quotation on p. 1049.

2. Children of the world. (1987, June 22). *Time,* p. 60.

3. Children's Defense Fund. (1989). *A vision for America's future: An agenda for the 1990s.* Washington, DC: Author.

4. Committee for Economic Development. (1984). *Children in need: Investment strategies for the educationally disadvantaged.* New York: Author.

5. Espanshade, T. (1983, February). *New estimates of parental expenditures on children.* Washington, DC: Urban Institute.

6. Finn-Stevenson, M., & Trczinsky, E. (in review). Infant, parental and family leaves: A state-by-state analysis of policies.

7. Kamerman, S., & Kahn, A. (1988). *Mothers alone: Strategies for a time of change.* Dover, MA: Auburn House. Quotations on pp. 178, 219.

8. Lawson, C. (1989, November 9). France seen as far ahead in providing child care. *New York Times,* pp. C1, C14.

9. Longman, P. (1987). *Born to pay: The new politics of aging in America.* Boston: Houghton Mifflin. Quotation on p. 80.

10. Moore, E.K. (1989). What we can learn from France. *The Black Child Advocate, 16*(3), 3.

11. Moss, P. (1988). *Child care and equality of opportunity.* Consolidated report to the European Commission. Final version. London: Child Care Network of the European Economic Community.

12. Penner, R. (1989). *Social security and national savings.* New York: Committee for Economic Development.

13. Philip Morris Companies. (1988). *Family survey II: Child care.* Conducted by Louis Harris and Associates. New York: Author.

14. Popenoe, D. (1988). *Disturbing the nest.* New York: Aldine De Gruyter.

15. Schorr, L. (1986). *Common decency.* New Haven: Yale University Press.

16. Sugarman, J. (1989, July 25). *The children's investment trust: For America's future.* Working paper. Washington, DC: Author.

17. U.S. Bureau of the Census. (1987). *Household after-tax income: 1986.* Current population reports, Special studies, Series P-23, No. 157, pp. 7–17. Washington, DC: U.S. Government Printing Office.

18. U.S. Bureau of the Census. (1987). *Who's watching the kids? Child care arrangements: Winter 1984–85.* Current population reports, Household studies, Series P-70, No. 9. Washington, DC: U.S. Government Printing Office.

19. Whitebook, M., Howes, C., & Phillips, D. (1989). *Who cares? Child care teachers and the quality of child care in America.* Executive summary, National Child Care Staffing Study. Oakland, CA: Child Care Employee Project.

20. Zigler, E., & Frank, M. (Eds.). (1988). *The parental leave crisis: Toward a national policy.* New Haven: Yale University Press.

Author Index

Subject Index